THE HALF LIFE
OF A
FREE RADICAL

GROWING UP IRISH CATHOLIC IN JIM CROW MEMPHIS

Clare Hanrahan

Celtic WordCraft
Asheville, North Carolina

Celtic WordCraft Books
Copyright 2016. All rights reserved
ISBN: 978-0-9758846-9-0

Printed in the United States of America
Ingram-Spark Publishing Services

Cover design: Jerri Strozier
Author's portrait: Julyan Davis - www.julyandavis.com
Photos and reviews on Author's website:
CelticWordcraftAVL.wordpress.com

Books available through your local bookstore, or from:
Clare Hanrahan P.O. Box 2551, Asheville, NC 28802
Hanrahan.celticwordcraft@gmail.com

Also by this author and available online at www.lulu.com:
Conscience & Consequence: A Prison Memoir
Celtic WordCraft Books, 2005
ISBN: 978-0-9758846-01-4

Jailed for Justice: A Woman's Guide to Federal Prison Camp
Celtic WordCraft Books, 2002
ISBN 978-0-9758846-8-3

Dissenting Opinions: Public Addresses on
 Justice, Peace and the Consequences of Dissent
Celtic WordCraft Books, 2009
ISBN: 978-0-9758846-7-6

To my Family —

All who have come before and all who may follow:

    May you be free
    May you be happy
    May you be at Peace
    May you be at Rest
    May you know we remember you.
       — From a Buddhist Blessing

Dear Dead Relatives

Father, Mother, Grands and Great
Long-gone brothers, three
Distant uncles, aunts
Hail to you
As the Season lifts the veil

Dear dead relatives
Ancient ones from generations gone
You live in my bones and blood
I honor your lives
Hail to you
As the Season lifts the veil

Dear dead relatives
You are the strengths and aversions
Talents and passions
I carry forward
Hail to you
As the Season lifts the veil

Dear dead relatives
I honor your lives
Forgive your failings
Invite your Counsel
Hail to you
As the Season lifts the veil
  — *Samhain*, 2015

Contents

Preface........................ 11
    A Dream in My Fiftieth Year

Acknowledgments...................... 14

About The Author..................... 15

1. Those Who Came Before............... 17
    Cracks in the System
    Jackson's Manifest Destiny
    "Fi Fie Foe Fum" English Roots
    Race from the Bottom
    The German Connection
    Jim Crow: Temper of the Times
    "Yellow Jack" Up in Old Pinch
    The Great Hunger
    Poor Paddy Works on the Railway
    Tennessee's Little Ireland
    Marriage & Mayhem in Memphis
    Tuberculosis: Number One Killer
    The River's Mighty Rampage
    A Literary Alliance
    Hanrahan's & Mahoneys
    In Sickness and in Health
    What's a Mother to Do?

2. North Memphis Meanderings. 45
Mrs. Birds Burgeoning Bungalow
Clutter and Chaos
Grandpa's Pipeline
American Snuff Company
Eternal Rest
A Courageous Coterie
A Point of Interface
The Bane of Alcoholism
The Loyal Order of the Moose
"And These Thy Gifts"
Perpetual Housework
Front Porch Life
Neighborhood Watch
Sweet Little Flowers
Shooing Away the Pets
TV Time
"Old Lady in the Shoe"
"The House is on Fire"
"Smoke, Smoke, Smoke that Cigarette"
Elvis Has Left the Neighborhood
Overton Park: The Grandest Time

3. Thou Shalt Not. 89
"My Most Grievous Fault"
Daily Mass
"Loss of Heaven & Pains of Hell"
"The World & Its Evil Powers"
"Failure to Quit"
Angel Guardians & Rosary Time
Oh Holy Night
A Separate Peace
Priestly Abuse & Cover Ups

Contents

4. School Days & Hood Ways............ 107
    Dear Old Golden Rule Day
    Reading & Homework Time
    Getting Mama's Message
    Falsely Accused
    Ring Leader
    Broken Bones & Busted Teeth
    Crab Apples & "Clean Dirt"
    North Parkway Gang
    Trick or Treat

5. "Lawyer Dan".................... 127
    "Tender Mercies"
    "Ask Your Daddy"
    A New Jersey Summer
    Daddy in Politics

6. Our Enterprising Mama............. 136
    Mama's Office
    Worms for Sale
    A Winning Way
    Rearing Saints
    St. Jude & Danny Thomas

7. A Culture of Racism................ 145
    Censoring Social Equality
    "A Very Worthy Negro"
    "Fair to Middling"
    King Cotton's "Bale of Fun"
    "The Land of Cotton"
    Neighborhood Changes

8. Crossing the Color Lines............ 156
    Blessed Martin Catholic Worker House
    From the Bus Window
    Desegregation and "Race Mixing"

"Kneeling In"
Gradualism

9. The Secret Vote. 166
Communists Coming Down the River
Murder in Dallas

10. Teen-Age Turmoil. 171
My First Kiss
And When She Was Bad
"We Are Daughters True"
Vanity and Charm
Grounded in Shame
"you're Crazy"
Public School Detour
"Lie Back and Enjoy It?"
"Do Not Fold, Spindle, or Mutilate"

11. "Next Stop is Viet Nam". 188
"Back Our Boys in Viet Nam"
Marine at the Door
"The Change is Forever"
The Fall of our Twin Towers
Rogue Romance
Murders & Rapists at Large

12. Marching in Memphis. 201
"Some Difficult Days Ahead"
Murder at the Lorraine
"How Long Will it Take"

13. "For Better or Worse". 208
"Miss USO"
"It's Not What You Think"
Liberated Betrayals

Contents

Angelic Intervention
"All my ex's Live in Texas"

14. Magna Cum Laude.................. 219
"We Ain't Got a Barrel of Money"
My B.S. Degree
Down, Down in Memphis Town
A Great American Smoke Out
"When in doubt, Love"

15. Off The Grid....................... .227
An Island Paradise
Clinch Mountain Tipi
Puget Sound Awakenings
Withdrawing Consent
Winds of Change
Mississippi Backwater
Stuck in the Mire
Mud Island Wilds
Gleaning the Backwater Bounty
Caught Red Handed
A Special Tribunal
Working for Peace & Justice
My First Arrest
Flowing with the River
Wide, Deep & Muddy
At Anchor in St. Petersburg

16. Solidarity & Resistance............... 261
Haphazard Community
Finding Home in Appalachia
Inmate No. 90285-020
Torn

17. "Requiem Aeternam"................ 273
"Hush Now, Don't You Cry"
Johnny's "Blaze of Glory"
Danny's Last Waltz
Tommy's Last Climb
Endless Wars
The Veterans' Truth
Mama's Last Goodbye
Mending Mama's Quilt

Reference Notes & Index

Preface

A Dream in my Fiftieth year:

I am high up on a narrow plank bridging a deep, cold lake. Inching along on my hands and knees, I follow close behind a crawling child. It is a long, long drop to the water. We are secured to the ledge with a make-shift clothesline harness. The toddler looks back and catches my eye. Her gaze is steady and clear as she carefully and deliberately loosens her harness, releases her hold and plunges far, far below into the murky deep. I feel the challenge in her gaze:
"Will you follow me down? Will you find me?"
I'm afraid to let loose of my precarious hold. I watch as she plunges down, down and disappears. The water closes around her and the surface becomes still again. It is quiet. Of a sudden it feels as though that child and I are one. The water surrounds us with a pleasant warmth and buoyancy. I look up toward the filtered light streaming from the surface and awaken.

Memories come hard. Writing now, well into my sixth decade, I again take up this account of my early years, retrieving the words from old diaries, the binders of yellowing papers, the various and obsolete computer disks, the outdated word processing files and the more recent electronic blogs.

Can I retrieve the authentic threads of memory from the chaos of my Memphis childhood? Will I find my place among this family of survivors, living and dead, who through the generations lived through famine and epidemics, occupation and exile, racism and war? I have tried to convey with integrity my experiences within a family that has endured dogma and repression, prison and poverty,

The Half Life of a Free Radical

addictions and depressions; a family gifted with keen intelligence, sustained by a warrior spirit, and inclined toward the good.

I cannot write of my life in Memphis in the 1950's and 1960's without also writing of my ancestors who arrived in Tennessee before the Civil War. Nor can I tell my story apart from the ugly truths of the apartheid years of Jim Crow and the racial injustice that continues long after the Sanitation Workers' Strike and the assassination of Martin Luther King, Jr. shook the city.

I live now in Asheville, North Carolina, a bio-region of the ancient Southern Appalachians, rich in natural diversity and beauty. I have spent the past quarter century in the powerful embrace of the Blue Ridge Mountains, yet distant from the family of my birth.

I write with a heavy heart for the living planet. The weather is erratic and record breaking in its intensity, with fires and floods, droughts and dust bowls, earthquakes and monstrous storms. Famine, wars and epidemics are widespread.

The triple threats of racism, militarism and materialism continue at home and abroad—fear driven and unabated—with drastic consequences now and into the generations that may follow. The world of our grandchildren, all the grandchildren, and that of all sentient life is in danger.

I had hoped to finish this autobiography by my fiftieth birthday. I wanted to neatly tidy up my tumultuous half century of life and move into my remaining years with a clean slate. But it is difficult to dwell in memory, to listen to parts of myself that still feel unhealed and unholy.

Now I am sixty-seven. My hair is as gray as the winter clouds, its silver strands glistening as my mother's did. My face is lined like the surface of a lake etched by the wayward winds. Now it is time to weave the story of times past, mending the tattered quilt of my family with these threads of memory, speaking my own truth, and finding clarity for the remaining years.

Have I gathered enough of the shards of our shattered and scattered family to weave a true story? Letting go of so much of the holding on is part of this process. Though much must be missing in the telling, now is the time to edit the dross and find the essence.

Would that my words could sing with the lilt of an Irish ballad, flow with the power of a Gaelic lament, dance with the sweetness of the fiddle, and resonate with the primal depth of a *Bodhram* drum.

My intention is that this work will give due tribute to my ancestors, to my parents, and to my siblings, whose memories and perspectives will surely differ.

Would that this story, my story, will help our children and theirs in the generations that may follow to understand, to forgive, and to claim some measure of pride in the roots that nourished them, that held the hard ground and pushed through to the light.

Acknowledgments

I have been supported in myriad ways over the years as I worked to complete this book. I am grateful to my sister Eileen, who added her keen eye to early manuscripts, delivering discerning criticisms kindly, and providing the benefit of her genealogical research. To my brother Robert, for reading early drafts and responding sweetly, and to brother Michael, for your gems of anecdote and writing. To my sister Regina, for keeping me mindful of how differently we each experienced our shared childhood, and that not all stories need to be told. For my daughter Jessica, a warrior spirit in her own right, who made it through. May the long-time sun shine upon you and all love surround you.

Special thanks to my writer friends Mike Hopping, Bill Branyon, and Ellen Thomas for your editorial comments and review, and for the suggestions and encouragement of other early readers: Chuck Fager, Catherine Gattas, Ken Jones, James Latimore, and Redmoonsong. To the ever-generous Monica Tilhou, for her friendship, confidence, and vital help with production needs, and to my counselor, Sandra Newes, for the compassionate support that kept me focused throughout this emotional journey. Thanks also to my good friend and colleague in peace action, Coleman Smith, who has stayed the course in organizing for a better world.

Here it is y'all.

About the Author

Clare Hanrahan lives in Asheville, North Carolina, where she settled nearly three decades ago after a nomadic and contrary life. She is a grandmother, writer, grassroots organizer and peace and human rights activist.

A *cum laude* graduate of Southern Methodist University, she deepened her education during a six-month incarceration in Alderson Federal Prison in West Virginia for peaceful protest.

She is a wayside gardener, planting the cracks and crevices of her uptown neighborhood. She gets around by bicycle and on foot as an everyday revolution and step-by-step solution to the environmental burden of automobiles.

"It does my heart good to know you remember the good things… like dandelions that always brightened my outlook when they came unbidden to smile up at me when I bowed my head in sorrow. Little bits of sunshine scattered at my feet."

Mama
From an email on her 80th birthday

1

Those Who Came Before

Neither the life of an individual nor the history of a society can be understood without understanding both.
—C. Wright Mills, *The Sociological Imagination*

The Mississippi River flows wide and deep past my hometown: Memphis, Tennessee. I have known those muddy waters through many seasons, passing countless hours with the river watching from the high bluffs or standing barefoot on sun-heated cobblestones as the cool brown wake of passing tow boats lapped against my feet.

Memphis' name translates as "Place of Good Abode" though much of its history tells a different story.

In Memphis today, paddle-wheeled riverboats still dock along the cobblestone bank near old Confederate Park where a bronze statue of President Jefferson Davis has stood since 1964. Nearby, a concrete block inscribed with the Ten Commandments is just a short walk from the flat-topped stone on Auction Street where human beings were bought and sold in the dark decades when Memphis was a leading slave market.

Confederate General Nathan Bedford Forrest, the first Grand Wizard of the KKK, still rides his cast-iron horse atop the grave he shares with his wife Mary in the Memphis park that bore his name since 1904. Not until 2013, when Memphis' African American population reached 63 percent, did the Memphis City Council vote to remove Confederate names from city parks, which for many residents "evoked a racist past."[1]

In 2015 Memphis Mayor A. C. Wharton called for removal of the monument to Confederate General Nathan Bedford Forrest:

"These relics, these messages of this despicable period of this great nation, it's time for those to be moved."[2]

Throughout my childhood I played in many of the parks where these Confederate statues stand, though I paid them scant attention. Those military leaders seemed as remote to me then as the Catholic saints whose statues stood in the alcoves of our church and school. My parochial education did little to inform me of Memphis' tumultuous past, and I had no curiosity then about the Civil War, and the horrific battles in which my maternal great grandfather fought.

Cracks In The System

I came of age in Memphis at a time when cracks in the systems of oppression were widening and the few but persistent seeds of social justice found fertile soil to take root. Throughout my childhood I witnessed the inequities of segregation and the cruelty of hardened racist attitudes backed by the force of law. I also witnessed many brave and determined efforts to bring justice, equity, and harmony to the Bluff City. Yet the foul stench of racism that has infected Memphis since its beginnings is as persistent now as the musky scent of the turbulent Mississippi.

In the 1950's Memphis was named the "quietest, cleanest and safest"[3] city in the United States. Memphis is anything but that now. Urban blight stalks the inner city and the crime rate is among the highest of the nation's fifty largest metropolitan areas. Suburban sprawl has eroded the city core and class and racial tensions persist in the frayed patchwork of Memphis neighborhoods.

My childhood home in North Memphis is on Faxon Avenue at Breedlove, just a few miles down North Parkway from the mighty, muddy Mississippi in what was then a racially-divided but otherwise ethnically-diverse neighborhood.

As a child in apartheid Memphis, I was curious about the many layers of separation between the "coloreds" and "whites," the rich and the poor, the Protestants and Catholics. Even the North-South regional tensions that were played out in our own home between my Brooklyn-born father and Memphis-born mother.

Public signs reading "For White Only" or "Colored" were the commonplace markers of the racial apartheid maintained by tradition, economics and the force of law. The so-called "coloreds" were a caste apart. In our neighborhood they lived in small, shotgun-style clapboard houses of weathered gray wood along the side streets and across Jackson Avenue, a commercial interface just a few blocks from our home. These humble dwellings were referred to by some in the vulgar language of 1950's Memphis as "nigger shacks."

One morning when I was quite young I remember gazing intently out our living room window across the street where some laborers were painting a house. I was sitting on the cold iron radiator beneath the window sill and behind the couch.

"Mama, do colored people really have tails?" I asked. Someone had told me they did.

"No, Clare, they don't have tails," Mama corrected.

Time after time Mama patiently corrected us if we expressed any of the racist attitudes that surrounded us in that divided city. Still, we southern children absorbed the racism we heard from our neighbors, at school, and in the daily reminders of legally-enforced segregation. Our parents taught us early not to repeat racial slurs. The "N" word was taboo in our lexicon. Even today I wince at its harshness. A word rivaled only by the vulgarities in common usage then to keep women and girls in a place of submission.

Jackson's Manifest Destiny

Memphis was founded in 1819 by Andrew Jackson, a Tennessee frontier attorney, revolutionary war soldier and slave-holder. Jackson and his cronies, John Overton and James Winchester, named Memphis after the Egyptian city on the Nile River.

The Mississippi River at Memphis was a major crossing into Indian Territory in what is now the state of Oklahoma. Jackson Avenue, a commercial thoroughfare just blocks from my childhood home, had been part of the main east-west Indian route across Tennessee, once known as Cherokee Trace. It was renamed for Andrew Jackson, whose ruthless campaign of Indian removals cleared

The Half Life of a Free Radical

millions of acres of land for settlement by European whites. This expanded the development of the Southern cotton plantations sustained with the labor of enslaved people.

The pervasive belief in the racial and cultural superiority of so-called white Americans, known as "Manifest Destiny," became the justification for the forced relocation and near extermination of the indigenous First Nation peoples.

At the forefront of this westward push were the Presbyterian Scots-Irish, who Theodore Roosevelt characterized as "a truculent and obstinate people." They formed "the vanguard of the army of fighting settlers," Roosevelt wrote, and "gloried in the warlike renown of their forefathers."[4]

Jackson's Scots-Irish Presbyterian parents emigrated from Ulster, a province in the north of Ireland occupied by Scottish and English settlers during the seventeenth century. At that time the native Irish, mostly Gaelic-speaking Catholics, were forced back to harsher lands in the west of Ireland where in the mid 1800's The Great Hunger took its harshest toll. According to some historians, the Plantation of Ulster became England's first successful attempt at empire.

As Andrew Jackson grew in power and influence, he applied English techniques of empire building in his dealings with North America's indigenous people, who like many of my Irish Catholic ancestors, were considered an inferior race. In 1838 he forced the relocation of the Cherokee Nation through the so-called Indian Removal Act, known as the "Trail of Tears."

Most of my early lessons in Memphis history came, not from school textbooks, but from frequent family outings to historical neighborhoods with our Mama as guide. One of my favorite excursions was to Hernando De Soto Park in South Memphis, named for the Spanish Conquistador said to have "discovered" the Mississippi river in the 1500's. The park is high above the river along the fourth Choctaw Bluff on the site of the old Chickasaw Indian village of Chisca, near the Civil-War era neighborhood known as Fort Pickering.

We children called it "Indian Mound Park," and delighted in scrambling up the two large earthen mounds, remnants of the native Mississippian culture. At the top we could look out over the wide Mississippi, and then slide to the bottom on flattened cardboard boxes. From my vantage point poised atop the Indian mounds, I tried to imagine what the First Nation peoples may have seen when the land was theirs to inhabit. They had lived along the wooded bluffs above the ancient river for centuries, calling the wide water *Misha sipokni*. *Misha* in Choctaw means "beyond," with the idea of far beyond; and *sipokni* means "age."[5]

Only now am I reaching back into Memphis history to learn about this place where my ancestors settled after the Civil War, and where many of my wonderfully colorful and diverse relatives still make their home, as our family has for seven generations.

"Fi Fie Foe Fum" English Roots

The first of my ancestors to arrive in Memphis, as far as I know, was Union Army veteran George W. Gardner. He was of English ancestry and born in Terre Haute, Indiana, in 1832. This maternal great grandfather is listed in an 1872 *Memphis City Directory* living at 201 N. Main Street. According to accounts of the time, it was "a thriving street with all types of shops and businesses, as well as numerous hotels, restaurants, and theaters."[6]

Conversations in Yiddish, Italian and Irish brogue could be heard all along the busy commercial area. The Memphis population then was about 40,000. It was a rough river town densely populated with "immigrants from Ireland, Germany, and Italy, Jews from Central and Eastern Europe, white cotton traders, scalawags and carpetbaggers, and former slaves up from the plantations farther south."[7]

Passenger steamers linked Memphis with river ports up and down the Mississippi, Ohio and Missouri Rivers. This helped the city to prosper, but also made it more vulnerable to the Yellow Fever epidemics that by 1878 had emptied the city of more than half the residents.

Before the Civil War, George W. Gardner lived in Terre Haute, where he left behind his first wife Mary and their children Ida Jane and George W. Gardner, Jr. to join the 2nd Illinois Light Artillery. By April 6-7, 1862, he was engaged in one of the bloodiest battles of the Civil War at Shiloh on the Tennessee River near Pittsburg Landing. The two-day Battle of Shiloh left 24,000 dead.

The Half Life of a Free Radical

As one survivor recounted: "The ground ...for half a mile was so thick with dead men one could walk the entire distance and step from one to another."[8]

My great-grandfather Gardner survived the war, but I have found no record of his whereabouts between 1862 and 1872, a chaotic decade in Memphis marked by much tragedy.

On April 27, 1865, the steamboat Sultana docked in Memphis to pick up coal. The boat was loaded to six times its legal capacity. Passengers included 2,300 just-released Union soldiers headed for home. Just seven miles north of Memphis the Sultana exploded and sank killing 1,700 of the crew and passengers.

Many Irish immigrants living then in Memphis provided the labor for cutting roads, erecting buildings, and constructing railroads, levees, and canals. Irish crews also staffed the area's trains and boats, and handled their cargoes.

Following the Union occupation of the city, the Irish made up the majority of Memphis' police force and fire companies. Conflicts were routine between Irish police and black Union soldiers. This was "heightened by ill-defined jurisdictions, since military patrols shared responsibility with the city constables for policing off-duty soldiers."[9]

The friction reached the combustion point in May 1866. A three-day riot ensued in the South Memphis neighborhood of Fort Pickering where many former slaves and black Union veterans had settled. Accounts vary, but all record a bloodbath:

> *The victims initially were only black soldiers, but the violence quickly spread to other blacks living just south of Memphis who were attacked by a white mob while their homes, schools, and churches were destroyed. White Northerners who worked as missionaries and schoolteachers in black schools were also targeted.*[10]

There is documentation of collusion and participation by Memphis police and firemen in the Memphis riots. Also among the rioters were the native-born artisans, professionals and small shopkeepers, intent on reestablishing the traditional social order and keeping blacks subordinate to white authority. In Tennessee then, the law enforcement and criminal justice systems relied heavily on "racist enforcement discretion to create a *de facto* Black Code," restricting many basic human and civil rights of black persons.[11]

Race From The Bottom

In the mid 1800's the Irish joined people of color in what has been called the "common culture of the lowly."[12] They soon discovered that the surest way to gain employment advantage in America required that they be seen as "whites." Irish were called "Negroes turned inside out," and blacks were derisively called "smoked Irish."[13] As they gained more electoral & political power, the Irish in America demanded that they be afforded access to the pre-existing construct of "white skin" privilege and all the benefits extended to other white men.

Back in Ireland, Daniel O'Connell, a leader of the Irish liberation struggle, recognized slavery for the evil it is and called on Irish in America to join the abolitionists. But for the most part, Irish immigrants failed to join the antislavery cause.[14] In this "work or starve" environment, "the Irish effort to gain the rights of white men collided with the black struggle to maintain the right to work."[15]

Congress passed a conscription law in 1863 subjecting men between twenty and forty-five years of age to the Civil War draft. Black men in New York were not drafted, and the rich could avoid conscription by payment of three hundred dollars, an amount far beyond the means of the Irish immigrant, most who lived in "pestilential misery."

For every Irish immigrant worker forced into the army, a black competitor would be next in line for the job. This volatile intersection of race, class and ethnic antagonism brought about the New York Draft Riots, a murderous assault by mobs of Irish immigrants on innocent blacks that took hundreds of lives and four days to quell.

It is sad learning now of this bleak history of collusion by Irish immigrants in the oppression of people of color.

My Hanrahan ancestors lived in Brooklyn at the time of the draft riots, but I heard no stories about that dark chapter of the Irish in America. It is a history that we must face to more fully understand the social and economic roots of racism. Yet it would not be until two decades after the Civil War before references to the Irish as a separate race disappeared from ethnological discussion.[16]

The German Connection

Richard Mayger, a maternal great-great-grandfather, whose ancestry was English, was born in Maryland in 1826. By 1848 he was living in Ohio County, Virginia, where he married Catharine Huff, born in Prussia in 1828. German was the most widely used language in the U.S. then, other than English, and is a language I never realized was an ancestral Mother tongue.

Germans immigrated to the United States between the 1830's to the 1860's for many reasons, including political oppression, religious persecution, and poor economic conditions. The arrivals before 1850 were mostly farmers who sought out the most productive land to apply their intensive farming techniques.

By the 1850 U.S. Federal Census twenty-four-year-old farmer Richard Mayger and his wife, twenty-two-year-old Catharine, are living in Wood County, Virginia, with Richard's siblings, Phebe E. Mayger, twelve, and Emma Mayger, nine. German-born laborers, John and Henry Huff, likely Catharine's brothers, ages eighteen and twenty, are also part of the household. The Census notes that neither brother could read nor write. Their daughter, Amanda Catharine was born in Virginia in 1852.

By the time of the 1860 U.S. Federal Census the Huff-Mayger family is living in Parkersburg, Virginia, a town situated at the confluence of the Ohio and Little Kanawha Rivers. Amanda Catharine, my great-grandmother to be, was seven then and her sister Phebe was four. They shared the home with Richard's sister, Emma, then nineteen. I do not know how Amanda made her way to Memphis from Virginia, perhaps through Kentucky. Amanda's early years are still a mystery.

In 1879, twenty-seven year-old Amanda Catharine Mayger married forty-seven-year-old Union veteran George W. Gardner. They became maternal great grandparents. How they met is also a mystery. I have yet to discover where Amanda's parents, Catharine Huff and Richard Mayger lived in their later years. Where did they die and where are they buried? I have found no record. What I do know is that Great-Grandmother Amanda Mayger Gardner lived in Memphis from 1880 until her death in 1929, and was an enduring influence in my Mama's early life.

Those Who Came Before

Jim Crow: Temper of the Times

Following the Civil War, Memphis' "Negro" citizens began to make political and economic inroads by registering to vote, establishing successful businesses and running for public office. Many in the white power structure sought ways to maintain authority and control.

During that time an estimated two or three black persons were lynched each week in the Southern states. Lynching became a specific "race ritual of terror."[17] It coincided with the systematic passage of state laws disenfranchising black voters and decreeing "separate but equal" civil and social facilities. This Jim Crow way of life was hardened into law with the Supreme Court 1896 *Plessy v. Ferguson* decision.

The term "Jim Crow," I later learned, has its origins in African folk culture. Jim Crow was a "trickster animal" incorporated into folk song and dance. In the 1830's, a New York minstrel performer, Thomas Rice, appropriated the song and dance he had seen in his travels down south. Back in Manhattan he performed in black face, mimicking the enslaved working man with a crooked leg and deformed shoulder he had seen dancing and singing: *"Weel about and turn about/ and do jis so/ Eb'ry time I weel about/ I jump Jim Crow."*[18]

"Jim Crow" later came to refer to the post-reconstruction exclusionary laws that prohibited equal rights for blacks.

In 1880, the same year Great-Grandmother Amanda moved to Memphis, the teacher and anti-lynching journalist Ida B. Wells also arrived. Wells was born into slavery in Holly Springs, Mississippi, in 1862. She and her seven siblings had been orphaned in the Yellow Fever epidemic. In 1889 she became part owner and editor of *The Memphis Free Speech and Headlight*.

Ida B. Wells was an effective critic of lynching, exposing "the racial and sexual double-standards that allowed white men to victimize black women with impunity."[19] Her writings give voice to the temper of the times in Memphis around the time my great grandmother was raising her children there.

In an 1892 editorial Wells wrote:

> *Nobody in this section believes the old threadbare lie that Negro men assault white women. If Southern white men are not careful they will*

The Half Life of a Free Radical

> *over-reach themselves and a conclusion will be reached which will be very damaging to the moral reputation of their women.*[20]

Her strong words incensed many white men in Memphis. The white publishers of *The Memphis Daily Appeal* printed a front-page story demanding that "the black wretch who had written that foul lie" should be tied to a stake at the corner of Main Street and publicly burned. Fortunately, Wells was out of town. White terrorists burned her newspaper office. She soon moved to Chicago as part of the great "Negro" exodus from the terrorist threats in the south. Wells continued her anti-lynching crusade throughout her long life.

As I write this today, the country is rife with racial tension. Structural racism persists. Reports of police killings of people of color are widely shared on social media, though no reliable official records exist, even today, of how many lives have been taken. Lynching by any other name is just as lethal.

In a January 1900 speech to a Chicago audience, Ida B. Wells-Barnett said of lynching:

> *It represents the cool, calculating deliberation of intelligent people who openly avow that there is an 'unwritten law' that justifies them in putting human beings to death without complaint under oath, without trial by jury, without opportunity to make defense, and without right of appeal.*[21]

A small memorial plaque to Ida B. Wells is prominent on Beale Street today. Yet this courageous human rights activist has yet to be honored with a statue in the Memphis neighborhood where her truth telling newspaper was published.

Today there is a statue of Elvis Presley, the King of Rock 'N Roll, on the west end of Beale Street and a smaller statue of W. C. Handy, the King of the Blues, a few blocks east. A proposal to Memphis City Council in 2012 to rename Nathan Bedford Forrest Park for Ida B. Wells did not carry.

Certainly my great grandparents Amanda and George Gardner had to be aware of Ida B. Wells, whose letters to the editor were frequently published in local papers. I can only hope that they also raised their voices against the racial violence. Their Memphis home was a little over two miles from the Beale Street Baptist Church basement offices of Wells' paper, *The Memphis Free Speech and Headlight*, "the most radical and talked about newspaper in Memphis."

"Yellow Jack" Up in Old Pinch

When Amanda and George Gardner married, Memphis was still in recovery from the so-called "Yellow Jack" epidemic, considered to be "a catastrophe of even greater magnitude than that experienced during the war or the reconstruction which followed."[22]

An epidemic of Bubonic Plague, Asiatic Cholera and Yellow Fever was widespread in Memphis in 1873 and again in 1878, when 25,000 of the rich and well-to-do whites, most living in the large Victorian homes along Adams Avenue & Jefferson Street, fled the city. In a 1946 article in the *Saturday Evening Post* about those times, the author noted:

> *Of the 20,000 who stayed, only 5000 were white, and, of these, 4,000 died. Of the 15,000 Negroes who had nowhere to go and no way to get there the Lord bestowed a certain blessed immunity. Only 7 percent of their number died.*[23]

Freed slaves and black Union Army veterans in Memphis had a strong immunity to these so-called "yellow jack" epidemics, carried by river traffic up the Mississippi Valley and transmitted by mosquitoes from human to human. It is likely that repeated exposure to Yellow Fever over many generations in West Africa provided many blacks with a higher resistance to the disease. Many remained in Memphis to care for the sick, bury the dead, and rebuild Memphis.

In 1880 Amanda Mayger and George Gardner lived at 365 Sixth Street. That year their first daughter, my Great Aunt Georgia Frances Gardner, was born. She shares a November 26 birthday with my daughter, Jessica Colleen. Next came May Blossom, on May 24, 1883. Then Novetta Catherine, my grandmother-to-be, born November 15, 1888, sixty years to the day before my own birth. Their brother, Mayger Leon, followed in 1889.

The Gardner family later lived at 195 Looney Avenue near Memphis' oldest neighborhood, the twenty-five-block area known as "The Pinch." The neighborhood was derisively so called because

The Half Life of a Free Radical

of the pinched-gut appearance of early Irish immigrants who settled there after fleeing The Great Hunger. Most worked on the railroads or on the river. Many made shanty homes using discarded lumber from old Mississippi river flat boats along Catfish Bay near where the Wolf River joins the Mississippi.

St. Brigid's Catholic Church at Third Street and Overton Avenue, founded in 1870 to serve Irish immigrants, by 1873 had lost over 800 of parishioners to the "yellow jack" fevers that ravaged Memphis. Many of the nuns and priests who heroically stayed to care for the sick also perished.

Pinch resident Mary Harris, who had already survived the horror of famine in Cork, lost her entire family to the fever in 1879. She wrote of the overwhelming grief of the times:

> *...The dead surrounded us. They were buried at night quickly and without ceremony. All about my house I could hear weeping and the cries of delirium. One by one, my four little children sickened and died. I washed their little bodies and got them ready for burial. My husband caught the fever and died. I sat alone through nights of grief. No one could come...*[24]

Mary Harris stayed on in Memphis to nurse the sufferers until the "plague was stamped out." She then moved to Chicago where more hardship waited. Tempered by adversity, she rose to become the legendary union crusader and fiery speaker against child labor and worker exploitation known today as Mother Jones.

I like to think that Great-Grandmother Amanda might have crossed paths in the neighborhood with Mary Harris, who became a hero of mine long before I knew of her Memphis connection.

We Memphis children of the 1950's were not taught the history of independent and fearless women like Ida B. Wells, who challenged racist terrorism, nor of Mother Jones, who crusaded against labor injustice. Neither did we hear of The Great Hunger in Ireland and the forced exile of many of our own ancestors, nor of the horrific reality of lynching. Instead, in our parochial school we were indoctrinated with stories of centuries-old martyrs of the Roman Catholic Church whose lives and times were far removed from the world we knew.

Those Who Came Before

The Great Hunger

Catholics in Ireland had for centuries resisted the English subjugation institutionalized in a series of racist codes known collectively as The Penal Laws. These laws, described in the 1790's by statesman Edmund Burke, were "as well fitted for the oppression, impoverishment, and degradation of a people, and the debasement, in them, of human nature itself, as ever proceeded from the perverted ingenuity of man."[25]

The Penal Laws imposed a caste status out of which no Catholic, no matter how wealthy, could escape. Though these anti-Catholic laws have long since been repealed, Ireland's "troubles," rooted in centuries past, persist even today.

During the terrible years of The Great Hunger (1846-1851), known in Gaelic as *An Gorta Mor*, a million Irish Catholics died of starvation and epidemic disease. Mostly-absentee landlords evicted as many as 500,000 impoverished farmers and their families.

Between 1845-1855, two million people were forced to abandon their homeland. Historian Jim Donnelly, who shares a family surname, writes:

> *There existed after 1847, at least an absolute sufficiency of food that could have prevented mass starvation, if it had been properly distributed so as to reach the smallholders and labourers of the west and the south of Ireland.*[26]

At the time, historians note, the city of Cork alone reported 5,000 beggars in its streets. All the animals were gone. The people were walking skeletons. Cork artist, James Mahony, traveled around the West of Ireland with sketchpad in hand documenting the horrors for the *Illustrated London News*:

> *I saw the dying, the living, and the dead, lying indiscriminately upon the same floor without anything between them and the cold earth, save a few miserable rags upon them. ...not a single house out of 500 could boast of being free from death and fever.*[27]

Poor Paddy Works on the Railway

In 1848 Cork was still reeling from The Great Hunger. My maternal great-great-grandfathers, John Donnelly and Patric Duffy, and their families, were forced to abandon their homeland. There were reports of a Cholera epidemic on the way. Death and despair, eviction and emigration was taking its toll.

John Donnelly traveled with his two young sons, John and Dennis, who was born in Cork in 1838 and would become a maternal great grandfather. John later sent for his wife, Margaret Martin, and daughters, Ann and Catherine.

As one family story goes, Dennis had been drinking whiskey during the cold ocean passage when he fell overboard. He appealed to the Blessed Virgin for rescue, promising he would never take another drink. Dennis was a teetotaler from that day forward.

The Donnelly men found work as railroad laborers, one of the most dangerous occupations at the time. They shoveled mud, blasted tunnels, laid track, spiked rails and graded and constructed trestles. A common expression heard among the workers then was "an Irishman was buried under every tie."

By 1854, the Donnelly family lived near the Tennessee River in McEwen, Humphreys County, Tennessee, about fifty-seven miles west of Nashville. They are listed in historical accounts among McEwen's early Irish Catholics and helped build old St. Patrick's Church.

My great-great-grandparents, Patric Duffy and Ann Kennedy, had been shopkeepers in Galway before they left for America in 1848. They traveled with their daughters Ann, Margaret, and Maria, who was born in Galway in 1844. Maria would become a maternal great grandmother.

The family took passage among wailing children and emaciated bodies, crowded together on a disease-ridden "coffin ship."

"A more motley crowd I never beheld; of all ages, from the infant to the feeble grandsire and withered crone," wrote Protestant traveler Robert Whyte, describing the Irish passengers in his 1847 on-ship diary.[28]

According to family stories, during the ocean crossing a child about Maria's age fell sick and died, likely from Typhus. Passengers made a small box for her casket, tied it in burlap and weighed it down

Those Who Came Before

with coals before sliding it overboard. With little time for more than a Hail Mary, the child sank beneath the waves. Burial at sea was the fate of as many as thirty percent of those taking the five-to ten-week ocean passage. Some ships never arrived.

The so-called "coffin ships" were small and ill-equipped, and often not seaworthy. Many were insured for more than they were worth, so the captains paid little heed to the well being of their human cargo. As many as 300 persons were crowded into steerage on six-by six-foot tiered bunks, each bunk shared by four desperate travelers.[29]

Typhus, Dysentery, famine and despair were deadly companions. So many bodies were disposed at sea that sharks would follow the ships in anticipation. A passenger on one such ship gave voice to the despair:

> *We thought we couldn't be worse off than we war; but now to our sorrow we knowt be differ...the minit the breath is out of our bodies, flung into the sea to be eaten up by them horrid sharks.*[30]

The Duffy family lived for a time in Pennsylvania where their son, Thomas, was born in 1855. By 1857 the Duffys had made their way to Tennessee where they joined the Donnellys in McEwen.

Whenever a train rumbles past sounding its haunting whistle along the tracks, I think of my Donnelly-Duffy ancestors and the hard labor that they endured to make their way in America. The Irish chantey, "Paddy on the Railway," captures the spirit of the times:

> *In 1841 the corduroy breeches I put on*
> *Me corduroy breeches I put on*
> *To work upon the railway, the railway*
> *I'm weary of the railway*
> *Poor Paddy works on the railway.*
>
> *I was wearing corduroy breeches*
> *Digging ditches*
> *Pulling switches*
> *Dodging Pitches*
> *I was working on the railway.*[31]

The Half Life of a Free Radical

Tennessee's Little Ireland

In the early 1800's, as many as 300 Irish-Catholic immigrants were offered Tennessee land for a mere twenty-five cents an acre as an inducement to settle in the area around McEwen. By 1860 the population of Humphreys County included 9,096 whites, 1,463 enslaved persons, and fourteen free blacks. Most residents were farmers who settled along the rich river bottoms and fertile valleys. They cultivated wheat, rye, oats, tobacco, and cotton. Indian corn was a major cash crop.

At the outbreak of the Civil War, only twenty-four miles of track for the Nashville and Northwestern Railroad had been laid from Nashville to Kingston Springs. Federal troops camped at Johnsonville to oversee the 1,118 laborers who completed the line to the Tennessee River, opening it up to Union supplies.

"Much of the labor came from free blacks and escaped slaves joined by Irish immigrants."[32]

Many of the blacks, impressed into labor by the Federal troops, would become part of the Twelfth and Thirteenth United States Colored Infantry. They camped at Yellow Trestle, less than a mile from McEwen and guarded the railroad from Confederate attacks. Union troops referred to the area around McEwen as "Buttermilk Station," because of the fresh buttermilk sold by the local Irish farmers. By the end of the Civil War the area became known as "Little Ireland."

I traveled through McEwen and Waverly in 2014. It was my first visit to the Tennessee lands where my Duffy and Donnelly ancestors had lived. In the Waverly County archives I found records listing Great-Grandfather Dennis Donnelly with real estate holdings valued in 1870 at $3,000, a considerable amount of property at the time.

I don't know what role my Duffy and Donnelly relatives may have played in the Civil War, beyond their work on the railroad, or on what side their sympathies may have rested. Many young Irish men in McEwen did join forces with the Confederates forming part of the 10th Tennessee regiment, known as the "Sons of Erin."

McEwen has celebrated its Irish heritage since 1854 with the annual St. Patrick Irish Picnic and Homecoming, the longest-running community picnic in the country. Most of the records of St. Patrick's Church were long ago lost in a fire, but the annual picnic carries

Those Who Came Before

forward the spirit of the hard working Irish Catholic immigrants who settled there before the Civil War.

My maternal great-grandparents, Maria Duffy and Dennis Donnelly, met in McEwen and were married in Nashville on May 14, 1863. At the time, Nashville was occupied by Union troops. Maria was only nineteen and Dennis was twenty-five. Their first-born daughter, Margaret (1864), and twin sons, James and Tim (1865), died soon after birth.

The family was listed in the 1870 Census of Humphreys County, Tennessee, where Dennis was a farmer with land on the South Fork of Blue Creek on the Duck River. Dennis and Maria Donnelly had nine other children born in McEwen, including my maternal grandfather, Thomas Joseph, born in 1880.

In 1894 digging in the area around the Duck River uncovered what is known as the Duck River Cache of prehistoric Native American art. The ancient settlement was a center of prehistoric trade, though it had declined and disappeared by A.D. 1500, long before my Irish ancestors settled there.

In 1886, Dennis sold the land in McEwen and moved the family to Nashville where he built the family home on Cedar Street (now Charlotte Avenue) behind a knitting mill. I've been told it had a long porch where neighbors and family spent much of their leisure time. The family attended St. Joseph Catholic Church, long since demolished and replaced by the Nashville Electric Service.

Family friends remember that Great Grandfather Dennis wore a well-trimmed beard and was a very gentle person, and that Maria smoked a corn-cob pipe, which she knocked out quickly when visitors arrived.

Marriage & Mayhem in Memphis

Thomas Joseph Donnelly moved to Memphis from Nashville in 1910. He found work as a foreman with the American Snuff Company. The tobacco firm had relocated from New York at the turn of the century, and occupied a block long, two-story brick building at 46 Keel Street. The structure is still standing up in the old Pinch neighborhood near the Mississippi river. The Memphis population then was more than 100,000, nearly twice the pre-Yellow

The Half Life of a Free Radical

Fever census, and "a hotbed of machine politics" under the direction of E. H. "Boss" Crump.

Grandfather-to-be Donnelly lived on Looney Street, a neighbor of his soon-to-be wife, Novetta Catherine Gardner, who worked then as a bookkeeper at the John Gerber Department Store. Novetta lived with her parents, George and Amanda and her older sister Georgia. Another sister, May Blossom, by then had moved to Birmingham, Alabama. Their brother, Mayger Leon, was soon to become a "doughboy" in World War I.

In 1912 the Wolf River overflowed its banks and flooded The Pinch neighborhood. Hundreds of homes and businesses were destroyed and as many as 1,200 people were driven from their homes. The flood waters brought more disease and pestilence to the city. After the flood, Tom Donnelly moved to 887 Seventh Street, in a house still standing today, though boarded and vacant in the now blighted neighborhood.

On May 21,1915, Thomas Joseph Donnelly married Novetta Catherine Gardner in a civil ceremony in nearby Somerville, Tennessee. The couple set up housekeeping at 695 Sixth Street. Novetta and Thomas had two daughters, Novetta Katherine, who the family called "Dee," and my mother-to-be, Alice Elizabeth, born in Memphis on October 29, 1917.

In my research of family history, and of the history of Memphis, I have learned much that was never taught in school nor shared in family stories. In a recent article in the *Memphis Flyer*, the author contends:

> *We have a responsibility to reckon with the whole history of our home places, even the stories deliberately left out of the history books, even the places left unmarked, the names we no longer know.* [33]

The writer, Martha Parks, recounts an horrific murder near Memphis in May 1917— the year of my Mama's birth:

Black woodchopper Ell Persons was "burned alive before thousands of spectators." The mob acted in broad daylight.

I cannot know how my grandparents, Novetta and Thomas Donnelly, who lived in Memphis then and who could not have failed to read the lurid press reports— I cannot know how they responded. Did they know that the charred and severed head of Ell Persons was photographed for postcards, and then taken to Beale Street and thrown into a group of black pedestrians?

As I write today, this nation's newspapers and social media report frequent vigilante and police murders of people of color in circumstances every bit as racist and deadly.

We have a responsibility now not only to reckon with "the whole history of our home places," but to challenge the deadly echoes of racist terrorism in the present time, however it manifests. The recent movement of whites, Showing Up for Racial Justice, is one such effort.

Tuberculosis: Number One Killer

It wasn't just racial terror that claimed lives in Memphis in the early 1900's. Tuberculosis was a number one killer. My maternal grandmother, Novetta Catherine, died of the airborne, contagious disease on November 28, 1919. She was just thirty-one years old.

The only treatment for TB then was bed rest and fresh air. When the dread disease hit the Donnelly family, the whole household was quarantined. Mama later recalled that her daddy was permitted out of quarantine only to go to work. He had to go and come through the back door to walk to his job at the nearby American Snuff Company. Novetta's mother, Amanda Gardner, by then a widow, helped to care for the two motherless Donnelly sisters.

On January 10, 1922, tragedy again darkened their lives. Mama's older sister, Novetta Katherine, died of tubercular meningitis. She was only six-years-old. The obituary printed in *The Commercial Appeal* read, in part:

> ...*white winged visitors made a short stop at the motherless home of Mr. T. J. Donnelly. ...so soothing was their presence that the gentle pure soul of his little 6 year old daughter, lured by the sound of their heavenly music followed them forward to the great White Throne.*[34]

The Gardner-Donnelly homes were at 919 N. Third Street, and later at 193 Bickford Avenue in North Memphis. Today many of these houses have been demolished or stand boarded and vacant among the still-occupied homes of African-American poor. Bickford

Park, where Mama played as a child, is still a block of green amid the urban decay.

With tuberculosis taking such a hard toll on the family, Mama's health was closely monitored. As a means of fortifying her, family physician Dr. E. C. Ham prescribed a home-brew remedy. Tennessee had a strong Temperance Movement then outlawing sale of liquor.

"My daddy, a teetotaler, made a vat of home brew regularly, bottled it in Coca-Cola bottles, and stored it on the floor of his bedroom closet to ripen then placed it in the icebox on the back porch to chill. I drank one bottle per day after school," my mother wrote.35

When she was nine, Mama attended the Lions' Open Air School, one of several so-called "preventoriums," where the classroom windows remained wide open in the unheated building. The ample fresh air and sunshine was considered a remedy for children who had been exposed to tuberculosis.

Grandpa Donnelly never remarried. Mama told me her widowed daddy had a "lady friend," Miss Florence Furr. I found her name in the 1921 *Memphis City Directory*. She was working as a clerk and living then at 681 Keel Avenue in the same North Memphis neighborhood where the Donnellys lived.

The River's Mighty Rampage

When Mama was ten, the great Mississippi River flood of 1927 inundated the homes of nearly one million in the Delta lowlands. It swept over the banks all along its course in what *The Commercial Appeal* called "its mightiest rampage."

Chicago-based Blues musician Blind Lemon Jefferson recorded the scene near Memphis in his song, "Rising High Water:"

> *Water in Arkansas, people screaming in Tennessee*
> *Oh, people screaming in Tennessee*
> *If I don't leave Memphis,*
> *Backwater spill all over poor me*
>
> *People, since its raining,*
> *It has been for nights and days*
> *People, since its raining,*

Those Who Came Before

Has been for nights and days
Thousands people stands on the hill,
Looking down where they used to stay.[36]

The flood displaced over 200,000 people, two-thirds who were black field laborers and their families. People of color in the Delta were herded into camps and denied adequate food, medical treatment, and shelter. Relief administrators siphoned off funds and supplies.[37]

After the flood waters receded, tens of thousands of black families moved to the big cities of the North, particularly Chicago. There are tragic similarities in the treatment of people of color in the 1927 Mississippi River flood, and those impacted by the 2005 tragedy of Hurricane Katrina. In both disasters, the levees broke and the Mississippi river inundated the homes of African-American communities. In New Orleans, the flood refugees were directed to the Louisiana Super Dome, and then abandoned for days without adequate food, medical treatment or shelter in what many likened to a concentration camp.

In 1937, another catastrophic flood hit the Mississippi Delta, filling Memphis with 20,000 refugees from low-lying rural areas in Arkansas and Mississippi. Mama lived then with her daddy on Jefferson Avenue near Crosstown and the old Curb Market. It is a neighborhood our family is well acquainted with, and a crossroads in our goings and comings from school and church and home throughout the years.

A Literary Alliance

Mama shared many stories of her Grandmother Amanda, who she described in her memoir: *In the Pinch: Memphis Memories*, as "the loving presence that held things together."

She remembered her Grandmother Amanda as an avid reader, a talented needle crafter and skilled basket weaver. Amanda wore her hair very long, and tied in a bun. When fashion went to short hair she cut it and "it sprang into beautiful waves."

Mama and her grandmother would read together every night, snuggled by the fire in the black-leather Morris chair in the home they shared with Grandpa Donnelly on Bickford Street. She writes of the time in her memoir:

The Half Life of a Free Radical

> *Learning to enjoy reading, to learn the authors' message, to dissect the methods used to create a mood or a scene, to thrill to the smell of print and new books, to make daily news an integral part of my daily life was the legacy she left me. She was financially a poor woman but rich in love, wealthy beyond belief in love and intelligence.*[38]

Sometimes Mama and her grandmother would take the trolley to the Lyceum Theater at Second and Jefferson Street. Mama remembers seeing the play, *Abie's Irish Rose*, there. It is the story of an Irish Catholic girl and a young Jewish man who marry despite the objections of their families. The Lyceum and other Memphis landmarks ultimately fell to the wreckers' ball.

Mama attended St. Brigid's Catholic School in The Pinch for her first few elementary grades. Both the school and church have long-since been demolished.

She occasionally spoke of her Grandmother Amanda's interest in the women's suffrage movement and of her grandmother's friendship with Elizabeth Lyle Saxon, a one-time president of the Tennessee Suffrage Movement, and author of *A Southern Woman's War Time Remembrances*, published in 1905, "for the benefit of the Shiloh Monument Fund." Saxon, wrote:

"I saw slavery in its bearing upon my sex. I saw that it teemed with injustice and shame to all womankind, and I hated it."[39]

Grandmother Amanda occasionally attended the First Congregational Church, Mama remembered. Many women in that Protestant denomination had been recruited south by the American Missionary Association, an integrated organization that worked along with the Bureau of Refugees, Freedmen and Abandoned Land, commonly called the Freedmen's Bureau, to build schools and colleges for freed slaves and to encourage their participation in the political process. Perhaps it was through such an organization that my great grandmother found her way to Memphis. I don't know.

In 1929, Mama's Grandmother Amanda fell sick while on a Donnelly-Gardner family vacation in Warm Springs, Kentucky. She died in Memphis on August 7, 1929. The family doctor, E. C. Ham, listed the cause of her death as "lobar pneumonia and nephritis." Mama was not quite twelve, and once again, a motherless child. Her childhood was marked with illness, grief, and separation.

Those Who Came Before

Grandpa's Nashville sister, Mary E. Connelly, and her nineteen-year-old daughter, Ann, moved to Memphis to help out. Grandpa was fifty, his widowed sister was sixty-eight. The arrangement didn't last very long. As Mama remembered, they missed the farm in Nashville. The old Connelly farm house is still standing at Sawyer Brown Road, right off of Charlotte Pike.

The years of the Great Depression hit hard in Memphis. However, the American Snuff Company continued to prosper. Grandpa Donnelly's 1929 Income Tax return lists wages from the Snuff Company of $3,190. Stock sales and real estate income brought his earnings that year to $8,275.36. It was a sizable income during the Great Depression.

Grandpa was the president of The Christian Sentinels, a charitable group that eventually became the St. Vincent de Paul Society. Often on Sunday mornings after Mass, Mama recalled, her daddy would go to the rectory and talk with the pastor at St. Brigid's church, Father Whitfield, about requests from families in distress. Then, with addresses in hand, he would visit the homes and offer what help the group could.

Around this time grandpa enrolled Mama in boarding school at Sacred Heart Academy in Helena, Arkansas, sixty-five miles southwest of Memphis. She later attended Nazareth Junior College and then Cardome Academy in Georgetown, Kentucky. She returned to Memphis in 1937 to attend St. Agnes College, soon to be renamed Siena College, and taught by nuns of the Dominican Order.

Mama became deathly ill with Typhus before her last year of college and was not expected to live. She was cared for night and day by two nurses, Miss Rose Bayer, an Austrian immigrant, and Mrs. Bluin. She stayed in touch with these women throughout their lives.

Mama recovered and graduated from Siena College in 1941 with a B. S. in English and a minor in Journalism. She then worked at a variety of jobs, including City Editor for the *Clarksdale Daily Register and Daily News* in nearby Clarksdale, Mississippi. She also attended flight school and learned to fly a two-seater, single-engine prop airplane known as a Taylor Craft.

I don't recall Mama telling me about the April 29, 1944, crash of a U.S. Army B-25 bomber in the densely-populated mid-town neighborhood where she lived. According to press reports, the pilot desperately tried to land in the parking lot behind Southern Bowling

The Half Life of a Free Radical

Lanes on Cleveland before the plane smashed into a two-story home at 222 North Claybrook behind the bowling alley. The plane exploded into a fireball that burned for hours. Seven people died that day in one of the worst disasters in Memphis aviation history.[40]

At that time, Mama worked as an air traffic controller at the airport, and her uncle, Mayger Gardner, was a fireman. It is likely they would have had stories to share had I known to ask.

My Mama was keenly intelligent, well educated, accomplished and refined, with a kind heart for others. Her life was soon to take a dramatic turn with her marriage in 1945 to my Brooklyn-born father, Daniel Gerard Hanrahan.

Hanrahans & Mahoneys

My paternal great-great-grandparents in the Hanrahan family line, Timothy Hanrahan and Ellen Cooney, emigrated from the west of Ireland. I have found few records of their lives. They fled Ireland in the pre-famine years. Perhaps they were among the almost 400,000 Irish people who left for North America between 1828 and 1837 when the British government repealed all restrictions on emigration.

Throughout the early 1830's Cholera repeatedly ravaged the poorest classes in Ireland. The potato crop failed on a local level in eight out of ten years and the winter of 1838 was so savage that cattle froze to death in the fields.[41]

The poorest among the emigrants who made the transatlantic crossing endured horrific conditions on the ship. They had a lower priority than baggage or livestock. As many as 2000 people crowded onto an open deck in all weather, clinging to each other to avoid being washed overboard.

Timothy Hanrahan, born in Ireland about 1815, is listed in the 1840 U.S. Federal Census living in Ward 13, New York City, as head of the household that included four "free white persons (males) under 20." Timothy's son, Daniel James, born in New York in 1843, became my paternal great-grandfather.

Daniel James married Josephine G. O'Shea about 1872. Josephine O'Shea's father, Michael O'Shea, was also from Ireland. Family stories tell that Josephine's mother, Eleanor Lloyd, was related

Those Who Came Before

to the famous "Lloyds of London" who had disowned Eleanor for marrying an Irishman.

Daniel James and Josephine O'Shea Hanrahan had seven sons and three daughters: Charles, Josephine, Daniel Francis (my grandfather-to-be), and Frank, Alexander, George, Estelle, Walter, and Percival. By the 1905 U.S. Federal Census, the family were living at 642 Prospect Place in Brooklyn near the newly-completed 526-acre Prospect Park, designed by Frederick Law Olmstead.

Great-Grandfather Daniel James worked as a flag man in the Brooklyn Rapid Transit yard. In the summer of 1907, when he was sixty-five, he was killed on the tracks of the "L," or elevated train. The story made the *Brooklyn Daily Eagle*.[42]

His death certificate notes his broken ribs, legs and crushed skull from the front wheels of the train. At the time of his death, the family lived in a brownstone apartment still standing at 448 Fourteenth Street in Brooklyn. My paternal grandfather, Daniel Francis, was educated at The Cooper-Union in the East Village neighborhood of Manhattan. The tuition-free private school for the "Advancement of Science and Art" was open to students of "superior intelligence" independent of their race, religion, sex, wealth or social status.[43] Daniel Francis became a chemist, and was perhaps in the first Hanrahan generation to benefit from a university education.

My paternal great-great grandparents in the Mahoney family line, Michael Mahoney, born in Ireland in 1816, and his wife Margaret, emigrated from Cork in the pre-famine years between 1830-35. They made their way to Utica, New York, at the foot of the Adirondack Mountains. They had five daughters and three sons. Roseanna, Hannah, Ellen, Mary, and Margaret. Their first son, my great-grandfather James Mahoney, was born in New York in 1838. His brothers were John and Thomas.

James Mahoney married Katherine Flynn. They had nineteen children! My paternal grandmother-to-be, Cora Elizabeth, born in Utica, New York in 1877, was their eighth child.

In the 1910 census, Katherine Flynn Mahoney is listed as "head of household," with thirteen "living" children out of nineteen "born." I add their names here, as that is all I have found about these great aunts and uncles: Julia, Frances, Nellie, Timothy, Frank, Catharine, Clara, Mary, my Grandmother Cora, George, Cecilia, William, Pearl and Freida.

The Half Life of a Free Radical

Daniel Francis Hanrahan married Cora Elizabeth Mahoney on April 15, 1908. They had six children. My father, Daniel Gerard, born in Brooklyn July 18, 1911, was their first, followed by siblings Rita (Dolly), William, Mary, Raymond and Regina. The family later moved to Fairview, New Jersey, where as noted in the 1920 U.S. Federal Census, Grandfather Hanrahan was employed with the New Jersey Coloring Company.

It took the mobilizations of World War II for the New York-New Jersey Hanrahan-Mahoney clan of my father, Daniel Gerard, to connect with the Tennessee Gardner-Donnelly clan of my mother, Alice Elizabeth. Much of this story now will take us back to Memphis on the high bluffs above the Mississippi where Mama and Daddy raised their nine children.

"In Sickness and in Health"

Daniel Gerard Hanrahan arrived in Memphis in the Spring of 1942. He was thirty-one and a staff sergeant in the Army Air Force. He had worked in the Pentagon before being stationed in Memphis. Alice Elizabeth Donnelly was at Memphis' Union Station, a volunteer with the United Service Organization (USO) welcoming soldiers arriving for duty at the nearby Millington Naval Air Technical Training Center.

"Your daddy caught my eye when he first stepped off the train," Mama once told me. "He asked me where to go to Sunday Mass," She laughed as she recalled first meeting her husband-to-be. "He showed up at Sacred Heart Catholic Church the very next Sunday," she said. "He sat just a few pews behind me, and then followed me down Jefferson Avenue as I walked home to the apartment I shared with my Daddy."

Dan Hanrahan not only caught our mother's eye, but her heart as well. They married on May Day, 1945. Mama was a brown-eyed beauty of twenty-seven, lean and tall, with an elegant stature she carried throughout her long life. She wore a white satin wedding gown with a long veil that covered her shoulder-length raven hair. Daddy was handsome in a James Cagney kind of way in his Army uniform. They walked from the church into their long marriage through an honor guard of crossed swords held by Daddy's Army colleagues.

Those Who Came Before

Thirty-five years later our family gathered in that same Sacred Heart Catholic Church for Daddy's funeral Mass. All my eight siblings, except John Vincent, sat with Mama in the front pew. Johnny, the family bard, was somewhere in Arkansas in a wandering mood and did not get the word in time.

Mama wore a simple green dress printed with small black shamrocks. Bearing her grief with characteristic dignity, she took my hand as we walked together down the center aisle she had walked as a bride, this time to say her last goodbye.

My parents' marriage "in sickness and in health ...till death do us part," was not an easy alliance. They began their life together in Asheville, North Carolina, surrounded by the same ancient mountains that shelter me now. Many of my childhood drawings included mountain silhouettes, somehow imprinted on my young mind long before I made my home here.

Daddy was stationed with the Army Air Corps Weather Intelligence Service. He worked in what he said was a secret project breaking Japanese weather codes. Recently I heard that government workers in Asheville may have played some part in the highly-secret Manhattan Project that developed the atomic bomb, though I have not been able to verify if that is so.

Like many who lived through World War II, my parents may have shared the belief that the atomic bomb, developed in the nearby "Secret City" of Oak Ridge, Tennessee, hastened the end of the war. I do not know. I have for many years joined others at the gates of the Oak Ridge bomb plant to stand in opposition to the continued production of nuclear weapons.

When I first arrived in Asheville in 1989, after years of wandering, I felt at last that I had found my place. My home is in the Battery Park Apartments on the thirteenth floor of the 1924-vintage former hotel. My view of the surrounding Blue Ridge Mountains is more beautiful than my childhood drawings could ever have depicted. And who could have guessed that I would come to live just across the street from the Grove Arcade Public Market, the building taken over in 1942 for use by the Army Air Corps., and the very building where my father worked during his time in Asheville.

On Mama's final visit to Asheville in 1997 we drove around until she found the house she and Daddy had shared on Gracelyn Avenue. She reminisced about her daily walks around nearby Beaver Lake and lamented the commercial highway Merrimon Avenue has become, replacing many of the beautiful homes she remembered.

Beaver Lake is a bird sanctuary now. I sometimes retreat there when I need a quiet spot away from the asphalt and traffic of the cityscape. As I walk the paths, I often think about Mama and her early days of marriage before alcoholism took its poisonous toll on our family and the burden of nine children sapped her vital energy.

What's a Mother to Do?

Daddy was discharged from the Army on February 8, 1946. Mary Alice, their first child, was born at St. Joseph Hospital in Memphis on February 25, 1946. Soon after they moved to Daddy's hometown, Belleville, New Jersey, where they lived at 116 Division Avenue. Mama told us she could almost see the Empire State Building, about five miles from the house.

Daddy took the train to Fordham University and St. John's University School of Law in Brooklyn, and then to a night job, while Mama stayed home in Belleville with Mary Alice.

Our oldest sister Mary was not yet one year old when the twins, Thomas Patrick and Daniel Joseph, were born on February 18, 1947.

Less than two years later, I joined the family. Mama told me that it was quite late that winter afternoon of November 15, 1948, when Daddy made it home and she was able to make her way to the hospital delivery room in Newark, where I was born.

As Mama once told me: "All the way to the hospital, I was thinking: What am I going to do with this one!"

I'm not sure my Mama ever figured that out.

2

North Memphis Meanderings

*Like a sad old melody/ Tears you up but sets you free/
That's how Memphis Lives in me.*
— Chad Kimball

I was not quite two years old when our family returned to Memphis in 1950. My five younger siblings were born in swift succession: Eileen Maria, Michael Francis, John Vincent, Regina Marian, and Robert Anthony. They joined Mary Alice, Daniel Joseph, Thomas Patrick, and me, Clare Marie.

As is common in Irish Catholic families, we each were given the name of at least one saint whose influence it was hoped would direct our lives on the right path. Each girl's name was some variation of Mary, the Virgin Mother. Such a large family is the almost inevitable outcome of the church law that forbade the use of "artificial" birth control "under pain of sin." Catholic women were expected to rely on what was called the "rhythm method."

"If I get pregnant again, I'll kill myself!" our Mother wrote in her "Ladies' Fare" column for the Catholic newspaper, the *Tennessee Register*. She went on to explain:

> *The basic conflict is the woman's will with what she may think is the will of God. ...You may feel God is asking 'too much' when He expects you to endure again the barbed words, unkind glances, the discomfort*

The Half Life of a Free Radical

and disfigurement of pregnancy, the pangs of birth, and the demands of a newborn child. Don't reject your special graces, use them while prayerfully meditating on the story of the Annunciation. Imitate Mary's boundless trust in God and kill yourself to attain supernatural life.[44]

"Kill yourself ?" This attitude of submission to the will of God may have carried Mama through her many difficult times, but it has been at the root of some of the conflict between us that continued throughout my adolescence. I was willful, and not inclined to obedience. Reading over surviving clips of Mama's published writing, I get a sense of how she may have felt during those years when, one after the other, she bore her nine children.

I know Mama endured the judgment and "barbed words" of many because of her adherence to Catholic dogma regarding birth control. One time when we were quite young, a pair of women came to the door offering literature on birth control. Mama was not amused. She called all her children around her to the porch and then challenged the women: "You choose which ones I should not have had."

In the days prior to my own impetuous and ill-fated marriage, the week after my twenty-first birthday, Daddy took me aside to remind me: "Birth control is against the church." Mama's counsel consisted of a dire warning delivered as she stood in the cellar sorting the laundry piled at her feet: "If you're getting married for sex, it won't be what you think it is." She was right.

Mama always wanted a large family, Eileen told me. "She said she had dreamed of it since she was a child." By the time that dream was realized, though, it may have lost its luster.

Regina remembers one of Mama's oft-repeated expressions: "Oh, the joys of Motherhood..." followed after a pregnant pause with the clincher: "they are few and far between."

Now and again Mama would proclaim to her children:

"Don't bring your screaming babies home to me." But in time she became a most loving and available grandmother to the twelve grandchildren and six great-grandchildren lucky enough to have known her.

North Memphis Meanderings

Mrs. Bird's Burgeoning Bungalow

Faxon is an avenue of tall oaks standing two by two in almost every tiny front yard. Throughout our childhood, these trees provided blessed breezes and cooling shade in the summer and the sparkling beauty of ice-sheathed branches in the winter. Several generations of Hanrahans have posed for photos marking First Communions, Confirmations, Graduations, and other special occasions in front of these still-standing, sentry-like oaks.

The two-bedroom, red-brick, 1920 vintage house at 1063 Faxon, which became our Memphis home, is located in Speedway Terrace, a North Memphis working-class neighborhood just a few miles east of the Mississippi river. We shared the home with our Grandfather Thomas Joseph (T. J.) Donnelly.

Mama often mentioned that our house had once been home to Mrs. Bird, a family friend who died before my birth. I recently found a listing for a Miss Marion Bird in the 1915 *Memphis City Directory*. She was employed then at the American Snuff Company where our grandfather worked, and her home was at 285 Looney, a neighbor of my Donnelly grandparents. The 1942 *Memphis City Directory* listed Josephine Ella Bird and her husband, George W. Bird, living at 1063 Faxon. Eileen remembers hearing that George Bird may have been a river-boat captain.

Mama and Grandpa inherited the Bird's 1,437 square foot bungalow. Grandpa signed over his half interest to Mama in 1955. She kept the property in her name from then on, until she moved to her retirement apartment in the 1980's. Over the years Mama had to mortgage the house from time to time to pay bills, but eventually she sold it to our youngest brother, Robert, and his wife Vernua. They live there today where they raised their children and grandchildren. Mrs. Bird's gift has already sheltered four generations of Hanrahans.

Clutter and Chaos

As the fourth child of nine, I was seldom able to find a quiet place to call my own amid the clutter and chaos of our close quarters. Our living room was just large enough for a two-piece sectional sofa, one or two upholstered chairs, and a bookcase. Two single-pane windows faced the street, and two more, on either side

The Half Life of a Free Radical

of the mantle, faced the driveway. Over the mantle was a copy of Monet's *Bouquet of Sunflowers*. An antique black clock, wound with a key, added a touch of times past. There was a small, open-flame gas heater in the fireplace and a tiny stone hearth. In the early years, a child's swing hung in the open doorway between the living room and dining room.

For decades, a mahogany desk that had belonged to Mrs. Bird stood in one corner until Michael claimed it as his own when he moved to his Nashville home. In another corner was our small black-and-white television on a rolling metal stand. A large print of Renoir's *Girl with a Watering Can* held a place on the wall beside the front door. The art prints came from the Quality Stamps redemption store, a Memphis-based enterprise on Union Avenue. Mama collected stamps from each purchase at the neighborhood Pic Pac grocery. We kids spent many afternoons licking them and placing them carefully in the booklets.

Our dining room was barely large enough for the green Formica-top table that seated six. When one of the table legs gave out, Eileen remembers, we stacked books in place of the broken leg to keep the table on level. Three decorative plates, one a still life of fruit, hung on one wall, and a framed print of Eric Enstrom's *Grace*, illustrating an old peddler with his head bowed in a mealtime prayer, decorated another.

The quiet reverence of a man at prayer was not at all like the scene in our dining room when nine hungry Hanrahans competed nightly for a space at the table. We usually ate in two shifts, then cleared the table for homework time.

The kitchen floor was tiled in a black-and-white checkerboard pattern of linoleum squares. There were two windows over the sink, and always a sweet potato or some other plant rooting in a small glass jar on the window sill. The large pantry held stores of canned goods and on the high shelves Mama's Kodak Speed Graphic camera and other not-to-touch items.

At some point the kitchen was remodeled to add more counter tops and cabinets, including the corner cabinet that became my favorite hiding place. When I was still small enough, I could crawl inside the metal "whirl-a-round" where the potatoes and onions were kept. Going in one door, and then, after some time, tumbling out the other.

North Memphis Meanderings

Mama's "cooking cabinet" always held a five-pound bag of Domino Sugar, Pillsbury Self-Rising flour, sweet spices, semisweet chocolate pieces, shredded coconut, food color, nuts, and other cookie-making treats, as well as a variety of flavors of Jello. It was supposed to be off limits, but I know I found my way into that cabinet on more than one clandestine occasion, usually to eat a spoonful or two of granulated sugar for its instant energy boost.

A full-length mirror hung in the hallway beside the bathroom door. If I lingered there too long, Mama would soon admonish me: "Quit staring at yourself. Don't be vain." The hall closet overflowed with towels and sheets, blankets and quilts, along with a few embroidered linens. The closet was another of my hideaway places where I could nest for a time, safe from the fray, sometimes nursing a bottle of souring milk lifted from a younger sibling.

Our black rotary-dial telephone sat in an alcove in the wall. Our phone number was BR5-7876. Beneath that was a low cedar chest always piled high with clean laundry in need of sorting and folding. The living room, dining room and kitchen led one into the other and back to a tiny hallway between the sun porch, with its perpetually leaky roof, and the small basement area where the old coal chute emptied. We all tossed our dirty laundry into a pile at the foot of the basement stair in front of the Maytag washer. I had many conversations there with Mama as she loaded the machine, standing ankle deep in the family laundry.

The only room in the house where there was any hope of privacy was the one bathroom that served us all, and then only if you took care of your business quickly. There was a deep porcelain-covered iron tub, and a small pedestal sink with a mirrored medicine chest mounted above. The toilet was in constant use with a lineup of siblings waiting a turn, especially on bath night. We would announce our bath time claim with the ditty, "If anybody has to go, speak now or forever hold your pee!" To fail to make such an announcement was reason enough for an impatient brother to barge in, with the accusation "You're hogging the bathroom." There was no lock.

Sometimes if I went too long between baths Mama would order me to take one. I was always afraid someone would bust in and see me naked, so I would defiantly run the water and swish it around with my toes to make it sound like I was taking a bath. It's no wonder I got the nickname "cooties" in those days.

The Half Life of a Free Radical

In the enclosed back porch that looked out on our backyard, the black-and-white-tiled floor was often damp with water plunking into the pot from the leaky roof and spilling over in hard rains. When we were very young, our red wooden rocking horse was kept there until all the springs wore out from repeated use.

There was a large chest freezer against the back wall, often filled with day-old Wonder Bread with the slogan: "Helps build strong bodies eight (later twelve) ways." We bought a dozen loaves of bread at a time from the Colonial Bread Thrift Store and used up an entire long loaf for our baloney, peanut butter and jelly, egg and olive, liverwurst or pimento cheese sandwiches that we took to school in brown-paper bags.

Michael remembers the old "Mathis Cooler" that Daddy brought home one hot summer day and mounted in the back room. Daddy's large fish tanks lined one wall. He stocked them with angelfish, guppies and neon tetras. A catfish cleaned the algae from the glass. In two separate glass bowls he kept Siamese fighting fish, with their brilliant colors and flowing fins. I could gaze on that watery world for hours. Much to Daddy's dismay, we kids were always messing with the thermometer on the tank, and I remember once finding most of the fish floating belly up. Daddy was not happy.

Mama speculated that the algae would be used in the future as food and she experimented with adding the green slime to her oatmeal cookies. Eileen tried an experiment mixing the algae with sugar and freezing it like a Popsicle. I don't think it turned out as well as she hoped. Eileen's specialty was fudge and she spent many hours in the kitchen stirring the pot until it thickened. I didn't have the patience or focus for such a task and burned many a pot in the process.

The opening to the crawl space under the house was behind the two wooden cellar stairs. Now and again Daddy and the twins, Danny and Tommy, would crawl in there to fix a pipe or repair some loose wiring. I liked to go under the house too, sneaking beneath the porch from the back yard, slithering on my belly, carefully avoiding the spiders and cobwebs, and inhaling the smell of rich, damp earth. I liked having my own secret places. Sometimes I would wander off around the block to North Parkway and burrow under piles of autumn leaves until the dark and cold drove me home.

North Memphis Meanderings

    Our pencil sharpener was mounted on a wall in the back hallway. On homework nights the sound of the wood grinding to a sharp point mixed with the smell of graphite. Above the pencil sharpener was our family version of a wailing wall. Scribbled there over the years was the sharp and pointed commentary of nine crowded and opinionated children. There were curses and confessions, blessings and threats, poetry and diatribe, limerick and lies. I added my point of view to the literary cacophony. Mama wisely allowed the graffiti without censure, and that wall became a safe and anonymous place to express our thoughts and feelings.

    At night, when most of the household was finding what peace we could in sleep, the cockroaches held forth. When I crept down from the attic and turned on the kitchen light on my way through to the bathroom, the huge insects would scurry across the floors and counter tops and fly about.

    Memphis has the big American Cockroach variety. They were terrifying. Crushing one would yield a thick white ooze of guts. But such killings did little to eradicate the pests. Sometimes with a childhood cruelty we would either put, or find, a dead or dying cockroach in a shoe or under a pillow, placed there in retaliation after a sibling battle.

    Once the entire house was fumigated and we each were given a turn with the broom to sweep the vermin out the door. The poison smell lingered for weeks. Despite the slogan "Real Kill kills every bug that crawls or flies or your money back!" the roaches kept coming back.

    The large attic where we children slept was reached by a narrow wooden stairway off the back hall, and served through the years as a dormitory for my three sisters and five brothers. There was often the smell of urine as one or the other of our younger siblings struggled to stay dry throughout the night. Mattresses developed a "wet spot" where the pungent dampness remained, despite efforts to cover it over with layers of old woolen blankets.

    When we were small enough, we delighted in wrapping up in one of the old Army surplus, olive-green blankets that Daddy brought home. We would then slide down the stairs head first, screaming at the top of our lungs. The eaves, accessed from either side of the stairs, were filled with itchy rock-wool insulation. This provided a great hiding place, early on claimed by the boys, who kept their stash of

The Half Life of a Free Radical

Marvel Comics, illicit "girlie" magazines, and candles to read by after "lights out."

We all shared one attic closet where we were supposed to hang our school uniforms. There was a chest of drawers for the boys and one for the girls, and a large "sock box" where we foraged for a matching pair before heading out to school. When Johnny could not find a matching sock, and especially if his shoe went missing, he would wander the house calling out, "Here shoe. Here shoe." Mama would calmly advise, "Ask St. Anthony." The patron saint of lost items was the go-to guy whenever anything was lost. Invoking the assistance of unseen allies is a habit I still employ when I misplace a needed item. It usually works.

Daddy mounted a large box fan in one of the attic windows. He set its rhythmic motion to draw the hot summer air through the house. I loved to sit there making my voice vibrate as I sang into the whirling blades. The breeze from the fan seemed never to reach into the corner where I slept. Sometimes in the hot summer months we kids would reverse the blades to "blow" to feel the relief as the cool air swept across our bodies. That respite would soon be interrupted by a bellow from below as Daddy ordered us to turn it back. His command would be met with a chorus of groans from his hot and sweaty children. Throughout the summer, we switched that fan back and forth many times over the course of the sweltering nights, eventually wearing out the motor. Downstairs, here and there in the house we had a few of the old rotating table fans.

Grandpa's Pipeline

Grandpa Donnelly was about seventy-years old when we all moved to Faxon Avenue. He had recently retired from forty-seven years at the American Snuff Company where he had been foreman of the tin shop. Mama remembered the day her daddy lost the tip of his right index finger in a Labor Day accident. She said he had opened a valve under pressure and metal fragments flew, embedding in his hand. His missing finger was always a curiosity to us children.

Grandpa was a quiet, somewhat taciturn man. He was tall and thin and often wore a light-colored seersucker suit with a dapper straw hat and thick, round, wire-rimmed glasses. He had been a

North Memphis Meanderings

Director of the Catholic Club on Adams Avenue and a member of the Knights of Columbus. After retirement he spent time playing poker with his friends at the Catholic Club, or he walked up to the barber shop on Jackson Avenue where he discussed his favorite baseball team, the St. Louis Cardinals. Grandpa was a founder in 1925 of the Memphis Irish Society, and we have an old newspaper photograph of when he was presented with a genuine Irish harp in honor of his service.

Mama always said that some of us had a "pipeline" to Grandpa's pocket. I never found the spigot. Tommy, his namesake, always seemed to have a way with his grandpa. Tommy's job was to give Grandpa his morning shave. If twin Danny went in to do the job, Grandpa would know, and send him away to wait until Tommy could come.

Grandpa had a soft spot for Eileen also. He called her "Eee Eye." Eileen remembers, "Grandpa would call me into his bedroom in his gruff voice: 'Come here, girl.' and I would stand at the head of his bed while he sat on the side. 'Reach your hand under that pillow,' he told me, and when I did, I would pull out a shiny dime." Grandpa had the front bedroom. His room was always neat, and we children were not allowed in unless invited.

One or the other of us was always put on lookout for when the black van arrived to deliver Grandpa's medicine. "Robinson's here!" we would proudly announce, and race to the door to meet the delivery man. The James S. Robinson Apothecary was one of the oldest pharmacies in Memphis, dating from Civil War days, and was the only one Grandpa used.

Robert was Grandpa's "living cane" when his eyesight failed. Robert's job was to walk in front, with grandpa's hand on his shoulder, and lead him to his place at the dining room table. Little Robert took his job very seriously. Sometimes Mama, or one of us older children, would read aloud the obituary column from *The Commercial Appeal* for Grandpa. He had cataracts and could not make out the fine print. I can still see the geometric pattern of deep wrinkles at the back of his sun-browned neck as I stood behind his chair at the dining room table. If there was a familiar name listed among the dead, there would be a discussion about that person's life. Mama would then get a card from the church and pay to have a Requiem Mass celebrated in their memory.

The Half Life of a Free Radical

Praying for the souls of the "faithful departed" was an important duty of the living. We children were irreverent about death and were always on the lookout for the drama of a funeral procession passing through the neighborhood. A sleek black hearse carried the coffin to the church, followed by a long line of cars, all with headlights shining. The procession was usually escorted by a motorcycle policeman. Whenever we saw a hearse pass, we would sing out:

Don't you laugh when a hearse drives by,
Or you will be the next to die.
They'll wrap you up in a big white sheet,
And throw you down six feet deep.
The worms crawl in, the worms crawl out,
The worms play pinochle on your snout.

American Snuff Company

By the time our family returned to Memphis, most of the white families who had lived up in old Pinch, the neighborhood where Mama was raised, had moved away from the pestilence and flooding of the river. Black families took their place in the deteriorating, gingerbread-trimmed wooden houses. Many other houses stood vacant and boarded. Racial polarization in Memphis was promoted and encouraged, according to some historians, to serve the interests of employers who were enriched by a "cheap, unorganized and racially divided" labor force.[45]

In late May of 1950, an explosion rocked the American Snuff Company and blew out the windows. This company where our grandpa had spent most of his working life, was engaged in a 185-day strike of the more than 300 mostly-white women employees. The union was asking for dues check-off, the automatic deduction of union dues from employees' paychecks, and a raise in pay. These demands would be echoed eighteen years later with the Sanitation Workers' Strike that brought Martin Luther King, Jr. to Memphis. I don't recall any family conversations about that strike, "the biggest and most violent conflict in the city CIO's history."[46]

One of Mama's childhood classmates at St. Brigid's parish school, George Dhuy, worked at the North Memphis plant of the Firestone Tire & Rubber Company. He was an organizer with the

CIO which supported the Snuff Workers' Strike. Although the strike had been heavily funded by the Steelworkers Union and supported by other CIO unionists, the workers eventually lost.[47] Years later, George Dhuy's daughter Sharon and I became classmates and friends, attending first through twelfth grades at Little Flower School and then Sacred Heart High School.

Eternal Rest

Grandpa died of lung cancer on July 18, 1958. It was Daddy's birthday. Mama moved Grandpa to a nursing home during the last days of his life, and had been spending a lot of time with him there. She woke us early that morning with the sad news. I was in the double bed I shared with Mary Alice. She let out a loud wail. I didn't cry. From a very early age I seemed able to contain my grief, withholding all but the briefest outward expression.

"Your Daddy and your Grandpa didn't get along at all," Mama told me on the Thanksgiving of her seventy-ninth year. We were visiting at Eileen's home near Rogersville, Tennessee.

"It made it very hard for us," she said.

In retrospect, that seems like quite an understatement given the tight quarters we all shared and the fact that Grandpa was a teetotaler and our Daddy was most certainly not.

All the way to the funeral Mass at Little Flower Church I wondered if Grandpa had been given Extreme Unction before he died. We were taught that this Last Sacrament would assure his safe passage to heaven. Mama always kept a cross-shaped wooden box by Grandpa's sickbed. Inside were a set of candles and a vial of holy oil for ritual anointing. Eileen remembers Father Leppert, our pastor, making a house call to bring Grandpa Holy Communion. He used the cross and candles when he came, she remembers.

Grandpa's wake was the first I ever attended. It was held at Memphis' J. W. Norris funeral home. I stood at the coffin for a long time gazing down at his body. It seemed to me that he was still breathing. I wanted to be sure he was really dead before they closed the lid.

The nuns had warned us of the sin of despair. They illustrated it with the story of a holy man who had been nominated for sainthood, but when his body was exhumed (God only knows why), there was

The Half Life of a Free Radical

evidence that he had been buried alive and likely had succumbed to despair, a Mortal sin. There were so many ways to go to hell.

The veil between the living and the dead seemed very thin in our home. Michael, who would have been about six when Grandpa died, tells of waking up to find Grandpa standing at the foot of his bed.

"He came to tell me that everything would be all right," Michael said. I remember feeling quite fearful of Grandpa's ghost, though Michael didn't seem to mind. I made the sign of the cross a lot, as a kind of shield, and I begged Grandpa not to show himself to me.

Eileen remembers waking up in the middle of the night nearly a decade after his death to see Grandpa standing beside her bed. She was about fifteen then, and sleeping on the back porch, which had been re-purposed into a bedroom.

"It was his presence that woke me," she recalled. "He was standing there in his suit. I knew that he loved me. As I watched he just kind of faded away."

Years later, when I was experiencing a dark night of worry for my daughter, Jessica, who lived far away, Grandpa came to me in a dream. He stood at the end of a long hallway. He was dressed in his seersucker suit and straw hat and just stood there looking my way. His presence was a comfort.

Grandpa visited me again in a dream in 2001 as I struggled through some restless nights in a prison barrack. I was imprisoned for six months for misdemeanor trespass in a peaceful protest in the year 2000 at a U.S. Army base in Columbus, Georgia. Night after night in that West Virginia prison, each of my long-deceased relatives whom I had known in life made a brief visit in a dream. In one way or another, they reassured me that I was not alone.

Eternal rest, Grant unto him, oh Lord,
And let perpetual light shine upon him.
May he rest in peace, Amen.

Mama would recite this prayer for the dead many times over in the course of her life for too many loved ones too soon lost. She kept an altar on her dresser with a growing collection of photos of her dearly departed.

In one of her "Ladies' Fare" columns entitled "Don't Canonize Coffin Dwellers," Mama wrote:

North Memphis Meanderings

"It takes little effort and costs us nothing to remember deceased friends with an aspiration. ..If they could speak they would be sure to say: 'Pray for me.'"

I keep that in mind whenever I pass a blooming dandelion in the Spring. I blow on the globe of seeds, dispersing them on the wind, as a prayer for the dearly departed.

A Courageous Coterie

Our parents had a lifelong circle of friends. Once a month in the late 1950's and early 1960's they visited for a game of penny-ante poker and conversation. Mama would prepare a buffet of homemade snacks. She wore one of her prettiest dresses, powdered her nose from her small round-plastic compact, and put on red lipstick. I remember lingering around the table to listen to the conversations and watch as the piles of red, blue and white plastic chips moved from person to person as the winning hands shifted. Smoke from Daddy's cigar and Mr. Porteous' pipe lingered in the room and the adult laughter was good to hear. As long as I didn't interrupt the conversations, I was tolerated for a little while before being ordered back to bed.

The discussions were always interesting, though I was still quite young and didn't understand then the social importance and bravery recounted across our dining-room table as the poker chips passed from hand to hand and the children listened.

These friendly gatherings were noted once in 1959 in Eldon Roark's syndicated "Strolling" column, a daily human interest feature in *The Commercial Appeal*. Roark wrote that the five families that gathered for poker and conversation every week, rotating from home to home, had a total of thirty-nine children between them, and one on the way. We were Catholics, after all.[48]

Clark Porteous worked for the *Memphis Press Scimitar* and was assigned to cover the Civil Rights Movement. He was a Mississippi native and a Neiman Fellow from Harvard. I recently found a 2011 article by former *Jet* magazine reporter Simeon Booker, in which he characterized Mr. Porteous as a "fair and square Southerner" with "calmness and keen judgment" throughout his coverage of the 1956 Emmett Till trial.[49]

The Half Life of a Free Radical

> *Clark Porteous of the* Memphis Press-Scimitar, *joined me and other black reporters on a high-speed, midnight manhunt through the backwoods of the Delta, led by local civil rights workers and law enforcement officials hell-bent on finding terrified blacks rumored to have witnessed aspects of the crime. In the end, despite these eye witness accounts and one defendant's confession to the kidnapping, the all-white jury let the killers walk free.*
>
> *Clark Porteous served as the main liaison agent for the operation and he did so unflinchingly in an atmosphere which was charged with tension and fear.*[50]

In Money, Mississippi in 1955, fourteen-year-old Emmett Till, visiting from Chicago, was savagely beaten and shot through the head for allegedly "flirting" with a twenty-one-year-old white woman. After a widely-covered trial, Emmett Till's murderers were acquitted. This travesty of justice was repeated with the acquittal in 2013 of the murderer of seventeen-year-old Travon Martin, who was pursued and shot dead in a case of racial profiling, and in numerous similar murders. The more recent "Black Lives Matter" movement has emerged from the long-simmering outrage at ongoing police killings of black persons, many unarmed and innocent of wrongdoing.

Clark Porteous was also in Oxford, Mississippi, in 1962, covering Air Force veteran James Meredith's attempt to break a 114-year whites-only tradition at "Ole Miss." He was covering that story around the time he stood as my sponsor for my Confirmation.

Mr. and Mrs. Porteous, as we always called Clark and Elizabeth, had seven children. We kids spent many summer afternoons at their home, a large two-story house on Forest Avenue. Tragedy struck the family in the mid-1980's. Donald, their middle son, died of AIDS, a disease as feared then as TB had been when Mama was a child. Donald loved to dance and Michael remembers he joined the Joffrey Ballet in New York City. A few years after Donald's death the youngest Porteous daughter, Sarah, was murdered on a Memphis street. Her death was one more of too many deaths in the violent city Memphis has become.

Genie and Fred Gattas also joined in the poker evenings. We Hanrahan and Gattas kids went to Catholic grade school together and ran the streets, alleyways and bayous throughout our childhood. The Gattas' third son, Donald, a gentle, gentle soul also met his death

North Memphis Meanderings

by murder in Memphis. The violence that surrounded us was so commonplace, we only took notice when it claimed someone close.

Also at the poker table were Bea and Bob Gantert. They had a large family too. Their son Ricky became a priest and offered the funeral Mass after our brother Tommy was found dead in his midtown Memphis apartment.

Many of these Catholic families had been part of the Outer Circle study group that supported the Blessed Martin Catholic Worker House in the 1950's. Our parents remained close throughout the years, and always sent a representative to family funerals, weddings or other special occasions.

Mama also stayed in touch with many of her college classmates, particularly Roberta Foster, our "Aunt Bobbie," who was the Chief Dietitian at the now-demolished Baptist Hospital where Elvis died. Aunt Bobbie had a bright smile and warm hug for each of us when she visited, even for Daddy, who seemed to light up when she arrived. Every year on January 6, a day we called "Little Christmas," she would come by the house with a bag of small gifts to mark the end of the holiday season. Aunt Bobby was Mary Alice's Godmother and their bond remained strong throughout her life. Both Mary and Regina were with her when she died. I always appreciated her loyal and kind presence in our lives.

My Godparents lived far, far away in New Jersey and I never heard from them. Sometimes I felt like a little waif destined to forge my way forward by dint of sheer determination. I didn't recognize the many allies and friends always around.

One of Mama's classmates and later a professor at Siena College, Dominican Sister Adrian Marie Hoffstetter, participated in the civil rights marches. During the Sanitation Workers' Strike, she joined others in a sit-in and hunger strike in Mayor Loeb's office. Not all of Memphis' nuns and clergy shared her convictions, nor were many willing to stand in solidarity with the sanitation workers. Siena College taught more than academics and had been an important part of Mama's life. I remember going with her to some of the alumni gatherings and holiday craft bazaars held on the grounds. This was before the school was sold and demolished to accommodate a shopping center. My friend Catherine's mother also went to Siena and her younger sister is named after Sr. Adrian Marie.

The Half Life of a Free Radical

Another of Mama's college friends, whom we knew as Miss Tucker, lived in a nearby apartment on North Parkway. She invited Mary and Eileen to travel with her to California. Mary went first, and the next summer, when Eileen was fourteen, she went. Eileen remembers that Miss Tucker had dropped by the house to see Mama just before leaving for California. On impulse she asked if she could take Eileen. Mama said yes, and Eileen recalls: "I gathered up some clothes and off we went." Though that opportunity didn't come round for me, I did enjoy several visits to a cabin Miss Tucker rented in Hardy, Arkansas, in the Ozark mountains. It was a great gift to get out of the inner city and experience the freedom and spaciousness of the Arkansas countryside.

A Point of Interface

Jackson Avenue was a point of interface in our racially-divided neighborhood. On my frequent walks to the Pic-Pac grocery store or the Speedway Terrace Drug Store on the corner of Jackson and Decatur, I passed a row of narrow wooden houses situated just a few feet apart from each other. On hot summer days, when the front doors stood wide open to the breeze, I could see straight through to the back of these so-called "shotgun" houses. Every house, it seemed, had a bed in the living room. Even as crowded as we were in our family, we never had to put a bed in the living room. Though by then I knew we were poor, I also knew that our "colored" neighbors had it even worse.

Mama would sometimes send me with a bag of "hand-me downs" to leave on the porch of one of the houses. These were the clothes that didn't fit any of us, gleaned from the packages of unclaimed garments Mama's cousin, Mary Thomas White, our Aunt "T," sent from her Nashville workplace, the Colony Cleaners and Launderers. Though I don't remember many children's clothes in the brown-paper-bag-wrapped parcels, I do remember some lovely women's dresses and our Mama's delight when one fit her well.

Kay's Bakery, on the corner of Jackson and Breedlove, sold fancy cakes, cookies, and glazed, chocolate and jelly donuts, cream puffs, and chocolate éclairs displayed in wide glass cases. Mrs. Kay wore her platinum-blond hair high in an elegant twist and always had a ready smile. Once a week Daddy would send us to the corner to ask

North Memphis Meanderings

Mrs. Kay for a bag of day-old bread. My favorite was the white crusty knot-bread. Sometimes Mrs. Kay would add a few sweet treats to the day-old bag.

On the outside brick wall of the bakery was a faint trace of a painted advertisement for Piggly Wiggly. Mama told us that this first self-serve grocery store was founded in Memphis by Clarence Saunders. His former home, known as The Pink Palace, had been turned into a museum that we often toured. One room was filled with the severed heads of large game animals, a gruesome display of his appetite for hunting.

A five-and-dime variety store was next to Kay's Bakery, and near that was the Greer's Sandwich Shop, a neighborhood bar renowned for its smoked barbecue sandwiches. Mama called it "a joint where the elbow bends," as it was a place Daddy frequented. Just across the street was Futrus Bros. Dry Cleaners, where Daddy took his suit and shirts for cleaning.

Mr. Rubenstein's upholstery shop was further up Jackson. One time Mr. Rubenstein covered our very torn and soiled sectional couch in a durable, tightly-woven brown fabric that provided decades more of hard use. Mama saved for a long time to get that couch fixed, and it sat in the store window for months before she could get together enough money to bring it home.

When times were good Daddy would take us to Hinden Dry Goods store to purchase new socks, shoes and underwear. Daddy showed me there how to tell my sock size by wrapping the sock around my balled-up fist. If the ends met, then it would fit my foot, he declared. It always seemed to work. Mr. and Mrs. Hinden knew each of us by name, and would carefully measure our feet with the sliding metal rule, and then fit us with sturdy, clunky and long-lasting Buster Brown shoes.

Near the corner of Jackson and Breedlove, I liked to peek into Joe's Shoe Shop where the smell of leather and boot polish was strong. The shop, as I remember it, was in a very small one-room concrete building that had been an old gas station. Joe was a large, muscular man with a hearty laugh and very coal-black skin. His radio was always tuned to the energetic music of WDIA with its "all-Negro" line up of disk jockeys. I found out much later what a special station WDIA was in 1950's Memphis. It consistently had one of the highest ratings of any independent station in the nation with black

The Half Life of a Free Radical

DJs such as Nat D. Williams and his Tan Town Jamboree. Blues musicians like B. B. King, Rufus Thomas, Dwight "Gatemouth" Moore, Muddy Waters, Lizzie "Kid" Douglas Lawlers (aka Memphis Minnie), Tina Turner and Bobby Blue Bland filled the airwaves. This so-called "race music" had some of the same soulful energy as the Gospel sounds that dominated Sunday radio, but with an exciting and somewhat forbidden edge.

Joe's Shoe Shop was where we went to get new soles on our well-worn shoes, which we sometimes held together with a rubber band to keep the soles from flapping when we walked. We also got another kind of soul at Joe's. The Delta Blues rolled out of Joe's Shoe Shop and round and round in my head as I walked home.

Gladys was the red-headed clerk behind the soda fountain at the Speedway Terrace Drug Store. She was the enforcer of the cruel rules that kept "coloreds" from sitting on the red-plastic upholstered rotating stools at the fountain. During one visit I overheard Gladys talking rudely to a "colored' boy who lived in one of the nearby shotgun-style wooden houses. He was about my age. I had just bounced up to take my place at the counter with never a question of my right to do so.

"Get on down, boy. You can't sit there," Gladys scolded, shaking her finger at the child who had just taken a seat at the counter.

"We don't allow race mixing here. Now go on out of here and get on home."

I was eight or nine then and beginning to notice the difference that skin color made in the lives of other children. Boldly I intervened.

"You're prejudiced," I said. "Coloreds have just as much right to sit here as white people do."

"Mind your own business," Gladys retorted, scowling at me with narrowed eyes. My dark-skinned neighbor left the store, shamefaced and head down. I left with him, feeling sorry for the boy, whose name I don't recall, and very angry with the clerk, Gladys.

I always spoke my mind, even if I got into trouble. Gladys never seemed to like me after that. "Nigger-lover" was a taunt we children came to expect whenever we stood up for a "colored" neighbor or challenged an adult about the way things were.

Eileen remembers one summer day she and our friend Catherine were sitting at the drug-store counter when a man came up and tried to set Eileen's hair on fire.

North Memphis Meanderings

"We ran out of the store and down Jackson Avenue. We found Daddy at Greers," she remembers. "He told us it would be okay, that the man was just a public nuisance."

There were a lot of public nuisances out and about on Memphis streets, and a lot of other characters that defied the social norms and moved through the neighborhoods living by their own light.

One of these was a man known by most folks only as "Monk," though he preferred to be addressed by his given name Tony. He was a familiar face in midtown for thirty years. He stood less than four feet tall, hunched over, and claimed to walk fifty miles a day selling pencils. He carried a large stick that he used as a cane and chewed on an unlit cigar that he held in the corner of his mouth. He wore an assortment of sweaters and shirts layered on, summer and winter.

Our childhood neighbor Tommy Joe, who became a Rock 'N Roll historian and disc jockey, remembers that Monk always wore a sweet-smelling gardenia stapled to his hat. Tragically, Monk was hit and killed by a car. Tommy Joe later told me:

"I was probably the last person to see Monk alive. I was talking to him less than five minutes before he was run over."

Brother Johnny also befriended Monk and prized a pint-size bottle of "Monks Magic Elixir," with a pencil sketch of Monk on the label. After Johnny died, we found it among his Memphis artifacts.

Another of Memphis' well-loved eccentrics is Prince Mongo, the self-proclaimed three-hundred-thirty-three-year-old Ambassador from the planet Zambodia. He is rumored to have a law degree and ran for Mayor several times. Prince Mongo's Pizza, and his anything goes nightclub, Prince Mongo's Planet, were favorite teen hangouts. I went to the nightclub on Front Street one time with my older brothers.

Much to the dismay of his neighbors, Prince Mongo decorated his yard with art that included mannequin heads, golf bags, signs, lampshades, traffic cones, coffins, and colorful cloth draping on trees and bushes. When called into court on the matter he didn't hold back. The judge, citing him for contempt, ruled that a defendant can't show up for trial wearing fur, bones, goggles and pale green body paint, even if he is from the planet Zambodia!

The Half Life of a Free Radical

The Bane of Alcoholism

"Grandpa didn't drink," Mama told me during one of our rare conversations about alcoholism. "He took the Pledge when he was twenty-one." Tommy shared with Eileen the story about Grandpa's last bout with alcohol:

"He locked himself in the pantry for three days, doing little else but drinking cheap 'Dago Red' wine." After that, the story goes, "Grandpa never touched another drop."

If our Daddy Dan Hanrahan took the Pledge, it was a vow he could not keep. Alcoholism was the bane of our family. My father carried the addiction and we all adjusted to keep a chaotic balance. Much of my life, in retrospect, has been reaction to those difficult years.

Daddy was less and less present to us as the years went by. When he did come home in the evenings, he paced back and forth in the living room, smoking his Roi Tan cigar. Mama would admonish him, "Sit down, Dan. You're acting like a caged animal." When he did sit down, usually in the upholstered living room chair, he kept his head buried in a paperback mystery.

I never saw Daddy drink at home, but I do remember the occasional times I heard Mama call Daddy a drunk. Alcoholism was never explained to me as an illness. It was an affliction wrapped up with the judgment of a moral failing and surrounded with deep shame. A book on the shelf in the living room had a title something like, "The Bane of Alcohol Addiction." I tried to read it, but it was far too complex for me to understand. I felt sorry for Daddy and was angry with Mama when she spoke of him in a derisive tone, although as the years went by I could understand more of the burdens she carried.

Long after Mama's death, as I was working on this book, a note fell out of an envelope mixed in with some of her craft patterns. On the note was this epitaph transcribed from a grave in Durham churchyard in England:

Beneath these stones/ Repose the bones/ Of Theodosius Grimm/
He took his beer from/ Year to year/ And then his bier took him.

North Memphis Meanderings

Mama was in charge at home. It was just something that was understood, and she did not hide her disappointment in Daddy. From what I could see, whatever Daddy had to say about anything carried little weight at home. In the winter he complained about the thermometer setting, and year round about the volume of toilet paper we used. Bills piled up on the mantle and his checks bounced.

"I'm worth more to you dead," was Daddy's oft-repeated maudlin lament. Mama knew that wasn't true. He had little to leave behind. I really hated to hear Daddy talk like that. His sadness was so deep.

"I saw a lot more of our Daddy's pain," Michael once told me. "Y'all worshipped our mother. She was good as far as humankind. How could you ask for a better mother than we had? But she could be mean," he said.

Sometimes Daddy would arrive home late at night, about the time of *The Tonight Show*. Soon the house would fill with the odor of beefsteak frying on the stove. Any of us who hovered around were invited to share in the after-hours meal by soaking a slice of Wonder Bread in the drippings left over in the cast-iron skillet. Daddy smelled of beer, slurred his words and left a mess in the kitchen. Sometimes though, he would break out singing while he cooked, leading us in a rousing round of "I've been working on the railroad," or "Its a long way to Tipperary." I often waited up for his return. Eileen remembers the first time she tasted the soft drink Fresca when Daddy brought some home to try with a few of Greer's famous hamburgers.

I found it much easier to approach Daddy than Mama. I liked to laugh and sing with him, but I did not like his hugs when I smelled beer on his breath.

"For God's sake, Dan, go to bed," our mother would cry out from their darkened bedroom. "Let me have some peace and quiet." She was always asking for peace and quiet. Whenever we asked Mama what she wanted for her birthday or Christmas, "Peace and quiet," was her reply.

Daddy was either at "the office" or at Greers, the neighborhood bar at 1037 Jackson Avenue, just two blocks up Breedlove. Greer's Sandwich Shop was small and dark and smelled of old bodies and stale beer. The parking lot was covered with years of accumulated metal bottle caps spread about in place of gravel. Michael remembers how hard it was to walk on the bottle caps with bare feet. Sometimes

The Half Life of a Free Radical

Mama would send one or the other of us children there to bring Daddy home for supper.

"Go up to Greer's and see if your Daddy is there," Mama would say. When it was my turn to go, I would creep into that dark place and look for him among the people laughing and talking in the three or four red-vinyl upholstered booths, or sitting at the bar, some with their heads hanging low as they nursed a drink. The juke box played country music or blues for twenty-five cents a song.

Sometimes Daddy would give me a quarter to pick out a tune. To my young eyes, everyone at Greer's seemed happy in a sad kind of way. Sometimes Daddy would heft me up to a bar stool, the ones that twirled around. On the bar were jars of pigs' feet and red sausage and packages of dried beef jerky, pork rinds and small bags of Lays potato chips. On a lucky day, Daddy would buy me a hamburger, cooked on the grill as I waited. He never seemed in a hurry to go home. I liked being with my Daddy, but I didn't like it at Greer's. My brothers seemed to have different experiences.

"Wally Greer made the best damn burger I've ever had," Michael recalled. "Greer's was like a neighborhood living room." Robert remembers the twenty-cent hamburgers cooked with a lot of pepper. He also liked the coleslaw and smoked barbecue. Robert's love of barbecue continues to this day and he is a regular participant in the annual Memphis in May World Championship Barbecue Cooking Contest at the river. I've been a vegetarian for so long that I avoid that Memphis ritual. The sight of whole hogs turning on a spit and the smell of roasting flesh keeps me at a distance.

"Greer's was the other woman," Mama said. "It was like being abandoned. I don't know why your Daddy married me. He just totally wanted to be alone." This revelation was the first time she had ever talked so openly with me about Daddy and his drinking. Mama was seventy-nine and Daddy had been long dead.

"He would go up to that Greer's establishment and he wouldn't leave," she said, with a familiar resignation. When I asked if Daddy ever admitted to a problem with alcohol she said, "No, he wouldn't face it. Your Daddy said he never drank more than 'a couple of beers,' that is all he admitted to. I really felt betrayed, and there was nothing I could do. That is a bald statement of my feelings."

North Memphis Meanderings

The old Greer's Sandwich Shop building is still standing, and now is home to a tire store in a neighborhood where few of the familiar landmarks remain.

On June 7, 1953, Mama was about to give birth to Johnny. Daddy wasn't anywhere to be found, and Mama had to get to the hospital in a hurry. She took a city bus the several miles to St. Joseph's Hospital. She made it in the nick of time, she said.

Somehow the story of this escapade found its way into the *Memphis Press Scimitar* under "City Briefs" on June 17 and went out on the wires all over the country. That evening, as we waited on Daddy to get home, our neighbors, Grace and Anne, taught us a song:

I went to the animal fair.
All the birds and the beasts were there.
The big baboon, by the light of the moon,
Was combing his auburn hair.
The monkey he got drunk,
And sat on the elephant's trunk.
The elephant sneezed, and fell on his knees,
And what became of the monk, the monk, the monk.
What became of the monk?

By then I knew it wasn't just the monkey who got drunk, and I wondered to myself what had become of my Daddy the day Johnny was born.

The Loyal Order of the Moose

During the summer of 1963, after public facilities were ordered desegregated, our segregationist Mayor Henry Loeb closed Memphis' public swimming pools rather than open them to all residents.

During that hot, hot summer Daddy would load us up in the Buick for the trip to the Moose club where there was a swimming pool. Mama could then enjoy a full day of rare and relative quiet at home. Daddy said his membership in the Loyal Order of the Moose was important for contacts for his law practice. He spent his time at the lodge drinking and visiting with friends. We kids were left on our own to swim for hours until Daddy called us in for the ride home.

The Half Life of a Free Radical

On the ten-mile trip back home down busy Jackson Avenue, I stayed on hyper-alert to make sure Daddy was driving straight and not weaving in and out of the lanes. Brother Robert remembers the ride: "Daddy was always three sheets to the wind and singing old war songs, like 'It's a long way to Tipperary.' It's a miracle we weren't all killed."

When the public pools were reopened, few white persons used them. We did. I remember well the first day we went and my hesitation at the edge of the pool filled with dark bodies. We had been so long kept apart from one another. I was wary.

"Dive in," Mama said. "Just dive in." So I did.

Not too long after that, Mama put her foot down with Daddy. As I remember, she decided to do without a family car rather than risk having Daddy drive after he had been drinking. If we wanted to get somewhere outside of the neighborhood we had to walk, ride the bus, or beg a ride from our friends, some of whom had the use of their parents' car. I came to hate having to ask for rides, and even today I have a hard time having to rely on others to get around. Living now, as I do, without a car as an ecological choice. I am fortunate to have a bicycle, good walking shoes, an apartment close to a bus line, and friends willing to share occasional rides.

"And These Thy Gifts"

Mama was an inventive cook. She was always making up recipes and trying out new desserts. She made breads and cakes and cookies from scratch, using her *Betty Crocker Picture Cookbook* or the *52 Fridays Meatless Menus and Recipes*. Fridays were considered Fast Days. We Catholics were expected to do without meat. This was not really a hardship as meat was not on the table every day anyway, and Catholics didn't consider fish to be meat.

I loved to watch Mama knead bread dough on a floured wooden board. The house filled with the yeasty aroma as it would rise, and any one of us lucky enough to be around would get the first slice of crusty bread, fresh out of the oven, with a pat of butter melting on top. Many meals we had biscuits. I liked to roll out the dough on a floured board and cut the biscuits with an upside-down glass.

Meal times were hectic. Supper was served in two shifts, one for the big kids and one for the "babies," as we called the younger five.

North Memphis Meanderings

Mama always tried to make a special Sunday dinner with ham or pork chops, meat loaf or fried chicken, but there were lean times too. We had many meals of white beans and catsup with raw onions and corn bread, or spaghetti and canned peas, or corned-beef hash, from a can opened with a key, and cooked in a cast-iron skillet with lots of potatoes and onions.

It was supposed to be Daddy's role to offer the standard Catholic blessing at mealtimes and he did so on the few occasions he joined us for supper.

Bless us, oh Lord, and these thy gifts which we are about to receive from thy bountiful hands through Christ Our Lord, Amen.

Other times, Daddy arrived home at supper time complaining. "I'm not hungry. My stomach hurts." Then he would retreat to the bathroom and lean over the toilet retching as we tried to ignore the guttural sounds and eat our supper.

Sometimes Daddy would send one or the other of us to the store for groceries. His list often included liverwurst or some vile smelling meat he called souse. It was a molded sausage made from a pig's or calf's head stewed with herbs and seasonings. One taste was enough for me.

My favorite sandwiches were thin slices of ham on white bread smeared with French's yellow mustard in the days after our Easter dinner, and breast of turkey with mayonnaise after our Thanksgiving and Christmas meals. I remember thinking that in heaven I would surely have as many ham sandwiches and chocolate ice-cream cones as I could ever want.

We celebrated birthdays with Mama's homemade cakes. She and Mary Alice made one that looked like a record. "It was for a 'Platter Party' for Mary's sixteenth birthday," Eileen remembers. Mama would buy a carton of three-flavored "Neapolitan" ice cream and cut it into slices with a bread knife. We would use the Sunday comic pages to wrap the birthday gifts, which usually cost well under $5. Mary, Danny, Tommy and Eileen have February birthdays. John's is in June, Michael's and Daddy's are in July. Mama and Regina's are in October. Mine is in November, and Robert's in December.

On my sixth or seventh birthday Daddy didn't make it home until well after dark. When Mama reminded him it was my birthday, we hurried to the five-and-dime on Jackson to get my present. I picked out a $5 doll from among the many "Princess" dolls arrayed on the high shelf in cardboard boxes with cellophane fronts. I don't remember now what name I gave her, or whatever became of that doll, but the special feeling of picking her out and then walking the two blocks home hand-in-hand with my Daddy is still with me.

When Mama's birthday came round on October 29, Daddy would get off the bus one stop early at the Speedway Terrace Drug Store and pick up a gift box of Evening in Paris cologne in the cobalt-blue glass bottle. It seemed to be his standard present for Mama.

On Daddy's birthday, July 18, we would give him tea or cigars or a handkerchief. Daddy would say something like "I don't deserve this. Don't spend your money on me," and would put his gifts away in the top drawer of his one chest of drawers, or on the high shelf of the closet he shared with Mama. Personal space was very limited in our house.

Perpetual Housework

Laundry and dishes were perpetual chores. The boys got away with doing less as they were often out throwing their paper routes or on the run somewhere in the neighborhood.

I don't remember ever seeing Daddy with a broom, and the only times I remember him in the kitchen were during his late-night cooking escapades or when he brought home fish and showed us how to scale them.

The boys and girls alike were expected to take a turn washing dishes. It usually took two sinks full of soapy water to finish the job. I had little patience for the chore and if I could not get the burnt-on food off the bottom of a pan, I would sometimes find a place to hide it. When it surfaced later, I didn't own up to my crime.

Every summer Mr. Jim McNulty, our blind neighbor, would be out in the neighborhood selling large straw brooms with wooden handles. He carried about six of them over his shoulder. Mama would always pick out the strongest one. They would then visit for a while on the front porch before he continued on down the street, tapping the sidewalk in front with his white-tipped cane. Our old broom would then be delegated for sweeping the walkway and the sidewalks in front of our house. This was the chore I most enjoyed. The rhythmic motion of the broom settled my mind. I much preferred outside jobs, like sweeping the walkway and raking leaves into big piles. I still recall the distinct aroma of the formic acid released by stinging red ants, whose hills I disturbed by the sweeping, and the pungent scent of damp leaves in the crisp autumn air.

Many years later, I was assigned the job sweeping sidewalks outside the barracks at Alderson Federal Prison in West Virginia. My good fortune reminded me of Br'er Rabbit in the old Uncle Remus tales: "Br'er Fox, oh please, don't throw me in that brier patch!"

Front Porch Life

Most everybody in the neighborhood spent a lot of time on their front porches, especially throughout the hot Memphis summers. This was before air conditioning was common. We had a few metal glider chairs, and long concrete banisters where we could sit. There was a square of concrete atop one of the brick corner posts. I liked to sit there shaded by the Crepe Myrtle tree and use it as an outdoor table.

Brother Tommy gouged his initials, TPH, with a pocket knife on that same banister long before the American war in Viet Nam maimed his hand, stole his youth, poisoned him with Agent Orange, and eventually took his life and that of his twin brother Danny. The banister was later knocked down by a speeding car that careened into the porch stopping just short of the front bedroom.

In the summer of 1956, my school project was to memorize all the U.S. Presidents. With the confidence of an eight year old, I was sure that my Daddy was the best man for the job so I always recited his name at the end of the list.

Throughout the summer, dramatic afternoon storms thundered by leaving torrents of rain rushing through the gutters. Memphis rain is soaking, long-lasting, drenching, flooding, cooling rain. The thunder rumbles and rolls, and water drips from the eaves in silver beaded curtains bright in the flashing light.

One evening, just before supper, I was on the porch watching a gathering storm and feeling the power and excitement in the air. Then, of a sudden, with a flash and a crack, lightning struck the tall oak tree next door. Wood splinters flew on the wind landing on the porch where I sat.

Our next-door neighbor, the Rev. Slaughter, was the pastor at Epworth Methodist church. He had also been outside when the lightning struck the tree in front of his house. Shaken, he walked over to see if I was okay. We kids made a lot of jokes after that about why lightening would strike the preacher's house.

Sometimes Michael and John invited neighborhood friends to our house to trade comics on the front porch. They had stacks of *DC Comics* featuring "The Justice League of America" and *Marvel Comics* with "The Fantastic Four," among others. They had not been trading for long when the preacher came over to see what was going on. The boys were sitting in a circle with the comics spread out in front of them. Mama was probably at work, and Daddy wasn't home either. I must have been in charge that day.

"Your mother wouldn't like this," The preacher warned me when I came to the door to see what was up. I knew what he meant. But I also knew he really didn't know our Mama, who wasn't worried at all about our "race mixing." When he realized we were on our own, he scolded us and told our friends, "Get on out of here, boys. Go on home now."

We probably called the preacher "prejudiced," which was the word we used to identify such bigotry. I really don't know what the preacher's views were on race relations, but he seemed rude to our friends that day. Everywhere, it seemed, the grown-ups' rules tried to keep us apart from the "colored" children in our neighborhood. But children find a way, as we did on many occasions, to play together, despite taunts of being "nigger lovers," from the crudest adults, and the stern looks of disapproval from the more genteel racists.

In 1964, when Presidential candidate Lyndon Johnson campaigned in Memphis, Michael recalls that it was Rev. Slaughter who gave the opening invocation at the foot of Monroe Avenue at Riverside Drive. We all went down to see the spectacle of this Texan who took over after Catholic President Kennedy was murdered. Michael also remembers that he and John scaled a street-light pole to get a better view. They were delighted to pick themselves out in the crowd in the large photo that appeared in the newspaper the next day.

North Memphis Meanderings

Neighborhood Watch

Mama looked in after the elderly widows on the block when she had the time, and neighbors kept a watchful eye out on her wandering children in return. Mama once showed me a folding metal grocery cart that she used when she walked the few blocks to the store. Years ago a neighbor had seen her struggling to balance heavy bags of groceries on her hips as she made her way home and gave her the cart. It had belonged to the widow, Mrs. Harrington, who lived across the street. So much for my fantasy of the wealth the neighbors would bestow on my long-suffering mother.

The Kernodle family were our other next-door neighbors. Their two boys, John and Leslie, were close in age to my younger five siblings. Their daddy was always taking photographs and home movies of them. Some nights when he showed slides on the window shade in their dining room, I would watch the show in reverse from our bathroom window as I perched on the narrow iron radiator.

John Kernodle later became a free-lance photographer, like his father. I have occasionally talked with him at gatherings of the Oak Ridge Environmental Peace Alliance where he photographs the protest vigils at the nuclear weapons plant. Life circles back on itself more often than not.

One of Grandpa's oldest friends was named Mr. English. He lived with his daughter Margaret a few doors down on Faxon next to the Weber's house. The family had owned a furniture store on North Main Street where we bought some of the beds for our attic dormitory. I couldn't understand how a man named Mr. English could be Irish. Somehow I got the idea that being English was not such a good thing. "Fee fie foe fum, I smell the blood of an Englishman," an old chant in the Jack and the Beanstalk story, still comes to mind when I think about that family. Sometimes when they argued, Daddy would hint about Mama's English blood. Michael remembers hearing Daddy call her a "half breed." I never heard such a charge. Mama's great-grandmother, Catharine Huff, was a German immigrant. Her grandfather, George Gardner, and her great-grandfather, Richard Mayger, were both of English ancestry. But her daddy was Irish, and in our view, that made us all-Irish.

One time Mama asked if I could stay at the English house while Miss Margaret went out for the evening. I was to keep an ear out for her father who would be sleeping. I was happy for the chance to earn a little spending money. The house was filled with heavy mahogany furniture and elegant upholstered chairs and sofas. I was still wary of ghosts, and worried that Mr. English might die while I was alone with him. I was quite relieved when Miss English returned.

Mr. and Mrs. Vincent Heffernan were good neighbors too. They shared their home with Mrs. Heffernan's sisters, Grace and Anne. It had a large, red-tiled front porch where Mr. Heffernan liked to sit in the afternoon. Often when we walked past, Mr. Heffernan would call us up to the porch. After a short visit he would give each of us a nickel. A nickel then would buy a Milky Way, a box of Luden's cherry cough drops, a colorful roll of Necco sugar wafers, or a box of candy cigarettes with the pink 'lit' tips. All too soon, and well before I graduated from eighth grade, I was addicted to the real thing.

Every year the Heffernan's got a new car. I remember particularly when they replaced their old black sedan with a new Chrysler with the jaunty tail fins that seemed so shockingly modern.

Jeff and his sister Jeanette Calhoun, lived next door to the Heffernans. The family owned a paint company on Front Street. Every Christmas in the Yule Parade Jeff would ride his huge white Palomino horse and wave his cowboy hat to the crowds as he pranced down Main Street. We children sat on the curb on old newspapers watching him go by. Jeff also had a pet chipmunk and to our delight he sometimes let it loose in the front yard to play while his caged parrots chattered away on the porch. He had a low concrete wall marking his front yard. I loved to balance on it as I walked by on my way to the grocery store.

Mr. and Mrs. Martin Stephenson and his mother lived next to the Calhouns. Fifty years later, the couple shared a room on the same floor as Mama in the St. Peter Villa nursing home. I always stopped to visit with them when I was in town, as we had so many years before as neighbors on Faxon Avenue. We knew most of our neighbors in those early days. The husband & wives, the spinsters, the widows, the siblings and parents of most of our playmates.

Sweet Little Flowers

Sometimes Mama would take us girls downtown to the Woolworth store to look for dress patterns in the huge

North Memphis Meanderings

Simplicity and *McCall* catalogs. She set up her Singer sewing machine in the dining room, and we helped pin the tissue-paper patterns to the material and then cut them out with pinking shears.

One Easter Mama sewed beautiful dresses for Mary, Eileen, Regina and me. Each was in a different pastel color with a raised velveteen flower pattern on the sheer organza material. We posed for a color photo in our neighbor Mrs. Fisk's garden, which bloomed brightly from early spring and throughout the long, hot summers. Tiny phlox blossoms carpeted the lawn and tall spikes of gladiola grew nearly as tall as I was then.

We were lovely young blossoms ourselves, my sisters and I, but we were not safe at Mrs. Fisk's house. Her brother, who we called "Uncle Buddy," was a Korean War veteran. He had lost a leg in combat and spent most of his time sitting out on his front porch watching the goings and comings of the neighborhood. Uncle Buddy would sometimes call us kids up to the porch. He gave the boys money to go up to the corner store to buy Lucky Strike cigarettes or Bull Durham tobacco in a pouch, and tipped them enough to get a candy bar. He kept treats on hand for us girls. But this was only the lure.

Whenever I tried to pass him on the porch, he would grab me and heft me onto his lap, then holding me tightly by the waist he worked his finger up into my panties, pushing, probing, and hurting me. It was a silent agony made even more painful if I squirmed to get away. I wanted to scream:

"No. Leave me alone. Stop hurting me. No. No. Let me go. Leave me alone!"

Instead, trapped on his lap with his grip strong around my waist, I endured. We had been so well trained to be polite and to respect grownups, that I was afraid to tell on him.

I didn't know how to talk to Mama about why I didn't like Uncle Buddy, and I don't remember talking to anyone else either about what he did to me. Eileen remembers: "I knew not to get within arm's reach of him. I don't know how I knew this, and I had no clue why. I just knew we were supposed to stay away." Someone must have sounded the alarm. Before that summer was over we were forbidden to ever go up on that porch again. I missed visiting with Mrs. Fisk but was relieved finally not to have to endure the tight grip and hurtful probing of her younger brother.

The Half Life of a Free Radical

For a long time after that I would watch from our attic window where I sat beside the window-box fan listening to the vibrating tones of my voice as I sang into the rotating blades. I could see Uncle Buddy sitting there alone on the porch, watching and waiting. I never went back on that porch, and I still recoil when I recall the helpless feelings of that painful childhood experience.

Shooing Away the Pets

Pets were rarely allowed in our house. Mama would shoo away any stray cats with a broom. Dogs didn't have a chance.

"We've got enough mouths to feed," Mama would say. Nonetheless, many times one or the other of us would sneak a cup of milk to feed a stray. We were always bringing home kittens. Regina recalls a litter born next door at the preacher's house.

"You and Danny brought them home," she told me, "We named them Inky, Dinky, Cinders and Sphinx." She and Johnny tried to rescue another litter Johnny had found in an old shed on his paper route.

"We went in and chased them down and got them," she remembered. "They tore our asses up. We had little scratches up all over our arms and faces. Then we decided they were from the devil, and we let them go."

On another unfortunate occasion, a mother cat abandoned her scrawny kittens in our falling-down garage. Their eyes weren't yet open. When I came home from school and went out to check on them, I was horrified to find them dead.

"Maybe the rats got them," Mama explained. We buried them in the back yard in the compost heap beneath the old peach tree, whose fruit seemed to always be hard as a rock.

One or the other of our older brothers one time fashioned a make-shift parachute for stray kittens and launched them from the high branches of the crabapple tree, despite his sisters' pleas for mercy. The excuse was always the test to see if cats really did have nine lives. Some of them were probably on their last life.

When I was about six, I had two pet turtles named Myrtle and Bert. They were the subjects of my first poem "Myrtle and Bert Meet." I entered them that summer in the pet parade at Overton Park. Mama made a tall white chef hat for me to wear, and I carried my turtles in an old soup pot labeled "Green Turtle Soup." I didn't win the contest, but enjoyed taking my turtles to Overton Park and walking in the pet parade. Another time I let them out in the backyard so I could watch them crawl, and they wandered off under the old fig tree. That fig tree had itchy leaves, but it was worth the discomfort to reach the sweet, grainy fruit with a pink center that supplemented our daily fare. I never saw my turtles again.

TV Time

Our first television was a small black-and-white set with rabbit-ear antennae. In the 1950's, we could tune-in two commercial stations, WMCT and WREG, and the "educational" station WKNO. On Saturday mornings we all crowded around to eat our Wheaties, Shredded Wheat or Kelloggs Corn Flakes, generously doused with skim milk, and watch Looney Tunes cartoons and later *The Rocky and Bullwinkle Show*. I liked *The Howdy Doody Show* with Clarabell the Clown, *Captain Kangaroo*, *The Little Rascals* and *The Three Stooges*, who were always slugging one another. We sang along with *The Mickey Mouse Club* jingle, and really loved *Leave It To Beaver* even though their family life was a world apart from our reality. On Saturday nights I watched *Your Hit Parade*. The show was sponsored by Lucky Strike cigarettes, with the jingle, "Be happy, go Lucky. Go Lucky Strike today." I especially enjoyed the song, "Oh the wayward wind, is a restless wind. A restless wind that yearns to wander." I so wanted to wander.

Your Hit Parade was where I first heard most of the popular tunes of the 1950's. We laughed a lot with *I Love Lucy*, *The Dobie Gillis Show* with beatnik Maynard G. Krebs, and Alan Funt's *Candid Camera*. Watching *The Millionaire*, I could fantasize what we could buy with one million dollars if the star, Michael Anthony, were ever to knock on our door. When Jack Bailey bellowed, "Would YOU like to be Queen for a Day?" we would all shout "YES!!!!" with the audience. On *Queen for a Day*, harried housewives shared their sad stories with a live TV audience. The housewife whose story seemed most pathetic was judged the winner measured with the "applause-o-meter." She was crowned, draped with a royal robe, and showered with prizes. I always believed Mama would win if she ever had the chance to appear.

The Half Life of a Free Radical

Eileen remembers Grandpa liked to watch *The Jimmy Durante Show*. Mama always watched *The Huntley-Brinkley Report* and game shows like *The $64,000 Question*. Her favorite drama was *Perry Mason* and, with Mama, we all wished Daddy could have been as prosperous as the handsome TV lawyer Perry Mason. Mama also liked the impish *Mr. Magoo*, sponsored by General Electric, and *The Lawrence Welk Show*.

When we were older, we would stay up late on Saturday nights to watch WHBQ TV's *Fantastic Features* show with the vampire Sivad as the "Monster of Ceremonies." *Tarantula* and *Godzilla* were monster mutants who emerged after the atomic bombs annihilated Hiroshima and Nagasaki, and were scary to me. There were also a lot of war movies that contributed to prevailing racist attitudes toward the Japanese, who were always the bad guys. I didn't know then about the internment camps, or the real costs of war. Later we all enjoyed the more sophisticated cartoons in T*he Rocky and Bullwinkle Show*.

My first glimpse of romantic love was on the *Early Movie* which featured old-time classics from the 1940's. I longed to be whirled around the dance floor in a lovely gown, waltzing the night away in the arms of the likes of Jimmy Stewart, James Cagney or Gene Kelly. Once I pulled a chair up to Mama's tiny bedroom closet and took down the box from the top shelf where she kept her wedding gown. I draped the yards and yards of heavy satin fabric around me, dragging it across the dirty floor as I pranced about. I can still feel the coolness of the satin against my skin. It was an unaccustomed elegance in our house.

I liked to stay up late after most everybody else had gone to bed to watch the TV sign-off, usually after *The Tonight Show*. I loved to hear "The Star Spangled Banner" and I stood at reverent attention with my hand over my heart, as we were expected to do in the classroom when we recited the "Pledge of Allegiance." When the screen turned to the black-and-white Indian-head test pattern, I turned it off and went to bed.

Later, as the dark truth of U.S. Government crimes and lies became evident to me, I could no longer pledge such allegiance. I miss the feeling of national pride that I had when I believed we were the best of the best.

North Memphis Meanderings

"Old Lady in the Shoe"

The year 1960 was a Census year. Mama must have known that a photographer and reporter from *The Commercial Appeal* would be coming to our home because she had us all get dressed in our Sunday clothes. We children crowded around our parents in the tiny living room for one of the few photographs we have with all of us together, from fourteen-year-old Mary Alice to the youngest, Robert Anthony, who was about four.

The article was headlined "Recall Old Lady in the Shoe? Well Meet the Hanrahans."[51]

Mama hardly looked like an old lady to me, though we had taken to pulling out the silver strands that were beginning to show in her mid-length black hair.

"Leave them in," she protested. "I've earned every one." The hook of the news story was the fact that Mama could not fit all her children's names on the census form that year. In the photo Mama is seated, pen in hand, filling out the form. Daddy stands behind her with his ever-present Roi Tan cigar in the hand that rests on her shoulder, and with his other hand he is counting his children.

One of census questions asked, "Did you work at any time last week?" Mama's answer was telling:

"I rise every day about 6 a.m. and work about three-fourths of the time until near midnight. That's about 16 hours a day and times seven for the week."

Thinking back on those days, I wish now I had been a more cooperative and helpful child, and had done more to ease her burden. I was doing all I could to hold my own in the midst of the chaos, and running free and wild in the neighborhood kept me out of the fray.

It is amazing, over a half-century later, to see the personalities of my siblings already reflected in their youthful faces in that newspaper photo. Michael, Johnny and Robert with their buzz-cut hair and striped t-shirts, are still the little boys. Michael is gazing up at his Daddy seeming to seek what he later called, "the tender mercies" of his attention. John has the mischievous look I remember well, and Robert, sitting on Danny's lap surrounded by his older siblings, looks warily at the camera.

The Half Life of a Free Radical

Both Danny and Tommy, their thick, black hair slicked and parted, are already quite handsome at thirteen. Danny, in his Boy Scout uniform, seems pensive; while Tommy, in a white dress shirt, leans forward scrutinizing the census form.

Mary is wearing a simple but elegant dress, much like the one Mama wears, and is poised and smiling. I'm wearing a plaid jumper and white blouse. My hair has the remnant curls of a permanent wave. I'm smiling too, looking right at the camera. Eileen, with her brown hair neatly pulled back with a nylon headband, looks quite serious and determined. An unsmiling Regina is perched on the arm of the couch, holding on to Mary's knee and looking a bit lost.

Regina recently texted me with her concerns about my publishing a book about our family. I didn't know how to allay her fears. But in the midst of her long text message was her own fine tribute to our parents:

> *We may have been poor but it was because our parents did without everything to make certain that we received an excellent formal education. At home we were taught modesty, morality, empathy, compassion, charity, love and confidence. We were taught to use common sense and we were given the skills necessary to make it through this world.*

We children then were like a globe of dandelion seeds, barely holding together before being scattered by the wayward winds.

"The House is on Fire!"

One hot summer afternoon in 1963, Michael burst into the house shouting,

"The house is on fire! The house is on fire!"

I was working at the ironing board set up by the front door to catch the breeze that was pulled in and through the house by the attic fan. I was the oldest sibling around that day and "in charge" by default. I usually chased all my younger siblings outside when I was the boss. It was the only way to keep the house clean until Mama came home from work. Daddy wasn't home either. I didn't believe Michael at first. He was only eleven, and I didn't smell any smoke or see any flames.

North Memphis Meanderings

"Fire is coming out the upstairs windows," he insisted, his panic rising.

"Everybody out of the house," I screamed, to no one in particular. Then I ran up the narrow wooden stairway to the attic. Sure enough, flames were leaping up toward the attic ceiling and being drawn out through the window fan. I ran back down the stairs to the phone in the front hallway and found the number for the fire department on the cover of the phone book.

"Come fast! Our house is on fire!" I said. Michael couldn't wait. He raced the two blocks to the fire station where our Uncle Mayger used to work and pleaded with them to come. I waited on the porch. In what seemed like forever, the fire engine pulled up out front. The firemen dragged heavy hoses through the house and up the stairs to the attic, soaking everything in the way.

Word of the fire spread fast throughout the neighborhood and a crowd gathered curbside. We kids watched from the sidewalk as the firemen tossed our clothes and bedding out the window followed by boxes and boxes of Johnny's prize collection of first-edition *Marvel* comic books.

Regina was two doors down visiting at the Weber's house. She remembers:

"I was sitting at the kitchen table with Suzie. When we heard the fire engines stop nearby, we came running out to see. The firemen were shoveling Johnny's smoldering comic books out the window. Johnny would get these old, old comics from bookstores," she remembered. "He had the little books, dime novels. He had every *Spiderman*. He had them all stacked up neat. They all burned up. Johnny got real depressed."

Michael took the brunt of the questioning after the firemen found an ash tray in the crawl space along the eaves where the boys would hole up in the itchy rock-wool insulation between the rafters.

"We hid our cigarettes under a board near the window fan, but that isn't what caused the fire," Michael told me. "The motor on the old attic fan burned up." Perhaps that old window fan was worn out from all the switching to reverse directions to direct some cool air our way on those hot Memphis summer nights.

I had been smoking that day too, downstairs as I worked at the ironing board. I didn't own up to it, and I wasn't interrogated by the firemen with the same scrutiny as Michael had been.

The Half Life of a Free Radical

Mama soon made it home from work. Later we watched as Daddy nearly ran the two blocks down Breedlove from the bus stop. The fire engines were still parked out front and the neighbors crowded around. Though the fire was put out quickly enough, the upstairs dorm where we all slept was badly damaged, and the downstairs rooms were ruined by the smoke and water. We were all put up for a week at the famous King Cotton Hotel near the downtown riverfront until the house was habitable again.

"That was the best week of my life," Michael remembers, "We were in high cotton at the King Cotton Hotel."

"One of Daddy's clients was a carpenter," Michael said. "Daddy had helped him out of some bad trouble." He worked with Daddy and our brothers to fix the damage. The end result was a much improved sleeping area, mercifully divided into two sides, the boy's and girl's, with a wall and open doorway in between.

Smoke, Smoke, Smoke that Cigarette

Danny and Tommy were well on their way to becoming what grownups called "juvenile delinquents" by the time they started high school., Sometimes they supplied beer and cigarettes out the side door of the school auditorium to students who attended the highly-chaperoned Catholic Youth Organization dances. Most of the adult attention was focused on keeping boys and girls from dancing too closely.

My older brothers were enterprising businessmen. Both won a trip to New Orleans as top newspaper salesmen when they were thirteen. The *Memphis Press Scimitar* published a picture of the winning group as they boarded the Greyhound bus. We Hanrahans left quite a trail of newsprint in the local papers as we came of age in Memphis.

Girls weren't hired for paper routes back then, and babysitting jobs were not often available in the neighborhood, so I always had less money to spend than my brothers. Keeping up with my cigarette addiction was becoming a challenge and I often skipped lunch to buy a few fags to quiet the craving. I could buy a thirty-five cent package of Marlboro or Kent cigarettes on my way home along Jackson Avenue. Store clerks there didn't question the purchase.

Sometimes along the route home we kids explored the storm drains beneath the city streets (we called them bayous). We could hide out from adult eyes in the damp darkness and feel a measure of freedom and adventure. My nicotine addiction became so bad that when I had no money or could not bum a cigarette from another delinquent classmate, I looked for half-finished butts in ash trays (we called them "shorts"), or from the gutter.

Mama tried to coerce me to quit smoking, but by the time I was in eighth grade, I just could not stop. It seemed I was "grounded for life." I smoked from age thirteen until I quit, cold turkey, on my thirtieth birthday as part of the first "Great American Smoke Out." A year later Mama, who had by that time taken up the habit, also quit. She thanked me for my good example.

When Michael started to smoke, Mama took more drastic action. I remember one summer afternoon she had him backed up to the Frigidaire and forced him to smoke one cigarette after the other, perhaps on the theory that this would cure him of the habit. It didn't. Michael later explained:

"That refrigerator incident affected me greatly. After Mama was finished with me I went out to the broken-down car in the back yard and I sat inside and smoked my F'n cigarettes and read my porno. I measure that day as the day I never listened to anyone ever again."

Michael tells me now "I don't have our Mama elevated to sainthood. She pissed me off. She was always interfering with my love life. She tried to control me." I still laugh when I remember the day she discovered the condom that fell out of his wallet. It's a good thing Mama didn't try the same technique she used to try and curb his cigarette habit.

Elvis has left the Neighborhood

The Suzore theater on Jackson Avenue where we spent many Saturdays was just blocks from Humes High School where Elvis graduated in 1953. While he was in high school, Elvis lived with his parents in Lauderdale Courts, the nearby public housing project for "whites only" across from St. Mary's Catholic Church on Market Street, and not far from the North Memphis neighborhood where my grand and great-grandparents lived. Elvis was a truck driver before he signed with Sun Records on Union Avenue near the then Nathan Bedford Forrest Park.

The Half Life of a Free Radical

By the time we kids were running free in the neighborhood, Elvis was a grown man and had moved to a new home on Audubon Drive, near the Pink Palace Museum. Over the years, though, Elvis made many visits back to his old school, and he still bought records From Poplar Tunes, the R&B and Gospel record store owned by Joe Cuoghi, a brother of Mama's good friend, Amelia, who she affectionately called "Cuoghi."

Elvis' Humes High School friend, George Klein, who grew up in North Memphis, was the DJ at many teen dances and on WHBQ radio and TV keeping the Rock 'N Roll scene alive.

I loved to dance. Still do. I was quite young when Elvis performed in Memphis, and I never had a chance to see him in person at the Overton Park Shell, Russwood Park, the Mid-South Fairgrounds, or any of the other places he appeared around town. My sister Mary did, at least once, Michael recalls. She showed him her prized Elvis signature when he last visited with her at her Calgary home.

I watched Elvis on the *Ed Sullivan Show* in 1957. He sang "Don't Be Cruel," and "Hound Dog," I couldn't keep from dancing. It awakened something in me, perhaps viscerally stirring my own ancient "tribal energies" and emerging sexuality. There was much talk among Catholics and Baptist preachers then about the "vulgar" way Elvis moved his hips when he played his "race music." The Catholic attitude toward Elvis' gyrations was stern disapproval. The aged Chicago Archbishop Samuel Cardinal Stritch, who banned the music from Catholic schools, described Elvis' music as "a throwback to tribalism that cannot be tolerated for Catholic youth."[52]

The Fazio sisters lived on Greenlaw Avenue. They had all Elvis' records. Now and again they would call me up to the porch to listen. It was a guilty pleasure.

Elvis was often sighted around town after his release from the Army. Rumor had it that he might see you out walking in his old neighborhood and take you to a car dealer and buy you a Cadillac. It had been known to happen, but never to us. I did see his teen-age girlfriend Priscilla one time as she stepped from a black limousine as she was dropped off at Immaculate Conception High School on Central Avenue. This was the parish where the more affluent Catholic white girls attended high school. We were told that Priscilla was a

North Memphis Meanderings

chaste young woman who was saving herself for marriage. And that was the impression given with her Catholic school enrollment.

Elvis touched us all, and I felt the shock wave of his raw energy even as I swooned at the sound of his deep, resonant voice. His music reminded me of many of the Blues tunes I heard on WDIA rolling out into the sultry summer air from the open door at Joe's Shoe Shop on Jackson Avenue.

I was living in Dallas the summer of 1977 when I heard the news on my car radio: "Elvis is dead." It was one of those moments when you just know someone great is gone, like the recent death of the modern musical genius known as Prince. I pulled over to take it in. Elvis was a home boy, a real Memphis greaser, as we sometimes called those working-class white boys from Humes High with their duck-tail and Pompadour hairstyles greased back with Brylcream—"a little dab'll do ya!" Elvis was the sort of rock star who remembered where he came from. We loved him for that.

On one Memphis visit, shortly after Elvis died, Michael and I went on a tour of Graceland. I was astounded at the crowds hanging around the gates weeping and wailing as they touched the surrounding wall with a reverence usually reserved for saints and gurus. Inside, the house was decorated with artifacts that hinted at Elvis' working class roots, including velvet art on one of the walls.

Michael, with his typical irreverent wit, caused some of the grieving fans to gasp at his graveside remark:

"Elvis is buried in the back yard, just like a dead canary."

In 1960, when Chubby Checkers came out with "The Twist," I found a way to use some of the rhythmic moves I had earlier perfected with my Wham-O Hula Hoop. I practiced twisting with a towel around my hips, then I would take to the hardwood floor in the living room and join the dancing on Saturday night with Dick Clark's *American Bandstand*. That's where I first heard the mad pianist Jerry Lee Lewis, who eloped with his thirteen-year-old cousin, a big scandal. But he sure could tear up a piano. My favorites were "Great Balls of Fire," and "Whole Lot a Shakin' Going On."

When I was fourteen, the Beatles' "I Wanna Hold Your Hand," came out. It seemed to capture all my teenage yearnings for connection. I had a crush on Paul McCartney, as did millions of other girls my age.

The Half Life of a Free Radical

Overton Park: The Grandest Time

Throughout our childhood summers we walked together the two miles or so along North Parkway to spend the day in Overton Park. A convenient half-way mark and cool way-station was the Art Deco, fourteen-story Sears Roebuck with its high Gothic tower and air-conditioned spaces. Though I seldom had money to buy anything, I loved to browse the aisles.

The Sears building was closed in 1983 and stood empty for the next twenty years, a hollow monument to our changing city.

Krystal Burger was just across Cleveland. For ten cents we could buy a bite-size square bun with a thin patty of hamburger meat smothered in greasy chopped onions. A few of these would fill us up for the rest of the walk to the park.

Mama knew Overton Park well and she would use the occasion of our day trips for lessons in Memphis history. The park included the Memphis Zoo, Memphis Brooks Museum of Art, Memphis College of Art, a nine-hole golf course, The Shell, Rainbow Lake, the Doughboy Statue, and meandering hiking trails in one of the few remaining old growth forests in Tennessee.

At the Poplar Avenue entrance, near the Brooks Art Museum, Mama pointed out the life-size statue of E. H. "Boss" Crump, who she said used to run Memphis. Crump died in 1954, but his reign as political boss had lasted for decades. I had little understanding then of the scope of his power or its impact in maintaining the racist status quo.

The Crump political machine paid the 1890-era poll tax that had priced voting ($2) beyond the means of most blacks. Poll-tax receipts were distributed to Negro voters with instructions on who should get their vote. Among other things, for their cooperation, Crump promised to hold back white violence and terrorism. The Negroes were expected to remain deferential in tone and submissive in behavior to whites.

A song was often heard on the levees around Memphis in times of high water: "River up or river down, Mr. Crump he run dis town."

Even the great Blues master W. C. Handy's "Southern Rag," called "The Memphis Blues," was originally written as a campaign song for Boss Crump:

North Memphis Meanderings

Folks I've just been down,
Down to Memphis town,
That's where the people smile,
Smile on you all the while.
Hospitality, they were good to me.
I couldn't spend a dime,
And had the grandest time.[53]

I had the grandest time at the Memphis Zoo. We white kids could go every day but Wednesday. A Memphis Park Commission sign, depicted in an iconic photo by Memphis photographer Ernest Withers, was posted outside the front gates which were guarded by stone lions reclining atop two tall columns. The message was stark: "No White People Allowed in Zoo Today." It was yet another outward sign in the deadly sacrament of institutional apartheid practiced in our city.

There was a wild energy at the zoo, punctuated with the cry of peacocks and the occasional roar of the lions, and rich with pungent smells. I loved to visit the bird house, the aquarium and especially Monkey Island, a grassy hill surrounded by a moat of water and home to an assortment of chattering monkeys. It was another world. Sometimes I would stand for a long time at the gorilla cage and try to catch the eye of the animal that paced inside, much like Daddy did in our small living room. The gorilla seemed so close to being human. I was sure he understood when I sent him my sympathetic thoughts.

For a few quarters at the concession stand I could get a bag of salty popcorn and an artificially-colored snow cone. Another area had rides for the little kids and a photo booth with a backdrop of the zoo entrance. I still have a 1965 photo taken on an afternoon date.

A larger-than-life bronze statue of a World War I Doughboy charging up a hill with his bayonet drawn, still stands in the center of Overton Park. It was dedicated in 1926 as a memorial to Everyman who fought in World War I, particularly those "who gave their lives to their country in the "Great War." The statue was molded from millions of copper pennies collected from Memphis school children, Mama told us.

In the early 1960's Memphis citizens learned of the U.S. Interstate System plan for a 7.6 mile east-west segment of the six-lane Interstate 40 to cut through Overton Park, leaving a swath of destruction

The Half Life of a Free Radical

through its center. Many fine neighborhood homes were razed in anticipation of the road building.

Michael and John joined with the efforts of "Citizens to Preserve Overton Park." Family folklore holds that Johnny tied himself to a tree to thwart the destruction. The group took the battle all the way to the Supreme Court. After much effort to assure due process for citizens, fair hearings, and full disclosure, the people prevailed. Interstate 40 now abruptly dead ends at East Parkway on the perimeter of Overton Park's urban forest. In 2016, a PBS documentary film featured Overton Park in its list of "Ten Parks that Changed America."

The North Parkway entrance to the park is across from Southwestern University, now Rhodes College, with its Gothic architecture and one hundred acres of landscaped campus. We couldn't have imagined it then, but Tommy, Danny and Eileen all graduated from that private Presbyterian college. Tommy was the first combat veteran since Korea to attend. Eileen was able to get loans, including the now-defunct National Defense Student Loan. Eileen remembers the philosophy then: "The best defense is a well-educated populace."

At the time, all I knew about Southwestern was the common ditty, "Southwestern at Memphis out by the zoo, where the girls are girls and the boys are too." Homosexuality was not explained to us in any way that I remember. But we came to understand that it was considered a sin. Anyone suspected of being "a homo" was the subject of scorn and ridicule, or worse. There was no concept then of what young people today call "gender fluidity," nor any tolerance for anything but heterosexual sex within the bounds of marriage. Church complicity in the social sins of racial apartheid, war, and priestly sexual abuse, however, was widespread.

When I visited Mama in her last years, I often walked through Overton Park while she napped at the nearby St. Peter Villa. I stopped to sit on a bench near where a Japanese garden once thrived. I felt close to Mama there, in what had been a favorite place for her. She often spoke of how beautiful the garden had been. Then came Pearl Harbor, and in a rash act on January 2, 1942, the chairman of the Memphis Park Commission ordered the entire garden razed to the ground to "avenge Pearl Harbor." Mama always spoke of that destruction with sadness.

3

Thou Shalt Not

Mea culpa, mea culpa, mea maxima culpa.

I was not yet three-weeks old when I was baptized and "cleansed of Original Sin" and duly enrolled in the "One, Holy, Catholic and Apostolic Church" at St. Peter Church in Belleville, New Jersey. Daddy's sister Mary and her husband Paul Brennan were my Godparents.

By the time I reached "the age of reason" and was considered to be morally responsible for my actions, I was seven and in second grade at Little Flower School in Memphis.

The Sisters of Charity carefully prepared us for the sacramental ritual of our First Confession. First we walked the Stations of the Cross, perhaps to evoke sufficient penitence. Then we lined up at the confessional booth. I clearly remember my timid hesitation. I didn't want to step into that two-sided box to plead for forgiveness of the priest hidden behind the screen. I soon developed a pat formula to expedite the ritual.

"Bless me Father, for I have sinned," I began, and quickly recited my sins: "I disobeyed my mother and father," I confessed. "I fought with my brothers and sisters. I coveted my neighbor's goods."

There was a thread of truth in all those disclosures and I was a certain recidivist regardless of how faithfully I performed the penance.

The Half Life of a Free Radical

The priest blessed me with the Latin *Te Absolvo*, and then issued my standard penance: three Our Fathers and three Hail Marys. These weekly admissions of sin varied little over the years, and held me in good stead until the initial stirrings of pubescent sexuality had me timing kisses and marveling at the thin line between Mortal and Venial sins. By that time I was well along on the road to having "sinned exceedingly in thought, word and deed, through my fault, through my fault, through my most grievous fault," the *mea culpa, mea culpa, mea maxima culpa* of the Lenten prayer *The Confeteor*.

I was the shortest girl in our First Communion class so I led the procession up the marble floor of the center aisle in my brand-new white dress and lace veil. The grownups, sitting in the oak pews that reached to my shoulders, watched in silence as the altar boys, swinging incense censers, continued up the steps to stand behind the priest at the altar. I already knew I could not join the boys on the altar. My job was to turn into the front pew and lead my classmates to our places. I sat close to the edge of my seat and rested my toes on the vinyl-padded kneeler so my feet wouldn't dangle.

I remember the hush in the church as the priest held high the golden cross with the white host visible through a round glass window surrounded by a gilded frame, like a sun burst. The altar boys rang small hand bells to focus our attention. Every statue was bright with dancing light. Even the Virgin Mary's eyes seemed to be alive.

At the communion rail, I knelt, palms pressed together and fingers pointed to heaven. I closed my eyes, lifted my chin and stuck out my tongue to receive the "Body of Christ."

Is that really Jesus in that round, white piece of bread? I wasn't sure. We were supposed to adore Jesus. But there he was on that wooden cross, hanging by nails in his hands and feet. His side was cut and his face so sad. Is that Jesus? Is he really here and there and everywhere? I wondered a lot, and when I asked, I was told: "These are the Mysteries of Faith."

"My Most Grievous Fault"

Once in fourth grade a visiting priest spoke to us about the "seven deadly sins:" pride, covetousness, lust, anger, gluttony, envy and sloth. The missionary priest asked for a show of hands. "Who has ever felt angry?" Mine was the only brave hand that

Thou Shalt Not

went up. Why of course I felt angry. Every day. I fought tooth and nail with my eight siblings. Our household was an intense arena of competing needs. Early on I learned to wield the sharp tongue of invective as a shield for my vulnerable self.

"You can dish it out, but you sure can't take it," was the taunt that sometimes came back at me when I let loose with my barbed tongue, trying to hold my own in one battle or another. When my father's insobriety and mother's grim resignation erupted into open dispute, I felt angry and confused. I remember my early attempts to articulate my conflicted feelings. I asked the visiting priest,

"Can you love and hate a person at the same time?" Whatever his response may have been, it did not ease my guilt.

"Get that black look off your face," Mama would command. Whenever my anger was in danger of spilling over she would hand me a broom and direct me outside to sweep the sidewalk.

Our Religion classes had little to say about the chaotic world beyond the school yard. The nuns stressed the Ten Commandments with all the "Thou Shalt Nots," but what I really needed then was wise counsel on how to navigate the sometimes-volatile emotions that ambushed me throughout my childhood.

I never did obedience well and was often in trouble. I could cuss with the best of them, bringing to the classroom and schoolyard the foul language that had become common in our sibling conflicts. When our battles escalated into shouting matches and fists, Mama would intervene with another mantra: "Blessed are the peacemakers, for they shall be called children of God." We siblings are still in need of peacemakers.

The sibling abuse at home was mostly verbal and seldom erupted in physical assaults beyond the routine knuckle slugs to my upper arm that was a favorite means of control from my older brothers, especially if they saw me crying. I learned early on that crying was a dangerous indulgence and would tuck away the hurt and tough it out. If the fighting got too bad, Mama or Daddy would threaten: "I'll get the belt." I can remember a few welts across the back of my thighs, but they soon gave up on that futile technique.

When I was still too young to understand, Danny or Tommy would coach me to say words they thought would shock the nuns.

"Tell Sister Samuella to fuck off," or "Tell Sr. Amadeus to go to hell." These obscenities coming out of the mouth of such an innocent-looking child as I was then must have really created a stir. Challenging authority seemed to come naturally to me. At home, Mama attempted to curb the vulgar language.

"I'll wash your mouth out with soap if you say that again," she threatened. And on more than one occasion I was forced to take a bite from the thick bar of Ivory soap. I wasn't the only one to suffer that fate, but I remember the taunting of my siblings as I flushed out my soapy mouth with water:

"It floats, it floats. What floats? Ivory Soap, you dope." That early childhood ditty still comes to mind when I scan the grocery shelves and see the old standby.

Daily Mass

Every weekday morning before classes at Little Flower School, we were made to attend 8 A.M. Mass, seated by grades in the long oak pews. We girls had to wear our uniform beanie cap. On Sundays and Holy Days of Obligation, we wore instead a small lace doily secured by a bobbie pin. If we lost it, Mama had a packet of Kleenex handy as a substitute. It was considered disrespectful for a girl to go bare-headed into the church.

Our pastor, Father Joseph Leppert, offered Mass in Latin with his back to the congregation served by two altar boys in white cassocks. I paid close attention as he intoned the Latin phrase *Introibo ad altare Dei* and the altar boys responded, *Ad Deum qui laetificat juventutem meum*. The translation: "I will go unto the altar of God; To God who giveth joy to my youth."

We girls knew we could not "go unto the altar of God." This prohibition lasted until 1992, and is still controversial in some Catholic parishes. Like the nuns, we came second to the boys in the eyes of the church, and were made aware of this subjugation in both overt and more subtle ways.

Father Leppert was a benevolent presence throughout all my grade-school years. His white-haired parents attended daily Mass in a special seat up front on the left side of the church. We were all sure they were living saints.

I remember especially the time Father Leppert and I were photographed for the *Tennessee Register*. I was seated in a swing, wearing my oversize black-and-white, wool-plaid coat. My bangs were held back with bobbie pins as Mama always admonished me: "Get your hair out of your eyes." Father stood behind me on the blacktop playground between the church and the school. Mama snapped the photo with her Kodak box camera. I was six-years old and felt quite special to be singled out by our pastor for this honor.

In about fourth grade I received my own copy of the *Saint Joseph Daily Missal* to follow along with during Mass and to learn the Liturgical Feast Days of the church. The Missal was in both Latin and English with many colorful illustrations for each section of the Mass. I can still recite some of the parts of the liturgy and can remember the songs from the High Mass. The choir loft was in back of the church with a full view of all the pews. We learned many Latin hymns, Gregorian Chants, and the special Marion hymns for the May Procession.

Today as I write in my Asheville home, my window looks out on Saint Lawrence Basilica where the church bell tolls hourly and periodically plays many of the familiar hymns whose lyrics still echo in my mind.

During church processions we were lined up by grade and height behind the priest, who held high the consecrated host, and the altar Boys swinging the incense censors. The pungent smells, the haunting rhythms of the Gregorian chants, the Spring beauty of the May Procession, the somber purple cloth draped over the statues during Lent, the gruesome Stations of the Cross, and the dread Confession booth are all still-vivid memories of my Catholic childhood.

"Loss of Heaven & Pains of Hell"

I learned Catholic dogma from the little blue *Baltimore Catechism* and Christian ideals from revised editions of *Butler's Lives of the Saints*, with statements such as "the chains and prisons of the martyrs were their joy and glory and the source of their grace and crown."[54]

We were taught a selective version of church history with tales of heretics and excommunication for dissenters. So many times I had questions about spiritual issues that were never adequately answered by the dogma in the books or the simplistic explanations of the nuns. The only Bible reading was at Mass when the priest read the scriptures specified for the day. I learned little or nothing about other world

The Half Life of a Free Radical

religions or Christian sects, and our Protestant neighbors, I suspect, learned little of what Catholics believed.

Once, Mama took me with her on a visit to the Monastery of St. Clare in the nearby community of Frayser. We sat in front of a wooden grate and Mama whispered to a woman on the other side. She may have been bringing a donation. We were not allowed to see her face. Mama said the Poor Clare sisters chose to live a life of poverty, depending on others for their necessities. They rarely left the enclosure where they lived together in simplicity and prayer, much as St. Clare of Assisi, my namesake, had lived centuries before.

Our Catholic schooling not only set us apart from "colored" Catholics but also from the neighborhood children who went to the Memphis City Schools and disappeared all day on Sunday into the Protestant churches that seemed to be on every corner. My impressions of Protestants came mostly through the Sunday morning preaching of radio evangelists whose fervor we mocked as children, or from the downtown street preachers in Court Square who warned of hellfire and damnation to the unsaved. I worried a lot about my Daddy going to Hell because he often missed Sunday Mass and we all knew that it was a Mortal sin.

Memphis also had a set of restrictions called the "Blue Laws" that limited what could be bought or sold on Sunday. Anything that had to do with work, or the purchase of food that had to be prepared, was considered illegal commerce. As Catholics, we were also prohibited from doing "servile" work on Sunday, though Mama seldom seemed to get a break. I wonder if that prohibition also extended to the people of color who labored in the households of many white Memphians.

Sometimes Daddy took us to the noon Mass at old St. Patrick's Church located at Fourth and Linden near Beale. He would always stand in the back close to the door, even though there were many empty front pews, so he could direct the smoke outside from his ever-present Roi Tan cigar. It was very hot inside in the summer, so we kept the cardboard hand-held fans moving.

After Mass, Daddy would now and again take us to breakfast at the Arcade Restaurant on South Main Street or stop at Walgreens where we passed around a tall glass of "all you can drink" iced tea while Daddy flirted with the waitress.

Thou Shalt Not

There was a ditty we sang on Sundays, "You take the high Mass and I'll take the low Mass and I'll get to breakfast before ye!" In those days it was the rule to fast before receiving Holy Communion. Mama usually went to the early Mass and had breakfast ready when we got home from a later one. Oatmeal was a staple, often accompanied by the song, "Peas porridge hot, peas porridge cold, peas porridge in the pot nine days old!"

Robert's grandchildren attended grade school in the revived St. Patrick's parish. Sadly, most of the homes in the neighborhood are now gone, razed in 1969 during the frenzy of destruction called Urban Renewal, when 500 buildings were torn down in the heart of the Beale Street neighborhood.

"The World & Its Evil Powers"

During seventh and eighth grades, Mary Alice and I joined The Legion of Mary. It was a religious group founded in Dublin in 1921 and organized in the manner of the Roman Legions "for service in the warfare which is perpetually waged by the Church against the world and its evil powers."[55]

The purpose, according to the *Legion Handbook*, is to "...bring Mary to the world, and she will give light to the world and presently set it all ablaze."

We met in the front room of the parish rectory adjacent to the church to read passages from the *Legion Handbook* and discuss various spiritual exercises, perhaps designed to shape us into chaste and holy young women devoted to the Blessed Virgin. We also strung plastic beads on wire to make rosaries to send to foreign missions.

Mary Alice was the expert at rosary-making. I couldn't seem to focus on the task long enough to finish one, and I soon gave it up. Mama tried so hard to find ways for me to embrace the church, but I was a heretic from my earliest days–it was "my most grievous fault."

My Catholic education came at a time when the subservient role of women in the church was accepted. I could sing in the choir and join processions to honor Mary, the Virgin Mother, with her attributes of submission, obedience and service, and when I came of age, in order of value, I could enter the convent as a nun (becoming a "Bride of Christ"), enter into the Holy Sacrament of Matrimony (with birth control forbidden), or remain chaste and single (as a teacher, a nurse, or a secretary).

The seven gifts of the Holy Spirit: Wisdom, Understanding, Counsel, Fortitude, Knowledge, Piety, and Fear of the Lord, were granted only if we remained in the "State of Grace."

Whenever I expressed doubts about the dogma in our *Baltimore Catechism*, or admitted my unwillingness to be burned at the stake or suffer the fate of the martyred saints, or if I just could not envision the sorrowful mysteries, Mama would advise: "Just pray to the Holy Ghost." She often repeated a prayer that her friends in the Outer Circle Catholic Action group had used to open each meeting. It seemed we were always calling on the invisible presence of The Holy Ghost.

> *Come Holy Ghost fill the hearts of thy faithful*
> *And kindle in them the fire of thy love.*
> *Send forth thy Spirit and they shall be created*
> *And thou shalt renew the face of the earth.*

The Sacrament of Confirmation was the final childhood initiation into the life of the Catholic Church. Our sixth-grade class had been thoroughly drilled in the meaning of this Sacrament. The nuns filled our heads with gruesome stories of martyrs, who were variously killed by lions, burned at the stake, shot with arrows, and turned on the wheel, all for keeping to the "One True Faith" in the face of persecution.

On Confirmation day we knelt at the marble Communion rail as the visiting bishop approached. He wore elegantly-embroidered vestments with a pointed miter on his head and carried an ornate staff, or crozier. He anointed each of us in turn with the consecrated oil called chrism, and then delivered a sharp slap to our cheek. This blow was meant to confirm us as "Soldiers of Christ" willing to endure whatever persecution necessary in witnessing to the "One True Faith." My sponsor was newspaperman Clark Porteous. At Mama's suggestion I took the Confirmation name Thérèse, a 19th-century French child who became a Carmelite nun at age fifteen. She was the patron saint of Little Flower Parish, and known as the "Sacred Keeper of the Gardens." Like my Grandmother Novetta, St. Thérèse had died young of the dread Tuberculosis.

Thou Shalt Not

Failure to Quit

Twenty-five years later, in the winter of 1986, I stood outside the iron gate at the White House to witness my daughter Jessica, on what I've come to see as her Confirmation day. It was a very different experience than mine had been.

We were in Washington, D.C. volunteering with the Community for Creative Nonviolence. The group operated an emergency shelter for as many as nine hundred persons within sight of the U.S. Capitol. They were threatened with a Spring eviction. Thirteen community members, including activist Mitch Snyder, were engaged in a month-long fast to compel then President Reagan to honor his promise to renovate the building as a model shelter.

Jessica and I volunteered in the women's wing. Never had we witnessed such a concentration of human need. Some women came with broken spirits, confused minds and ailing bodies, limping about on swollen and ulcerated feet. Others were still strong and determined with a clear sense of the injustice that brought them there. Obscenity was commonplace. Alcoholics spewed angry accusations, crazed souls wandered the halls muttering inanities, and the silent ones rocked and stared out of incomprehensible inner worlds.

Jessica was profoundly affected by the experience. When the call came for participants willing to risk arrest in a series of Good Friday actions at the Capitol and the White House, she did not hesitate to volunteer.

"I have seen too many people suffering and I'm mad at people for letting others suffer," she explained. "I want people to know that children care too."

With the assured support of the organizers, I let her go. I could not have stopped her.

On Good Friday morning, 1986, the White House lawn was crowded with uniformed police holding huge German Shepherd dogs that strained at their leashes. I watched from outside the iron gate as Jessica joined others to bravely step out of the White House tour line and over the boundary rope to kneel in prayer on the lawn. I felt a strange mixture of anxiety and pride as I witnessed her courage. She looked so vulnerable as she knelt there.

Behind me in the street, arrests were being made from among the hundreds who stopped traffic on Pennsylvania Avenue. Inside the fence an officer took my daughter by the arm, lifted her to her feet and led her away. So many times before it had been Jessica who stood and watched as I was led away for an act of peaceful protest. Now it was my turn to wait in support. It wasn't easy.

After nearly an hour, I was called to the gatehouse by Secret Service. They photographed us together and turned Jessica over to a D.C. police officer for further processing. Her charge: "Unlawful Entry. Failure to Quit."

At the police station, Jessica had the officer in tears as she explained why she had taken such a risk. She was released with a warning, and Mitch Snyder came to the station to escort us back to where we were staying. My brave daughter had confronted "the world and its evil power" to speak on behalf of all the homeless persons, particularly the children.

"If I can just touch one other person by what I do," she said. "then maybe I can make them think about things as I have thought about them."

Angel Guardians & Rosary Time

Night after night when we were very young, Mama would sit at the top of the attic stairs while we settled into sleep. We would recite together our evening prayer. It was the same one printed on the back of the Holy Card I received at my First Holy Communion:

> *Angel of God, my guardian dear,*
> *To whom God's love commits me here.*
> *Ever this day be at my side,*
> *To light and guard, to rule and guide, Amen.*

Somehow this reminder that we had a legion of unseen guardians watching over us made life easier, certainly more mysterious. Many years later, I received a note in the mail from Mama with a Holy Card. It was a Guardian Angel standing protectively behind a young child seated in a wooded area on the edge of creek. Printed on the back was the prayer I remembered from childhood. Mama wrote:

Thou Shalt Not

You mentioned the Angel prayer from times past and this just fell out of a book. Is this the one you remember? You must have a very good Guardian Angel! Love from your Mama.

There were plenty of Holy Cards available to help us visualize the Virgin Mother, the Holy Family and many among the "Communion of Saints." The best cards were in full color with a gilded edge. The two saints most often invoked in our household were Saint Jude, patron of hopeless causes, and Saint Anthony, who had the power to find lost items. On the back of each card was a prayer with the promise that if we recited it faithfully we would receive a so-called "indulgence" and be relieved of some of the temporal punishment due for our sins. Without enough indulgences to reduce the sentence, we would be sent to Purgatory to burn off the punishment. Reciting the Rosary, especially as a family, would provide even more special indulgences.

Every night in the early years when we still obeyed we would hear Mama's call: "Rosary time!" We usually gathered after homework and before bedtime. We knelt together on the hardwood floor in the living room before a Plaster of Paris statue of the Blessed Virgin Mary, the centerpiece of the mantle. The ritual would begin with the Sign of the Cross and the Apostles Creed, and then we would recite together either the Sorrowful Mysteries, the Glorious Mysteries, or the Joyful Mysteries, opening each of the ten decades with an Our Father, and then ten Hail Mary's fingered on our own beads, likely purchased at Rogers Church Goods Company.

We prayed for world peace, the conversion of communist Russia, for all the people stuck behind the Iron Curtain, and of course, for the sobriety of our father. Sometimes our neighbor Tommy Joe would peek in the living room window and watch us at prayer. My friend Catherine remembers that any time she spent the night, she too had to kneel down for the Rosary.

Try as I would, I just couldn't connect with the ancient mysteries. I often tried to imagine what the Holy Ghost would look like, descending in a tongue of fire, neither male nor female, but in the form of a dove filled with holy wisdom to help us know the truth.

A silver embossed wall plaque, with a head and shoulders image of the Sacred Heart of Jesus, hung on the kitchen wall beside the stove in the corner where Mama kept the tall trash can and the kitchen

The Half Life of a Free Radical

broom. His tunic was open to reveal his pulsing heart, which he held in his left hand. He raised his right hand in the mudra of blessing. Below the image on this family relic was the promise: "The home where this image is displayed and honored will be blessed."

Mama kept this icon close by throughout her life. On many occasions during my childhood when I passed that image, I felt a sense of betrayal. Sometimes that promise seemed like such a mockery of the turmoil that reigned in our home.

On a Memphis visit in 2013 I helped Robert sort through some of Mama's meager possessions that he had held in storage for many years. Among the rosaries, holy cards and scapulars in one box, my hand fell upon that old wall plaque of the Sacred Heart of Jesus. I have this childhood relic now in my own small apartment as a reminder of Mama's deep faith that carried her through. Soon, though, I will pack it up and send it to Eileen, in whose keeping I think it will be most treasured.

"Your Mother is a saint. Be good to her," my fourth-grade teacher once told me. Everyone seemed to think our Mama was a saint. Maybe she was. But I knew for sure I wasn't, nor did I want to be a "virgin-martyr" or "Bride of Christ," as many women saints were said to be, or a long-suffering mother, as mine seemed to be.

If Mama was a saint, she wasn't like those saints we read about in the revised versions of *Butler's Lives of the Saints*. Sometimes she smoked, but not until her first four children were teenagers and we all had taken up the costly habit. Now and again she had a beer. "Damn you," was her strongest curse, "Don't be stupid," her meanest admonition, and "Where in the hell did you get that idea?" a frequent query.

Even now, when Mother's Day rolls around, one relative or another will attempt to sanctify her. Mama would laugh at the designation of sainthood.

One story we heard often during our grade-school years was of the fabled 1917 apparition of Our Lady of the Rosary to the three shepherd children at Fatima, Portugal. The Virgin Mother, the story goes, appeared to the children to warn the world that "war is a punishment for sins." Her counsel was to "Pray the Rosary daily!"

Mama was a member of the Third Order of St. Francis and always wore a small (one by two-inch) brown-felt scapular, beneath her blouse. A scapular is a remnant of a modified habit for secular members in the ancient monastic and mendicant order. Historically, members were prohibited from bearing arms. Those who faithfully wore the scapular also earned at least some "remission of the temporal punishment due to sin."

Pope Pius XII, declared that the Third Order was instituted for this purpose: "to satisfy fully the sincere desires of those who had to remain in the world but who did not wish to be of the world. ...those who burn with the desire of striving for perfection in their own station in life."[56]

Mama heeded the call throughout her life. I remember being gifted with a scapular when I was about fourteen. I wore it for a while, but as with other religious artifacts, I didn't keep it long.

When Mama moved to her retirement apartment at St. Peter Manor around 1987, she continued praying the Rosary, holding weekly gatherings with a small circle of women residents. During one poignant moment in her final days, with her memory fading, she whispered to me, "I can't remember the words to my prayers." All I could tell her was that as far as I was concerned, her entire life had been a prayer.

Though she didn't live to see the "world peace" she had so faithfully prayed for, or the racial justice she tried to bring about, Mama was finally able to find the "peace and quiet" that had so eluded her while she was busy raising nine hooligan Hanrahans.

Oh Holy Night

Midnight Mass with Mama was a Christmas tradition. We girls wore our brand-new Christmas dresses and the boys wore a jacket, white shirt, and clip-on tie. The church was decorated with poinsettias and twinkling lights, with a life-size manger scene outside. We were hurried up to bed after Mass and the long night of waiting began. Christmas morning there was a small pile of gifts for each of us children arranged around the scraggly pine tree that Daddy brought home from Joe's Shoe Shop when they went on sale after dark on Christmas Eve. Daddy always expected us to wait until the price of a tree was down as low as $1.00.

Under the tree on Christmas mornings we always found books and puzzles and sometimes Tinker Toys, Lincoln Logs, Paint-by-Number sets, Crayola crayons and coloring books, harmonicas,

The Half Life of a Free Radical

Etch-a-Sketch, Vue-Finders with an assortment of tiny images on a circular cardboard, and other toys. There were new pajamas, socks and sweaters, and as we got older, baseballs, bats and gloves and roller skates. I remember one Christmas when I was in 7th or 8th grade I got a transistor radio so I could listen to my favorite songs.

"I got a black-velvet swan one Christmas," Regina remembers. "Its wings were lined in gold satin and it was big. Big enough where I could sit on it." She remembered that the neck was bent. That had been a slim year, and we older teenagers who worked during the Christmas holidays had bought it from the discount table at the Fred P. Gattas Co. store. Years later, when Eileen had a family of her own, she wrote about another frugal family Christmas for the Tennessee *Greeneville Sun*:

"It was already December 23rd and we still had no Christmas tree. Our family had no car, little money, and it looked as if Christmas would be bleak."[57]

With a few dollars she had saved from babysitting, Eileen walked the cold two miles down North Parkway to the Sears & Roebuck, but the Christmas trees there cost three times the amount she had to spend. Determined, she walked on. It was getting dark. At the 7-11 store in the next block, the clerk had just put a half-price sign out on the few remaining live trees. Eileen found one for just three dollars.

As she tells the story, she dragged that tree home in the cold and dark, cars whizzing by, but none stopping. Her arms ached "as they never had before." When she finally reached home, our brothers took on the job of setting up the tree, while we girls pulled out the old box of decorations, strung the lights and hung the ornaments, singing every Christmas Carol we knew. Regina found old boxes and a few rolls of wrapping paper left from the year before.

"We all pitched in, wrapped the boxes and put them under the tree. There were now so many packages they filled the whole corner of the room. And they weren't empty. They were filled with love."[58]

By the time I was a mother I had become far too alienated from the church to celebrate the holiday in the traditional manner. Somewhere along the line I became a Scrooge. That, together with my strong political opinions, wandering lifestyle, and vegetarian diet, has left me on the outside of most seasonal family gatherings.

One Christmas, when Jessica was thirteen, and we were living in St. Petersburg, Florida, we organized a walk to the manger scene in

Thou Shalt Not

Straub Park from the women's shelter we had co-founded.[59] At dusk, in the company of the homeless women and children who were our guests, we lay down next to the statues of Mary, Joseph, and the baby Jesus. We were met, not by gifts from the Magi, but with cold water from the municipal lawn sprinklers. It was a crime in St. Petersburg then for anyone "to lie down to rest or sleep in public" after 11 p.m. The demonstration became an annual event in the city to raise funds for the un-housed poor, called "Still, No Room at the Inn."

A Separate Peace

During a high school religious retreat, which was little more than a few days of intense instruction in church dogma, a visiting priest talked briefly about sexuality and the sin of "self-abuse." I guessed that by self-abuse he meant masturbation, though that was not a word in our family lexicon. But I already knew that it was considered a sin to touch yourself. I was guilty of this secret sin sometimes while soothing myself to sleep. The shame was always there. Sometimes I found myself repeating the *Act of Contrition* in the midst of my furtive efforts. There wasn't the privacy in our house to risk such indulgence often. Nonetheless, I felt I had to confess this sin of "self-abuse" to restore myself to a "state of grace."

I knelt in the dark confessional and told the priest of my sin while a long line of classmates waited their turn behind me. I was afraid they all had heard my whispers and that they all surely knew my secret. I was quite angry then at a God who would require me to humiliate myself by sharing my personal life with the strange man in the confessional booth. I decided then and there that it was none of his business. I was coming to a point of making a separate peace with God and another with the church. I seldom returned to the Confessional booth.

Even as my faith in the church and all its promises waned, I tried to remain receptive to the blessing conferred by the priest who turned to face the congregation in the closing ritual of the Mass: "May the Blessing of Almighty God, the Father, the Son and the Holy Ghost, descend upon you and remain with you forever."

In times when I felt most desperate, I repeated the prayer to the Blessed Mother known as the *Memorare:*

The Half Life of a Free Radical

Remember, O most gracious Virgin Mary,
That never was it known
That anyone who fled to thy protection,
Implored thy help
Or sought thy intercession,
Was left unaided...

But it often seemed I had been "left unaided." I carried a sense of deep alienation from the church. Try as I would, I felt no personal relationship with Jesus, who seemed but a remote historical figure, nor with the priests and nuns, who conveyed piety and prohibition and who I felt could not possibly understand me.

I continued with the urgent prayer to Mary:

...Inspired by this confidence, I fly unto thee, oh virgin of virgins, my mother.
To thee I come, before thee I stand sinful and sorrowful.
Oh Mother of the Word incarnate despise not my petition
But in thy mercy, hear and answer me, Amen.

Despite daily repetition, the answer I sought never came. I found little solace or help with the complex problems I experienced growing up in a family where alcoholism took its toll and where questions about sex were taboo. Words like masturbation, homosexuality, and divorce were ugly whispers. Alcoholism was an ugly word too, and one that carried a burden of shame. Abortion was "beyond the Pale." Little did I realize then that even the priests, ordained to confer the forgiveness of sin, had their own sexual struggles and dark secrets.

Priestly Abuse & Cover-ups

In the mid-1970's, with all her children grown, and most of us married or moved away, Mama found work as an administrative assistant at Holy Names Church. She attended Mass in the racially-diverse North Memphis parish with Robert, Vernua, and their children, Katrina and James. The parish priest was Milton Guthrie, a Memphis native who had been active in the Civil Rights Movement.

During this time I was working nearby at Lowenstein House as a social worker with persons just released from mental-health facilities. I knew that the neighborhood work was vital in that inner-city community.

In 1977 Father Guthrie was re-assigned to a different parish. When the new priest arrived, he fired Mama for "insubordination." She may have been advocating for a continuation of the neighborhood revitalization programs initiated in the desperately poor, mostly-black neighborhood north of Jackson Avenue. To my thinking, "insubordination" seemed an honorable charge. I was outraged when I learned of Mama's summary dismissal, but at her request, I held my tongue. I have no way of knowing now what the truth was about that situation.

Father Guthrie died in 2002, but his legacy of social service and civil-rights advocacy was marred in 2008 when a former parishioner filed suit against the Catholic Diocese of Memphis, alleging he had been sexually abused as a child by Guthrie in the 1970's. He further charged that the Diocese was part of a cover-up of such abuse by priests in general "at the highest levels."

In 2010, the Tennessee Appeals Court ruled the statute of limitations has run in the case, upholding similar Tennessee court decisions "that those alleging such abuse and claiming negligence have a year after turning 18 years old to inquire whether the diocese knew of other allegations and failed to act."[60]

I do not know what may have occurred in the rectory of Holy Names Parish, neither man had their day in court, but the ruling that an abuse victim has only one year after reaching adulthood to make a claim is itself a further abuse of power that does not serve truth.

Mama too had died by the time the allegations were made public. She spent her last years in the Catholic nursing home, St. Peter Villa. On some visits with Mama there I accompanied her to Mass in the first-floor chapel. It was the highlight of the day for many of the mostly-octogenarian women residents. It took a good deal of effort for the staff to get them dressed and transported on time. Sometimes the priest arrived late. Sometimes he didn't show up at all.

Once I suggested to the waiting women that they circle up their wheelchairs and hold their own service. But they had for so long deferred to priestly authority that most assured me they would rather "just wait until Father comes."

One of the Catholic chaplains I met at the Villa was from Viet Nam. His youthful presence seemed a welcome change from his somewhat perfunctory predecessor. Little did we know that this priest was under investigation at the time for alleged sexual abuse of young girls in the Confession booth in his parish church. I guess reassigning him to duty with octogenarians seemed a safe bet. I only learned of the allegations much later, in 2010, when *The Commercial Appeal* reported information from the unsealed court documents.[61]

Like many Catholic dioceses, the Diocese of Memphis covered up and reassigned its share of sexual abusers. Many offending priests were moved from parish to parish to avoid scandal. Another Memphis priest I knew, Father James Murphy, has been implicated on the controversial website: BishopAccountability.org.

Well over a million dollars has been spent on out-of-court settlements, and at least fifteen priests in the Memphis Diocese, some who I knew in childhood, have been accused of sexual misconduct over a period of four decades.[62]

Even a fraction of these millions paid to silence or settle these cases of sexual abuse would have gone a long way to improve the quality of life of Memphis' elderly poor and to alleviate the crowded conditions and over-worked staff at the Catholic nursing home where my Mama, and so many other loyal women parishioners spent their last years.

I spoke about these issues recently with my brother Michael, who like his older twin brothers had been an altar boy.

"Our Mother worshipped priests like they were elevated individuals," Michael said, "but I questioned everything they did. Priests were giving us wine back stage before we went out to serve Mass, and then taking us out to breakfast."

Michael was "fired" as an altar boy, he said, because "I had a hole in my shoe and was not cooperative. By fifth grade I had stopped being a Catholic."

4

School Days & Hood Ways

We've got a dollar, we've got a dollar, We've got a dollar, hey, hey, hey hey.
— Buckwheat, "Our Gang"

I held tight to Danny's hand as he walked me into the classroom for my first day at Little Flower School. The hardwood floors creaked in the empty classroom as I set my book bag down on a front-row desk, as Mama had suggested. Then we joined the others at the church for 8 A.M. Mass.

Our efforts at securing a front-row desk were defeated by the alphabetical arrangement of our seating. The small oak desks, each attached to the one behind, were lined up four across and six deep. The desk had a pencil slot and a round hole for an ink well. The hinged top opened to a storage place for books and papers.

Sister Frances Genevieve, my first-grade teacher, sat at an oak desk centered in front of a wide blackboard framed with placards for each letter of the alphabet. She called us to attention throughout the day by ringing a wooden-handled brass bell. A large crucifix was mounted above the blackboard and an American flag hung from a pole in the corner of the room.

Tall windows filled one wall looking out on the blacktop playground with swings, slides and the wooden whirl-a-round. On the hottest days Sister opened the window to the cooling breezes. I was admonished often for gazing out the classroom windows. It was hard to sit still. My mind was always taking flights of fancy and my gaze often followed a dust mote out through the glass to freedom.

The Sisters of Charity of Nazareth, Kentucky, in the spirit of Saint Vincent de Paul, were our teachers at Little Flower Parish. Their habit, which was what their uniform was called, consisted of a long, black gabardine skirt with a wide-sleeved black top under a starched white bib. On cool days, they draped a short cape around their shoulders. A white-fluted head covering, also starched, framed their face. Not a strand of hair was visible. Heavy wooden rosary beads circled their middle, with a large silver crucifix hanging down in front. We giggled at the thought of a big wind blowing off their bonnets and proving our suspicions that they were all bald.

I started school in Mary Alice's hand-me down navy blue uniform jumper with the embroidered emblem "LFS" (We called it " Let's Forget School") on the front and worn over a white cotton shirt. I was not quite six. My light-brown, chin-length hair with a fringe of bangs framed my dimpled cheeks. My blue eyes, wide with excitement, matched the color of our uniform beanie with the same embroidered "LFS" patch.

Even in school uniforms there was no hiding the poverty of our circumstances. Most of the girls wore white blouses with a Peter Pan-style round collar purchased at Goldsmiths Department store. I usually wore the pointed collars on yellowing hand-me-down shirts borrowed from my brothers, with the buttons on the wrong side. I hardly noticed this until the later grades.

Dear Old Golden Rule Day

As I soon discovered, everything at school was to be straight lines and order, piety and obedience.

I remember most of the names and faces of the nuns who taught me: Sr. Frances Genevieve, Sr. Margaret Ellen, Sr. Samuella, Sr. Ann de Paul, Sr. Loretta, and our principal, Sr. Amadeus, who was rumored to have a "spanking machine" in her small office. These nuns seemed indomitable, and "woe be-tide" any of us who failed to stand in unison with the greeting, "Good morning Sister," when they entered the classroom.

The first order of the day was the morning prayer with the Sign of the Cross: "In the name of the Father, the Son and the Holy

School Days & Hood Ways

Ghost." The Pledge of Allegiance came next, with our right hand placed reverently over our heart.

Before we began an assignment we carefully printed the initials A.M.D.G. at the top of each piece of lined notebook paper. Spelled out in Latin, *Ad maiorem Dei gloriam*, it is the Jesuit motto: "All for the Honor and Glory of God."

There were a few so-called lay teachers, Miss Reedy, Miss Narrowmore and handsome Mr. Rhem, who taught fourth or fifth grade. All the girls had a crush on him. Many years later, when I was back living in Memphis with Jessica, I met Mr. Rhem again. He was every bit as handsome as I remembered him.

Not all the teachers were nice. One time in seventh grade, a nun sent me home with a bottle of Clorox to give to my mother as a not-so-subtle hint that she might be falling behind on her job to keep us in snow-white pressed shirts. I felt ashamed and angry when I brought it home, and Mama was none too pleased either.

I usually made straight A's, except in "conduct," where it would be either "S" for satisfactory, or a "U" for unsatisfactory, never " E" for excellent. We had to bring the index-size report cards home every few months for a parent's signature. Mama always signed mine in her lovely cursive script, "Mrs. D. G. Hanrahan" or sometimes " Alice D. Hanrahan" or "Alice Donnelly Hanrahan" or "Mrs. Daniel G. Hanrahan." Mama had many variations, depending on the type of document before her, or which sweepstakes she had entered. It was one way she kept track of where the mail came from, she explained.

We were taught The Palmer Method of penmanship with its well-formed cursive letters. By fourth grade we were allowed to write with ink and had to provide a fountain pen and ink cartridges as part of our yearly school supplies.

We supplemented the school library with frequent trips to the Memphis Public Library. Mama made sure we each had our own library card. We were expected to take good care of the books we borrowed and to return them all on time. If we lost a book, or had overdue fees, Mama made sure we paid the fine in person from money we earned by doing a chore.

The day I got my first library card Mama photographed me standing in front of our brick bungalow, my head not yet reaching the bottom of the front windows. My shoulder-length brown hair is parted every-which way. The bangs that I just cut myself with dull

The Half Life of a Free Radical

kitchen shears are choppy and slanted. I'm smiling as I clutch a new library book. My "hand-me-down" plaid wool coat feels heavy and itchy. It is way too big. But it is warm. My brown shoes are scuffed from dragging the toes across the concrete. They are laced up with cotton string. Both my feet are close together, one sock has disappeared, bunched up inside my shoe, somewhere beneath the heel. The shoes don't quite fit yet, either, but like the coat, I'll soon grow into them. But now, clutching the book I feel big already. A library card in my pocket and winter coming on.

I remember how cold my fingers were on the walk home from the bus stop. I had to keep them out of my pockets to hold my books. I could see my breath when I blew on my fingers. I walked fast the few blocks as Mama urged me on. At home the little kids peeked through the front window in anticipation of our return. Inside, the radiator was warm and I settled in on the brown couch to read aloud as my siblings cozied up close.

Many school days we kids would walk the two blocks to the corner of Jackson and Breedlove and stand in front of Kay's Bakery to wait for the Number 52 bus to take us the two miles to school. The fare was fifteen cents with a student bus card. Michael remembers how cold it was some winter mornings as we waited, passing the time by blowing our breath to fog up the bakery windows and write messages on the frosty panes. One time, on a dare, Johnny licked a light post and his tongue stuck fast on the cold metal. We had to run and find some water to pour over it to free it up as it had quickly frozen in place.

The bus passed the St. Vincent de Paul thrift store where our neighbor Miss English volunteered. It was near a short block of so-called "nigger shacks," interspersed with car repair garages and small corner groceries. Poverty was sorely visible. Most of this area was later razed for a shopping center, and now is an Interstate expressway interchange that further demolished the neighborhood.

Sometimes Mama would drive us all to school in Daddy's work car. The coveted position was a window seat with a finger to the automatic control. On warm afternoons I would often walk the two miles home, and save my bus fare to buy a single-dip chocolate ice cream cone or a cherry-phosphate soda at the Speedway Terrace drugstore.

School Days & Hood Ways

I varied my walking route. Sometimes I would go west on Jackson Avenue past the Rosemary theater at Jackson and Watkins and the small Montesi family grocery. Across the street there was an ESSO gasoline station, a liquor store, and further down, Mike's bar, where Daddy sometimes could be found.

A child-like man who everyone called Ronnie Rosemary often showed up after hours on our school playground. We had to be careful around him if we played on the wooden whirl-a-round because he would start spinning it so fast we would fly off, landing hard on the blacktop. He didn't realize his strength, or the danger of not stopping when we screamed.

Ronnie was always at the Saturday afternoon movie at the Rosemary Theater, which is how he got his nickname. Mama cautioned us not to tease him or call him a retard, as others did. We were to say hello whenever we saw him.

One time Mama slipped into a rear seat at the Rosemary theater. Word had gotten back to her of some rowdy play during the movie, so she went to see for herself. This later became the subject of one of her "Ladies' Fare" columns through which she counseled parents about their movie-going children:

> *He should learn to keep his hands to himself to avoid the elbowing and pushing that leads to scuffles. ...and above all, teach him to respect his own person by making him vitally aware that God sees all things and that we are accountable to Him for our actions.*[63]

That all-seeing aspect of God haunted me, as did the phrase in the *Apostles Creed* warning that Jesus "is seated at the right hand of God the Father Almighty, from thence He shall come to judge the living and the dead."

I imagined standing before the throne of God with all the men there knowing about everything I ever did. But, before too long, I came to the conclusion that God could not possibly keep his eye on everybody all the time. So I quit worrying and like Jiminy Cricket, I let my conscience be my guide.

The Half Life of a Free Radical

Reading & Homework Time

Our living room bookcase held the many volumes of *Childcraft*. The encyclopedia had bright orange, textured-vinyl covers and colorful illustrations. Mama always encouraged us older siblings to read to the younger ones. It was a way we could practice our reading, and keep an eye on them while she made supper. After we got our television, we read less and less.

I memorized several poems from the *Childcraft* books, including, "You Are Old, Father William" by Lewis Carroll, and Edward Lear's "The Owl and the Pussycat." Mama also encouraged us to make up Limericks, which were always a fun way to play with words.

Eileen remembers the day she sat beside Mama on the living room couch as she paged through the sample copies of the *World Book Encyclopedia* brought by a door-to-door saleswoman. It was an exciting day for us all when the boxes of books finally arrived. To most of our questions Mama would reply, "Look it up," and point us to the shelf with the *Thorndike-Barnhart* dictionary and the encyclopedias.

Eileen, who recently retired as director of the Hawkins County, Tennessee, Library system, was an avid reader as a child. I had too much trouble staying put long enough to finish even a chapter. Mama seemed always to chide me: "Finish one thing before you start with another." That lack of focus, what some folks characterized as being "scattered," has been with me most of my life.

One Christmas Mama gave me an illustrated copy of Rachael Carson's *The Sea Around Us*. I recently found a paperback version. I never finished reading it as a child so it is on my list to read today.

Mama encouraged a sense of exploration. "It's a big world out there," she would often say as if to open to us a universe of possibilities beyond the poverty and limitations of our chaotic home. Though I remember few hugs and scant praise, Mama kept a light alive for us all, and hope that we could move beyond the North Memphis neighborhood that seemed to be closing in around us.

Our front hallway bookcase held monthly volumes of *American Heritage* and art history from the *Metropolitan Seminars in Art* series, each with full-color classic and modern art prints. Some of the images were confusing; one I particularly recall was Poussin's "Rape of the

School Days & Hood Ways

Sabine Women" with its disturbing depiction of how women are treated in war.

When I was seven or eight, I read parts of the historical children's novels in the *We Were There* series. Most of this series was about battles and adventures with boys as the heroes in titles like *We Were There on the Chisholm Trail*, or *We Were There at the Battle of the Alamo*. *The Hardy Boys* series by F.W. Dixon, and *Nancy Drew* mystery stories were better. We also had some of the *Bobbsey Twins* series by Laura Lee Hope, which I never liked.

Eileen remembers when she had the measles and was confined to a dark bedroom. She was about eight.

"When I felt well enough to do something, I sneaked in a *Hardy Boys* book and read it in the dim light, hoping I would not go blind."

Getting Mama's Message

Mama usually had refreshments ready for us after school. We drank lots of Kool Aid, with or without sugar, with her homemade oatmeal cookies. Sometimes we would have Mama's special treat: vanilla ice cream layered with grape nuts and honey. Other times she offered Jello with mixed fruit.

On summer days we listened for the bell of the Popsicle man as he made his way through the neighborhood with his hand-pushed cart. Popsicles had two sticks so it could be split and shared. We saved the wooden sticks for making crafts. "Tastes good lick after lick. Right down to the Popsicle stick."

In the 1960's, the hand-pushed Popsicle cart gave way to the motorized Merry Mobile, a round metal vehicle with an awning painted in red, white and blue stripes attracting kids with amplified carnival like music. After refreshments, and whenever the weather allowed, Mama's usual order was:

"Everybody out of the house, all of you, and don't slam the door!"

We wandered the neighborhood at will as far as our feet would carry us. The neighbors provided a safety net of watchful eyes, occasionally a Band-Aid for a skinned knee, or emergency childcare when Mama went off to have another baby.

We stayed outside until dusk when we heard Mama's call: "Supper time!" It seemed to echo through the neighborhood. If we were out of range of her voice, we would just feel her calling in our minds and know we better get a move on. "Glad to see you got my message," she would say when we finally made it home. Mama used her mind that way, but she discouraged any conversation about psychic abilities. Such things did not meet with approval of the Catholic church. Although I do remember hearing that her own mother had been able to move items across the table with just the concentration of her mind. I tried, but never succeeded in budging a thing.

Spiritualism and the belief that one could communicate with the dead was in common practice in the early 1900's when our Grandmother Novetta was a young woman. Its popularity was likely a reaction to the terrible losses of World War I and the influenza pandemics. I remember Mama demonstrating the energy field we could feel when putting our finger tips together and flexing our palms rapidly back and forth, then pulling our hands slowly apart.

When Mary Alice traveled to Europe, Mama and she set times when they would try to connect their minds across the ocean. I'm not sure of the outcome of those experiments. The communication between them did not seem to work beyond death, however, as Mary was away from home and didn't get the message in time for Mama's funeral. She later reported noticing lights flickering on and off in her hotel room around the time our mother died.

Falsely Accused

When I was about ten, I walked up to the five-and-dime store on Jackson Avenue. I wandered the aisles trying to decide what to buy a sibling as a birthday gift. I may have had a plastic water gun, a yo-yo, or some other small item in one hand when I drifted toward the door, lost in thought and trying to figure out if I had enough money in the coins I gripped in my other hand to buy a gift. The clerk had been watching me and followed me toward the door. She grabbed me by the arm, accusing me of trying to steal. I was hurt and felt ashamed. She let me go with a stern warning but I never went back to that store. Even to this day, I sometimes imagine the eyes of the clerks following me around if I linger too long in a shop.

School Days & Hood Ways

One afternoon many years later, my high-school friend Phyllis and I stopped by Zayre, a department store on Poplar Avenue similar to a Target or K-Mart of today. We spent a lot of time looking at all the new swimsuits. We took an armful to the dressing room to try on. We just couldn't make up our minds. When we finally left the store, still undecided, we were confronted by two security guards who had followed us out. They accused us of stealing and ordered us into a back room. They would not believe us when we insisted we were not wearing a swimsuit under our school uniforms. Cowed into obedience, we submitted to a strip search. Finding nothing, they let us go.

When I got home, still shaken from the violation, I told Daddy what happened. He sued. We didn't have to testify in court, so he must have settled out of court. Phyllis' share was enough to pay for her dental braces. I never saw a dime of my share. It probably went to pay some family bill or another. Recently, a speaker told about her experience and that of many African-Americans, of whatever financial means, who are often followed around by store clerks as they shop. As a poor white child in Memphis, I felt a similar scrutiny, though as I became an adult it stopped happening to me.

Ring Leader

We never locked the doors at our house; there were just too many kids coming and going throughout the day. The big black flies buzzed right inside with us all summer long. Mama kept a wire-mesh fly swatter on hand, and its tell-tale swat added to the symphony of summer sounds.

We shared many different kinds of outdoor toys over the years including a pogo stick, a little red wagon, a blue-metal pedal car, a broomstick pony, a two-wheeled scooter, roller skates and the newest fad, a Whamo-O Hula Hoop, which I was quite good keeping spinning. When it was my turn with the roller skates, and I could find the key to adjust the length and tighten the skates around my shoes, I would fly down the sidewalk at high speeds with the key swinging on a string around my neck.

Our outside games included most of the neighborhood children, and there were dozens loose on the streets. We played Hide-and-Go-Seek, Kick the Can, Chase, and King of the Hill well into the darkness

The Half Life of a Free Radical

in our small front yard, or in the larger fenced back yard. We climbed the trees, built scrap-wood tree forts and dug a warren of tunnels down into the damp cool earth.

As a pre-teen, I spent a lot of time helping dig those tunnels or just hanging out in the musky coolness, leaning my back against the smooth dirt walls and enjoying the quiet. We covered the hole with old plywood boards and discarded window panes to let in light and to help keep us dry when it rained.

Out by the weathered gray wooden planks of the back-yard fence we could spy on the neighbors through the knot holes. I often wondered what went on inside other people's homes, and sometimes walked around the block after dark to see what I could through open blinds. I wanted to have X-ray vision, like Superman.

One time Daddy came home from the salvage yard with some large, hard-plastic dome-shaped tubs that had been a part of the cockpits of WWII airplanes. With a kid on either side we could rock back and forth, or spin them around on the grass, holding on for dear life. Danny and Tommy devised a more daring use. Our neighbor Tommy Joe recalls that they found some iron rails, perhaps from old bed frames, and leaned them up against the low roof of the back porch. Then, hauling one of the cockpit bubbles up with a ladder, we would ride them down to the ground at high speed.

"Your Mama put an end to that roller-coaster ride pretty quickly," Tommy Joe remembered.

After we tired of the cockpit bubbles, Mama re-purposed two as planters in the front yard. This was part of her ongoing efforts to bring the beauty of growing things to the space between the two oaks that stood sentry over our house. A less-trodden space might have become a lawn, but not during the years when it was the playing field for the Hanrahan children and our many neighborhood friends, including the Kernodle, Gattas, Baker and Holland kids.

Sometimes we played an after-dark game to test our courage called "monster." Regina remembers:

> *The monster, usually a big kid, would hide in the back yard. We would go back one at a time in the dark and walk around, never knowing when the monster would jump out. It wasn't just us playing Monster, it was every other damn kid in the neighborhood who could get out. Our yard was the place to be. It was fun, and Clare was a ring leader.*

School Days & Hood Ways

"Ring-leader?" Maybe. I do know that I loved the freedom we all had to roam the neighborhood with our gang of friends, and play until well after dark in our back yard. Such freedom to roam is rare today for children whose lives are scheduled and monitored in ways we could never have imagined.

Broken Bones & Busted Teeth

Our outdoor play was rife with casualties. One time in a game of Hide-and-Go-Seek I climbed on top of one of the barrel-like steel garbage cans in the back of a neighbor's house to get a better view. When I jumped down my hand landed on a shard of broken bottle. I remember screaming in fear as a neighbor washed the blood off in the sink while everyone hovered around.

"You might need stitches," she said, setting off my anguished howls. I don't remember if I had to go to the emergency room, but the thought of a needle in my hand terrified me. Mama always warned us about rusty nails when we walked barefoot outside. They were a sure way to have to get a Tetanus shot with what was rumored to be a foot-long needle.

We held marathon relay races to the corner and back, regularly falling and skinning our knees which Mama would douse with Mercurochrome or Merthiolate when we made it home for the night. Throughout much of the summer we had large black scabs on our knees and elbows, numerous itchy welts from mosquito bites, skin sticky with summer sweat, and a dark ring of dirt that filled the creases around our necks. Mama called this our "Grandma's necklace." When it lingered for more than a day or two, we were marched inside for a bath, though the gritty hardwood floors soon turned the soles of our bare feet black again.

Michael was about ten when he lost his front tooth.

"I was running through the preacher's back yard. I didn't see the wooden ladder sticking out from a window in the greenhouse. I ran right into it and knocked my front tooth out."

Danny's high-school friend Don was visiting that day and took Michael to the hospital on the back of his Vespa scooter.

"They wired the tooth back in my mouth," Michael told me recently. "It lasted all these years until 2013 when it finally gave way."

The Half Life of a Free Radical

Danny was the catcher in a backyard baseball game one summer when he was about fourteen. Whoever was at bat took a swing and let it fly as they ran to capture first base. The heavy wooden bat struck Danny hard across his face, breaking his nose. These casualties were not without cost, and I'm not sure if we ever had insurance to cover them.

When we were very little Mama's childhood physician, Dr. Ham, made house calls. We all had our bouts with mumps and measles and chicken pox. Eileen remembers the time he sat down on the radiator in the living room and one by one turned us kids over his knee to give us shots. Other medical procedures were left up to Mama. I have a very early memory of her rubbing Vicks VapoRub on my chest as I lay in bed. A humidifier humming nearby filled the air with steam. I don't remember many sick days over the years. We toughened up pretty fast.

When we had a toothache that wouldn't go away, Daddy took us up to his office in the Sterick Building near the Strand movie theater. The dentist across the hall drilled and filled many a tooth throughout our childhood years. After the trauma in the dentist's chair, we would sometimes stop for a treat at the Planters Peanut store where a large figure of Mr. Peanut, complete with top hat, monocle, and spats, tapped on the window with his cane.

Sometimes we all got boils on our butts and other body parts. Mama would hold us down across her lap to lance them. We screamed as she squeezed out the core when the sticky black salve that was the first remedy did not draw it out. Eileen remembers Mama saying that every time she had to go to the emergency room with one of us, we would all come down with boils soon after.

One afternoon, Mama beckoned us, one at a time, to a towel spread out on the bathroom floor. Enema time! I think we may have had worms. I remember hearing dire warnings after that day about the need to cook the pork chops through and through.

In 1955 the polio vaccine was declared "safe, effective and potent" after field trials on 1.8 million school children. Polio was highly feared and there was much talk about "infantile paralysis" and of children who had to live out their entire lives encased in an iron lung. I was about seven when Mama took us to Vollintine School where we waited in long lines for the dreaded shot in the arm. Then for weeks after we compared the gruesome-looking scabs that left a telltale scar. I remember saving dimes and slipping them into the cardboard cards provided by the *March of Dimes* campaign to end Polio.

When Robert was about three, he began having what we all called his "spells." He would be sitting at the table waiting for supper time when, all of a sudden, his eyeballs would roll back and he would slump over. His forehead banged the table to a chorus of cries from his older siblings:

"Mama, Robert's having another spell!" She would come running. Robert had epilepsy with petit mal seizures that soon progressed to grand mal seizures. One year, Robert said, the seizures were so bad he had to be home schooled. We all tried to help Mama look out for Robert. Eileen said she came upon him one time when he had passed out on the attic floor.

"I sat down beside him and listened for his heart to be sure he was still alive," she remembers. "I stayed with him until he woke up."

Mama and Robert made numerous trips to the hospital for tests and medications over the years, seeking the right balance of treatment for his "spells." They developed a close bond that continued throughout her life. He was her last child, and the only one of her nine children that did not flee Memphis to find a life elsewhere.

"They put wires on my head and glued them down," Robert remembers of the EEG testing he endured. He later outgrew the seizures. Somehow that affliction may have saved him from the alcoholism that overwhelmed his older brothers.

Crab Apples and "Clean Dirt"

When we were old enough to go beyond our block, we roamed the neighborhood streets gathering kids together for ball games on the great green field across North Parkway at Dunlap.

Years before, the field had been a favorite playground for Elvis when he and his Humes High School friends gathered for pickup ball games. We called it the waterworks, though it was officially called the Parkway Pumping Station. A family friend, Mr. Agnew, worked there. When we got thirsty we would wander inside the building among the water processing machinery to the fountain and drink long and deep of the water drawn from the artesian well that supplies Memphis.

The Half Life of a Free Radical

As I was more likely than not to strike out in a ball game I seldom was picked for a team. I usually spent my time flying down the grassy hill on a piece of flattened cardboard, or amused myself in the world of ants that navigated over humps of earth moving in long lines beneath clover leaf and grass carrying bits of brown leaves.

We wandered through alleyways and beneath the city streets in the open storm drainage ditches we called bayous that channeled rain water runoff. On snowy winter days we put on layers of clothing, wrapped plastic bread bags around our shoes, secured them with rubber bands, and put several old socks on our hands for gloves. We built snow forts, slid on great pieces of cardboard down the icy slopes, and embedded the spiky seed balls from the sweet gum trees into snowballs to give them extra punch in our neighborhood snowball wars with kids from the public schools.

"Back then we Catholics thought we were superior," Michael remembered. Rusty Holland lived just up the block. When Michael was about ten, he said, he told him:

"It doesn't matter what you think because y'all are all going to hell."

This declaration inflamed sectarian tensions with our Protestant neighbors, who Michael remembers, "didn't like the Catholics or the Jews."

During the summer time, one of my favorite places to climb, when I was small enough not to break the branches, was up in the smooth and flowering limbs of the pink crepe myrtle in the side yard. Eileen has a Crepe Myrtle offshoot from those trees growing now in her garden in Rogersville, Tennessee. I seldom pass a Crepe Myrtle today without stroking the smooth sinewy bark with affection. Jessica's home in Grapevine, Texas, has several Crepe Myrtles in the front yard. They were in glorious bloom on my last visit there.

I also climbed the old crabapple tree. Its large limbs reached over the garage roof and provided a view far across the back neighbor's fence to North Parkway. I liked to snack on the tart little green fruit with only a slight pink blush. Once I encouraged Eileen to climb up with me. Getting her down safely proved to be quite the challenge. I had her hold on to my back while I slid down the large branch until we were close enough to the ground to jump. My arms and belly were scratched raw from the rescue, but we both made it to solid ground.

School Days & Hood Ways

Another time, Eileen remembers, I jumped off the roof, landing with a roll on the grass below. I had a lot of derring-do then.

Sometimes when I was very small I would wander around the block to where a large shade tree grew in a narrow grassy strip between the street and sidewalk. After a good rain, rivulets of water would gather between the tree roots. I loved to watch the water meander and imagined it a tiny river that I would navigate on a piece of bark. I could sit for hours by that little strip of green lost in reverie.

Today, just outside my uptown Asheville apartment, I cultivate a similar tiny square between the sidewalk and street, planting hardy perennial herbs and flowers and placing figurines to create a miniature urban garden in the midst of the asphalt. It catches the imagination of many passersby and satisfies my inner child's need for outdoor play.

I ate dirt too. On the next block, soft silky clay washed down to the sidewalk after a hard rain. Eileen and I called it our "clean dirt." It had a particular feel and smell that we sought out. I'm not sure why, perhaps some mineral we may have craved. I would scoop up the "clean dirt" in my little hands and lick them clean. I can still taste its earthy essence. The tell-tale rim of dirt around my mouth always gave me away.

Sometimes I would sit out on the back stoop at dusk as the mystery in the falling darkness gathered around me. I liked to watch the night sky and listen to the katydids sing. Fat slugs crawled along the walkway or in the corners of the concrete step. The twinkling magic of the fireflies used to fill our small yard. Sometimes we would catch them in Mason jars and bring them inside, but that never ended well for the lightning bugs.

My brothers had a cruel practice that I tried out too, pouring salt over the slug and watching it crawl away to die, leaving a glistening trail behind. Some life had value in our world, and other life did not. Cockroaches, rats, house flies and slugs were among the least likely to survive.

On winter days when we were stuck inside, we played Blind Man's Bluff and Simon Says, or would twirl round and round until we were so dizzy we fell all over each other on the bare wooden floor with gales of laughter. As we became more sophisticated, we added marathon board games of *Monopoly*, *Parcheesi*, *Clue*, and *Scrabble* and

The Half Life of a Free Radical

various card games. Pick-Up Sticks and jacks tested our focus and patience.

The boys played at war with small green plastic soldiers. We girls had paper dolls. I remember especially the *Betsy McCall* and *Lennon Sisters* paper dolls. We would carefully cut out the dresses and bend back the tabs to hold the costume in place. Old *Life* or *Look* magazines were a good source for paper-doll clothes. So was the *Sears Catalog*. We also used multi-folded paper strips to cut out paper-doll chains. Daddy sometimes helped us make paper kites and we tore up old rags for the tails. He also showed us how to fold a sheet of paper into a paper airplane. Mama liked to save old newspapers so we could spend an afternoon tearing them into strips to make *papier-mâché* that we held together with a paste of white flour and water. We were endlessly creative with whatever materials we had on hand.

Some summers, before there were too many of us to manage, Mama would drive us to McKellar Lake to the fishing rodeo. The lake is an oxbow of the Mississippi River adjacent to the now toxic Presidents' Island. My brothers would take a bamboo pole and a can of worms dug out of Mama's worm ranch. They would sit for hours at the edge of the lake. I didn't have much patience with sitting still. I liked to walk around on the forest path, feeling like an explorer. Sometimes we would take a hiking trail deeper into the woods and find a thick kudzu or grape vine attached high in a tree. We could hang on, get a good push off and swing in a wide arc across a gully. Tarzan and Jane never had it so good. I got pretty good at the Tarzan yell as I leapt into the air.

Mama also took us to the Mid-South Fair. It was a sensual delight. The enticing aroma of burnt sugar swirled around onto a paper cone for melt-in-your-mouth "cotton candy," the unfamiliar accents of carnival barkers beckoning passersby to toss a coin or knock down a pyramid of bottles, and the flashing neon lights that drew us to the midway. We didn't have the money for more than one or two carnival rides, so I picked carefully. I liked getting lost in the House of Mirrors and the excitement of being in the driver's seat in the Bumper Cars. My favorite ride was the thrilling "Zippin Pippin." It had endured well over a half century of use by the time I was old enough to ride and was one of the oldest existing wooden roller coasters in the country.

School Days & Hood Ways

North Parkway Gang

Our neighborhood wanderings often extended across North Parkway and beyond. We joined up with the older kids in the Gattas family who lived in a two-story wooden house at 995.

Many times their large extended family of Lebanese relatives were visiting. I tasted many Lebanese specialties at the Gattas table, including unleavened flat bread and a kind of spicy, ground round steak with bulgur and minced onions called "kibbe." Uncle George Gattas was then a handsome bachelor who drove a flashy convertible, and Aunt Naz, a gruff-voiced, dark skinned, kind-hearted woman with a sharp wit and hearty laugh.

Of all the treats at the Gattas house, I liked the apples best. Unlike our home, there was always a bowl of fresh fruit on the Gattas table.

"Can I please have an apple?" I pleaded whenever I was over to play, only to be teased with a loud chorus of voices:

"Mama, Clare wants another apple!" They were so crisp and sweet and good, and much better tasting than the mushy figs or the dry and sour crab apples from our backyard trees.

Sometimes the boys would gang up to chase the big rats out from beneath the neighbor's back porch. They tried to hit them with sticks or shovels as they scurried past into the alley where the garbage cans were lined up. One time, Tommy Gattas remembers, they piled the rats in the alley, set them on fire, and then ran and hid with the police in hot pursuit.

The alley was our well-used route to the water works. It was a real gauntlet, as we had to pass a barking bunch of backyard dogs. Even though they were fenced in, they would lunge at us, barking ferociously as we passed. Once when I was very young I was chased by a big dog that had escaped his fence. The faster I ran, the faster the dog pursued until I made it safely to a neighbor's porch. I've been wary of unleashed dogs ever since.

One of the neighborhood boys, whose father was a preacher, had a BB gun. He would take aim from his second-floor bedroom. One day he trapped Tommy and some of his friends inside a garage. When Danny ventured upon the scene, unaware of the danger, the neighbor shot him. The BB hit Danny just above his eye. Another time the boys somehow set fire to the garage.

The Half Life of a Free Radical

"There was a lot going on in the neighborhood then," my friend Catherine remembers.

One summer, when Catherine's cousin Joe came up from Clarksdale, Mississippi, we had to correct him when he used the "N" word about our neighbors. We knew it was just the way white people talked in Mississippi, but we would not let him get away with using the "N" word in our neighborhood.

Whenever Stella Mae was working at the Gattas house, she kept the radio on WDIA at high volume rocking the Blues through the house. Then, when she had enough of our shenanigans, she picked up the broom or a shoe and chased us all down the stairs, around the house and out the back door where we made a point to run through the clothes hanging out to dry.

Catherine had her own room next to her older brother Pat. Her younger siblings were two to a bedroom. Catherine's bed was always freshly made. Stella Mae neatly stacked her laundered clothes ready to be put away. Sometimes Stella Mae sat at the big ironing machine in the back room where the air had a slightly scorched smell and was steamy from the freshly-laundered sheets pressed between the rollers until they were dry and smooth.

This was not how things worked at our house. Clothes fresh from the backyard line, or later from the dryer, were piled high on the cedar chest in the middle hallway. We sorted through them until we found something that would fit. Though we all had clothes of our own, there were plenty around that were interchangeable.

I loved to spend the night at Catherine's house. We kids all had supper together at the kitchen table or sometimes in the more formal dining room. In our early teen years, we played with Barbie and Ken dolls, which were the new fad then. We set up scenes with Ken and Barbie as we imagined what it would be like to go on a date, though that experience would be years away. At night we would give each other long back scratches before we fell asleep in her double bed.

Sometimes I watched as Catherine practiced piano. I wanted to learn too, but lessons were not in our family budget. I could hear music in my head, and if I had enough time alone at Catherine's piano, I could pick out songs I'd heard without reading music.

In eighth grade, Catherine and I climbed out her second-floor bedroom window to smoke on the roof that looked out on to North Parkway. We never got caught, though it was a daring feat. Catherine's cousin Laura Ann sometimes picked us up from Little Flower School and shared a cigarette with us from her package of Kents.

One afternoon our neighborhood pal Joe Bruno and I were visiting Catherine up in her room. Mr. Gattas was home that day with a bad back. We kids weren't supposed to be inside, and were tiptoeing around so not to disturb him. The phone rang and he headed down the hallway to answer it. We had pulled it into Catherine's room on the long cord. Joe and I rushed into her tiny closet to hide. We stayed there, crunched up and as quiet as we could be, until the long call was over. Catherine's father ruled the roost at the Gattas house and we didn't want to get him mad.

Joe and David Bruno lived on Forest across the back alley from the Gattas house. Their father was a plumber by trade, but he had quite a reputation around the neighborhood. Everyone called him "Jumping Joe Bruno." Stories abounded of how he had eluded capture and escaped from police custody a number of times. He spent more than a few years in prison, so was hardly ever home. His boys, Joe and David, were part of our gang. One time I joined in a game of spin the bottle at the Bruno house. I don't remember the outcome, but still recall the sense of the forbidden as we played. Wearing layers of clothes was the trick to maintaining some modesty, though that was not the point of the game.

Michael, who was a few years younger, remembers Joe for the time he rescued him from a sexual predator. As Michael tells it, "A pervert cornered me on the bus seat. Joe saw what was going on and threw the man off the bus." Years later I heard that Joe was killed in a boating accident on the Mississippi river.

Trick or Treat

Halloween is a time in between. A certain wildness is given its due as the veil between the living and the dead seems to thin.

When I was still quite small, I would hurry out to sit on the concrete steps by the front sidewalk in the crisp autumn air. As dusk settled around me, I hunkered down against the chill winds that raised the hairs and prickled the skin of my arms. The twin pin oaks flanking our house released slender bronze leaves that spiraled down covering the yard and collecting in piles along our neighbor's chain-link fence.

The Half Life of a Free Radical

The sidewalk was littered with acorns. I clutched my brown-paper bag, big enough to hold all the candy I hoped I would get, and practiced saying "Trick or Treat!" I could barely contain my excitement as the neighborhood kids gathered on corners in anticipation. Shadows darted here and there and strangely-dressed figures crossed up and down the street.

"Hurry up! Hurry up!" I yelled to my siblings who were still scrounging around inside for something to use as a costume. Sometimes we were ghosts, cutting eye holes in otherwise intact bed sheets, or we became gruesome monsters in masks made with brown paper bags and crayons. We crafted angel wings with coat hangers and scraps of fabric, wigs with old mop heads, and raided the rag bag to dress as a hobo, or made a robot costume with boxes covered in tin foil. We used whatever we could find. We were always a more interesting gang of goblins than our more affluent neighbors who wore the TV-inspired plastic Casper the Friendly Ghost or other such costume sold at the five-and-dime store.

When the cricket song was strong and the street lights came on, we ran free through the night, crisscrossing from one house to the next, kicking our way through piled leaves, crushing acorns beneath our feet, flattening the yellow-orange centers. We rang the doorbells and roused the neighbors, and when the doors opened, we screamed in unison: "Trick or Treat!" and thrust our bags forward. There were only a few doors that would not open to us, and a few houses we knew not to approach for fear of people rumored to be "perverts."

When our bags were loaded and the porch lights all around the neighborhood turned off, we knew Mama would soon be on the lookout for us. Back at home we poured our sweet loot into separate piles on the dining-room table and began the ritual of trading back and forth for one favored candy or another. We had Tootsie Rolls and Sweet Tarts, Double Bubble gum and candy corn, tiny chocolate Snickers bars, Atomic Fireballs and candy orange slices.

Halloween was the best of holidays, deeply rooted in ancient Celtic traditions, though I had no knowledge of that then, except the deep resonance that sometimes kicks in when our ancestral memories are stirred.

5

"Lawyer Dan"

We lived poor but I knew the score. Dad Gave. Dad Gave. So Do His Children. — Michael Hanrahan

Family economics fluctuated a lot in 1959 after Daddy left his job as a Claims Adjuster with Aetna Life Insurance Company to go into private law practice. Daddy was associated with several Memphis firms. Eventually he kept his own office in the Dermon Building at 46 North Third Street where he practiced criminal law, domestic relations, and probate law.

In 1959, Daddy's photo was in the *Memphis Press Scimitar* with other supporters of former Democratic Mayor Edmund Orgill who were organizing a "Dedicated Citizens Committee."[64]

Orgill was a member of the Memphis Committee on Community Relations, a group that attempted to deal with black demands for equality and justice.

I don't remember ever sitting in a courtroom where Daddy practiced law, and wish now that I had the opportunity. I do remember how proud I felt that he worked at the Shelby County Courthouse, cater-corner to where the old Catholic Club once stood, and across from Saint Peter's Catholic Church. The courthouse entrances are flanked with larger-than-life statues depicting the feminine embodiments of Blind Justice, Peace, Prosperity and Liberty, and the masculine forms of Wisdom and Authority, each sculpted from a single block of Tennessee blue limestone.

The Half Life of a Free Radical

Robert's son, James Daniel, once told me a story about "Lawyer Dan." In 2002, when James was a teenager, he attended a social function in Memphis with then newly-elected A. C. Wharton, the first African-American Mayor of Shelby County, Tennessee. When James introduced himself, the mayor asked:

"Are you related to the lawyer, Dan Hanrahan?"

"That's my granddad," James said.

The Mayor then told him how "Lawyer Dan" had been an early mentor in his career. The mayor later paid his respects at the funeral home after Mama died, among the wide spectrum of Memphis families represented there.

Daddy often took on the legal cases of so-called "Negroes" who lived across the color line in the neighborhoods north of Jackson Avenue and beyond Chelsea. They were the maids and the handymen employed as laborers, or as domestics in friends' and neighbors' homes or in the cotton fields of Arkansas and Mississippi. During that time, the caste system in Memphis labor kept people of color from most of the well-paid jobs, despite their skills and qualifications, and the legal system was not known for colorblind justice.

In the courtroom, Daddy had to fight the institutional racism and insist that his "Negro" clients be referred to with the dignity of the title Mr. or Mrs., rather than by first name only, as had long been the demeaning custom. It wasn't until the 1960's that Memphis newspapers began to capitalize the word "Negro."

I overheard people on the streets or around town using the word "nigra." It was a kind of verbal bridge between the vulgar racist insult "nigger" and the more respectful "Negro." The racist designation "mulatto" was also in common use then, and sometimes I heard the hurtful slur "pickaninny" to describe mixed-race children. I feel sad now as I write about those times and the hurtful ignorance of many Memphis whites and the institutional racism that sustained it.

"Tender Mercies"

Daddy was a smart man with a quick wit and ready smile. He had what someone once called an "eidetic" memory, and could quote large passages from the many law books that lined his office.

"Lawyer Dan"

When Daddy won a case all seemed well for a while. It was "fees or famine" it seemed. Daddy's payment for legal services would sometimes come in barter. Once someone left a basket of freshly-caught fish on the front porch; this led to a night of guts and gore in the kitchen sink as Daddy showed us how to prepare the Mississippi-river fish for the frying pan. Scales were flying all over the kitchen counters and floors, and the bloody water filled the sink. But the fish, when filleted, floured and fried were a most welcome and tasty meal.

Eileen remembers another time when Daddy's legal fee was paid with enough cucumbers to fill the bathtub, where we washed them off before slicing them and putting them up in jars of vinegar. We ate those sour cucumbers with many meals for a long time.

Michael befriended some "colored" men in the neighborhood whom Daddy may have represented in court for one reason or another. These men could be counted on to help him fix his bicycle, "as a favor to 'Lawyer Dan.'"

"Don't tell your dad who done it," they told him. That way, if any one of them needed a lawyer again, they could each say, "I fixed your son's bike," Michael remembers.

"The garbage men were my heroes. They had real integrity." Integrity carries high value in our family. In 2002, when email facilitated more frequent communications between us siblings, Michael shared a poem he wrote about his 1959 Memphis memories:

I have a place in this America.
I ate crackers on Decatur Street
With garbage men in '59
They fixed my bike.

They told me not to tell my Daddy they done it tho.
He was Lawyer Dan, my old man.
The black folk knew.
Me without a clue was protected by Lawyer Dan.

Next time trouble came in Memphis,
A black man would tell my dad he fixed my bike.
Lawyer Dan would smile and say:
All my sons have their bikes fixed. What can I do for you?

The Half Life of a Free Radical

We lived poor but I knew the score.
Dad Gave. Dad Gave.
So Do His Children.

"You wouldn't believe how many jammed up people Dad helped," Michael remembers. "He was just not very good at collecting his fees."

Like the rest of us, Michael didn't have as much time with our Daddy as he needed.

"The tender mercies he sent my way were tremendous. They were so few and hard to come by. My father, when he had time, was one of the most wonderful people in my world," Michael remembered.

Daddy was more of a mystery to me. He kept his own counsel. I didn't have the kind of conversations with Daddy that Mama would engage in with us as we sat on the front porch after dinner, or around the dining room table at homework time. With Daddy I learned to expect disappointment and forgotten promises. Try as I will, I cannot bring up many more memories of my Daddy. But I still feel his warm and lively smile, see his dancing blue eyes, and laugh at his ready wit. I also see him sitting with his head down, lost in a book while his children swarm about vying for his scant attention.

In a telephone conversation recently, Michael recalled an afternoon he spent with his Daddy at Mike's bar on Jackson Avenue.

"The bar was a real 1950's classic with red Naugahyde upholstered double doors, each with eight to twelve embedded buttons," Michael remembers. "The first beer I ever drank was a Falstaff with salt on the rim of the glass. Daddy told me not to tell Mama. I was just twelve."

For many years a small snapshot of Daddy had a place on the wall in Michael's Nashville home. In that photo, our Daddy is once again the young Army sergeant with the broad grin, dancing blue eyes, and curly brown hair that first attracted Mama's interest.

It was Daddy's curly locks, the family story goes, that his mother refused to cut until he was nearly six years old. According to Irish folk tales, this was a way to keep the *Sidhe,* the fairy folk, from stealing the first-born son.

"Lawyer Dan"

"Ask Your Daddy"

From the time I was old enough to board the bus alone, I loved to go downtown to browse in the bargain basement at Goldsmiths Department Store, to read in the big room at the old Cossitt Library, or sometimes to meet Daddy at the fountain in Court Square. We would then have lunch at Walgreens, still standing at the corner of Main and Madison, or in Britlings Cafeteria, long lost to urban removal.

Whenever I needed money for a school trip or wanted a dress I had seen in the Lerner Shop window, Mama would say: "Ask your Daddy." Meeting Daddy downtown at his office seemed to increase my chances of a "yes." But more often than not, Daddy would say: "Wait until I settle this case."

That was often a very long wait. We all knew when Daddy had money to share because on those rare occasions he would call us together in the living room and dish out quarters as we eagerly gathered around.

One time I was able to cajole a check from Daddy which I presented to the clerk at Goldsmith's Department store. After some scrutiny she refused to take it as payment. Our Daddy's checks had bounced before. I had to put back the dress I had wanted to retrieve from layaway and catch the bus home, embarrassed and empty handed.

Occasionally I did manage to acquire the money to buy a dress. The stylish Bobbie Brooks brand featured in *Seventeen* magazine cost about $15 on the low end. My favorite was a corduroy shirtwaist with a round collar. Mostly I wore the school uniform and changed into blue jeans and hand-me-down shirts after school. By the time I was earning enough in after-school work to buy an occasional dress, the styles had changed. Everyone was wearing old blue jeans rolled up at the ankle and long-tailed white shirts.

The shame was always with me around money matters. I wore it like a heavy cloak and it rests still on my shoulders when I am confronted by the insensitivities of those who always have had more than enough. Asking for help is not easy.

Perhaps it was during these years that I began to develop that false belief that I could never have nice things. Everything was too expensive. I decided to stop wanting. It was easier than always wanting and never getting. But I still felt angry at the unfairness of it all. It was a kind of freedom, perhaps, but a detachment born more out of thwarted desire. It seemed the easiest way to deal with the disappointments. I learned to live without rather than confront the feelings of shame involved in asking someone to share a ride, or help with the price of a movie ticket, a round of bowling or ice skating, or anything else that I might have wanted to have.

When I was old enough for baby-sitting jobs, and later after school and summer work, I had money of my own to spend, though by that time, much of it went to support a pack-a-day cigarette habit.

Mama and Daddy had strong differences of opinion about our earnings. Mama said "If they worked for it, the money is theirs." Daddy thought we should give him a part of everything we earned. Mama won that battle and we kept all of our own part-time earnings.

A New Jersey Summer

One summer Daddy took us four older children on a car trip to his New Jersey family's summer cabin on the Delaware river. I was about eight. It was a long, long trip. I remember baloney and mustard sandwiches on the Turnpike roadside, an overnight stay in a large hotel in some Northern city, and being warmly greeted by Daddy's family at their cabin on Packanack Lake.

Eileen remembers how much she wanted to go with us. She hid herself in the back of the car beneath the cardboard boxes tied with string that served as our suitcases. To her dismay, Daddy discovered the little stow-a-way just blocks from our house.

Throughout childhood, we heard from our New Jersey relatives through an occasional long-distance telephone call or a Christmas card. Eileen remembers an occasional visit from Uncle Billy's family while we were still very young. "They stopped in Memphis on the way to Louisiana where Aunt Marguerite's family lived," she said, "until there were too many children to fit in the car," as our cousin Bill, now a priest, told Eileen.

I have always sensed there was some estrangement between Daddy and his birth family, more than just the geographical distance. Eileen suggests it may have been that he felt ashamed at not having been more successful in his chosen career. Alcoholism takes a heavy toll on self esteem as well as family economics.

"Lawyer Dan"

Through the years, Robert and Vernua made frequent visits to New Jersey with their young family and they have come to know many of our northern cousins. Some have, in turn, come South to visit. The social media of *Facebook* has provided us all with more contact in recent years than we ever could have imagined in our childhood.

I have visited New York and New Jersey several times, but wasn't sure who or how to contact family then. From the train window, Newark seemed grim and depressed. As I emerged into the bustle and rush of Pennsylvania Station, I could imagine some of the feelings Mama may have had, leaving behind her more relaxed southern culture for life in the small city of Belleville, in the shadow of New York City.

I have vague memories of a visit from Grandmother Cora to our Memphis home. Eileen remembers it as about 1953, when John Vincent was the baby. I wasn't yet five. Our house was so small, there were by then seven children, and our Grandpa Donnelly lived with us as well. I can't imagine where Mama found room to put our New Jersey Grandma on her only Memphis visit.

In my most vivid memory, Grandma and I are standing at the kitchen sink. My head barely clears the counter top. She has me by the hand and is smearing mud on a bee sting. She says if I leave the mud on until it dries, it will draw out the stinger. I can tell that Mama does not approve of this folk remedy. I can feel the tension between them. I also remember Grandma Cora saying it was good to eat dandelion roots. Mama always loved the golden dandelion blossoms and didn't want them to be uprooted. Eileen remembers hearing that grandma learned about the uses of herbs from native Americans of the Iroquois Confederacy who lived around her childhood home in Utica, New York.

Grandma Cora had very blue eyes, as did my daddy. Regina, Michael, Robert and I also have blue eyes. Stories from our northern cousins tell that Grandma Cora was often called upon at family gatherings to recite poetry by heart. Now Jessica provides her well-crafted verse to mark many special family occasions. Grandmother Cora, who I met only twice, died in 1966, the year I graduated from high school. I wish I had known her.

The Half Life of a Free Radical

As I take my place now in the "senior generation" of surviving Hanrahans and look back at the generations before, I am amazed at the many relatives whose names and stories I never knew.

What became of Grandmother Cora's eighteen siblings? or Grandfather Daniel Francis' nine? or Grandfather Donnelly's eleven siblings? or Grandmother Novetta's three? Mostly, the story of their lives has been lost to me. Perhaps some of their hopes and dreams, fears and sorrows, joys and talents are somehow echoed in my own life, and in the lives of their many descendants. We each carry so much forward from our ancestors, most who we may meet only in our dreams.

Daddy in Politics

Daddy was an Assistant City Attorney during the tenure of Mayor William B. Ingram, from 1963-1967. Ingram was a liberal Democrat with some support in the black community. Daddy had been Ingram's campaign manager.

Robert remembers riding around town with Daddy in a car mounted with a loud speaker as they campaigned throughout the neighborhood.

Ingram lost the election and Daddy lost his job. Henry Loeb, a wealthy Brown University graduate and former Naval officer, was elected again in 1968. Loeb, like many in Memphis, upheld the genteel form of structural racism practiced by many wealthy whites. Loeb was an avowed segregationist whose obdurate ways would be especially harmful during the Sanitation Workers' Strike of 1968.

In 1975, Daddy tried to pursue a long-held dream and entered the Division VI race for City Court Judge. I didn't share in the campaign excitement as I was living then in Dallas. Though Daddy lost the election, he received over 11,000 votes.[65]

There were some dirty politics afoot when opponents attempted to publicly discredit him. I never knew the details. It must have been hard on both my parents to face such public scrutiny.

Our Daddy was a Brooklyn-born and-educated attorney who tried to practice law in Memphis, and attempted to give equal representation and dignity to all who came before the courts. But Memphis was then, as it is now, a city steeped in racism. It could not have been easy.

"Lawyer Dan"

The closest I came to understanding Daddy's work as a Memphis attorney was in his last years when Mama asked that I help to organize his office files. Daddy was not cooperative with my efforts, perhaps realizing that this was being done in anticipation of his death, as the cancer and cirrhosis were taking their toll. In a desk drawer that he usually kept locked I found dozens of airline-size empty whiskey bottles. It was a sad sight. I usually waited until Daddy was out of the office for lunch or coffee and then, little by little, I systematically went through each and every file, organizing the papers and reading the briefs, so I could assure Mama that all was in order.

Michael remembers Daddy's counsel: "Son, apply yourself. Apply yourself. Read."

Instead of the shame and blame around our Daddy's alcoholism, I wish I could have better understood the nature of the disease. I wish there had been a way out for our Daddy, and our brothers, and others.

6

Our Enterprising Mama

Poverty is hereditary—you get it from your children. — Phyllis Diller

With all the demands of a rapidly-growing family, and a husband largely absent from the domestic realm, our Mama was remarkably productive and disciplined in her writing life.

"Writing was a way I could do something to make a mark while raising you kids," she once told me.

Mama's writing time was only a fraction of her days which were mostly spent cooking, washing, hanging clothes, helping us with our homework and later, working at various jobs to keep the roof over our heads.

We called the tiny room off the front hallway "The little room." It was just large enough for a single bed, and served as the baby nursery until we were all old enough to move to the attic.

One of my earliest memories is in The Little Room. I'm alone in my bed below two big windows that look out to the enclosed back-porch. Something startles me awake. There seem to be particles of light moving toward me through the panes of glass, as if from another world. I can't make sense of them and cry out.

It's my Daddy who comes. I'm small enough to nestle against his chest, smelling the familiar cigar, as he rocks me back to sleep while singing his favorite lullaby: "Too-ra-loo-ra-loo-ral, Too-ra-loo-ra-li, Too-ra-loo-ra-loo-ral, Hush now don't you cry!"

Our Enterprising Mama

I don't remember being held by my Mama. Surely I had to have been, before my memory awakened. But I remember Daddy and how safe I felt when he soothed me back to sleep with his sweet lullaby.

Mama's Office

When we were all past toddler stage, "The Little Room" became Mama's office. She retreated there for an hour each day, no matter the mayhem outside the door. Her large steel army-surplus desk had deep drawers where she kept Carter's Midnight Blue carbon paper, onion skin, and white bond paper. She had an Underwood manual typewriter and a three-drawer file cabinet where she kept articles, ideas for articles, and clippings of published writings.

Mama was a good photographer too. She bought film at Ed's Camera Shop on Madison Avenue. Film development was costly, particularly color, but she did capture some special moments of our lives through the years. Sometimes she included photos with the articles she sent to various magazines for publication. "The Little Room" served as Mama's office until I was a teenager. Then, to keep the peace between Mary and me, I had a chance to call it my own.

Mama wrote about subjects familiar to a young mother. She sold one article in 1949 to *Parents* magazine titled "How to Use Skim Milk," and another in 1954 titled "Your Child's First Lunch Box." She later told me that the $60 payment for the skim milk article came just in time to cover the house note that month. We drank a lot of dried skim milk, stirred up with tap water in the large plastic pitcher.

Mama also wrote a column titled "Ladies' Fare" for the *Tennessee Register*, a Catholic monthly published in Nashville. For thirteen years she wrote book reviews for *The Commercial Appeal* and the *Memphis Press Scimitar*. Our hallway bookcase held many books she had reviewed. I remember seeing a copy of Dostoevsky's *Brothers Karamazov*, though I have yet to read it.

Mama never got a byline for her book reviews. When I asked her about that she said:

"I never wanted a byline. I wanted the writing to stand for itself."

Mama joined an effort to publish an alternative weekly newspaper called *The Sunday Times*. I remember well her distress when they found that all the bundles put out for distribution had been stolen from the racks the first day of publication. The paper soon folded. Perhaps the Scripps-Howard newspaper monopoly didn't take well to the competition.

Worms For Sale

Mama often worked out in the yard digging, planting, and coaxing life out of the small patch of earth around our house. The remainder of our tiny yard was pounded smooth and bare by the feet of so many children at play.

She planted a peach tree from seed in the rich compost pile out by the back fence, much like the one she planted as a child after her mother died. She explained that her daddy would bring home tobacco stems to place around the tree to kill insects. After WWII, tobacco stems were processed into Hot Shot, an insecticide which we sometimes used on wasps and hornets that threatened to sting us. Eileen remembers picking large, juicy fruits from the old peach tree.

"They did have worms," she said, "but it was a simple matter to cut them out."

I remember trying to eat the small hard fruit. Maybe, as Eileen says, I was just too impatient to let them ripen.

Mama also kept several barrels of rich soil thick with fat earthworms out by the old fig tree. She called it her "worm ranch," and would turn it with a pitchfork, proudly displaying the worms knotted up in thick clumps in the leafy mulch. Fishermen were always driving past our house on the way to the Mississippi river. Mama put a sign out front, "Worms for Sale." This was just one more example of her survival enterprises and of her inventive mind and resourceful approach to our cash-poor circumstances. Though that home business never really flourished, it was an early example of making the most out of what was available.

Mama had little time for leisure while we children were young, but I can see her now, with silver strands gleaming in her thick black hair, wearing her bi-focal reading glasses, and sitting down with a book or a crossword puzzle while chaos swirled about her. Our Mama was smart and wise and reliable. She had a ready laugh, but a stern edge. Her sometimes wry smile brightened with a touch of her red lipstick. Her high cheeks were sprinkled with freckles and just a hint of the powder she dabbed on from the round-plastic compact with

Our Enterprising Mama

a mirrored lid. Her eyes were a deep brown, and when we were sneaking around, she would warn us:

"I have eyes in the back of my head." There wasn't much that Mama missed.

She showed her love in the constancy of the daily tasks she did for us. She always had dinner on the table, and lunch and bus money for school, seven nickels stacked in a row, one stack for each school child, pocketed on our way out the door.

A Winning Way

Mama's faith in what she called Providence was time and time again affirmed.

"God works in mysterious ways," she was fond of reminding us. But to help Providence along, Mama tried her luck with sweepstakes, raffles and jingles. She also entered many of her unique casserole and dessert recipes in cooking contests, including the Pillsbury Bake-Off, and encouraged her children to do so.

In 1958, when Mary Alice was thirteen and in eighth grade at Little Flower School, she was one of fifty finalists for Junior Cook of the Year in a cook-off contest sponsored by Kroger Food Foundation. I remember the excitement in the house when the newspaper reporter and photographer came to do a story. It is nice now to have these old clippings, and the quotes of our mother, who was justly proud of her firstborn.

"Mary Alice has loved to cook since she was a little girl," Mama said. "Before she was much more than a toddler she carried my cookbook under her arm everywhere she went. Both back and front of the book came off-but she still clutched it under her arm."[66]

That year, Mary won $100 and a trip to Cincinnati for the cook off finals. We all went to the Memphis airport to see Mary and Mama off to Ohio. A story in *The Commercial Appeal*, pictured Mary and Mama as they boarded the airplane to Cincinnati. Daddy held Regina in his arms and Eileen and I stood nearby. Later, the Westinghouse electric stove she used in the competition was delivered to the house.

Just before her fifteenth birthday, Mary Alice was a "Grand National Junior Winner" of the Pillsbury Bake-Off in Washington, D.C. In her photo in the *The Commercial Appeal*, she looked poised and confident, wearing the small Elgin watch she received as an eighth

The Half Life of a Free Radical

grade graduation present, and a small clip-on velvet hat with netting on her short, black, permed hair. Her scoop-neck shirt-waist dress with three-quarter length sleeves had a touch of elegance with a patent leather belt cinched around her narrow waist.[67]

The next year Mama entered Danny and Tommy, who were thirteen, in the Kroger-Westinghouse Junior Cook of the Year contest. They were featured in a story in the *Memphis Press Scimitar* on October 1, 1959, and were photographed making ravioli in our small kitchen.[68]

Cooking didn't ever interest me, but Mama entered a casserole recipe in my name and I won last prize: a record album by the The Platters with songs such as "Twilight Time," and "Smoke Gets in Your Eyes." I memorized the entire album. It was the only record I ever owned as a child, and Mama let me play it over and over on the small RCA turntable she kept in her bedroom.

One summer Mama loaded us all in the Buick and we went to the Klinke Bros. Dairy and Creamer on Madison Avenue to pick up a $100 check, her prize for naming a new flavor of ice cream. She called it Santa Clara Apricot.

"It was Providential," she later told me. "I wondered how I would ever be able to afford the school books you children needed. The check was just enough to cover the costs."

Mama most likely purchased our text books from Burkes Book Store, one of Memphis' oldest book stores founded by Walter Burke just after the Civil War. I remember going with her on many occasions to the downtown store, and later, when it moved to Madison Avenue, a few blocks from her senior apartment. Most recently I visited the store in its new location in the Cooper-Young neighborhood.

When I was ten, I won a "Space Trainer" as a sweepstakes prize. It consisted of two hollow aluminum hoops, about four feet in diameter, with a seat suspended in between and hooked to a stationary frame. I could sit inside, push down on the center rod, and turn over and over, front wards or backwards, until I was dizzy. Soon we kids devised a more daring use. We detached it from the stationary frame so it could roll freely down the sidewalk with the screaming passenger inside. A sibling running alongside was the only safety against sure disaster should it roll into the busy street. It never did.

In June 1959, Mama entered Robert's name in the "Popsicle Railroad Sweepstakes." He won the best prize of all: the "Popsicle

Our Enterprising Mama

Red Ball Express," a child-sized, battery-powered train engine that pulled several flat metal cars with wooden sides. The metal track circled the back yard. We held neighborhood carnivals and sold five-cent tickets to ride around the track. We ran that train almost non-stop until the track rusted and the battery no longer held a charge.

I also won a yellow fiberglass boat. It was large enough to hold one child, but too large to be allowed in the swimming pool, and not safe enough for the river or lake. One time Mama loaded it into the car and we took it to the wading pool at Overton Park, but the water was so shallow it wouldn't float. My toy boat withstood the rugged dry-land use of us neighborhood kids for many years, before finally being crushed and hauled away in the big orange garbage trucks that picked up curbside trash on Wednesday. The "garbage men," as they were commonly called, hung on either side at the back of the truck, jumping off to pick up piles of debris to pack into the barrel-like compactor. These same men would soon be marching along Main Street in 1968 as part of the Sanitation Workers' Strike and carrying signs reading:

"End Dismal Working Conditions Now."

The one prize I really would have liked came for Tommy. He won a brand-new bicycle. I settled for a used one that somebody acquired for me. I had no instructions how to repair and maintain it, little patience with figuring it out, and never enough money for all the needed bike repairs. Eileen remembers a shop on Jackson Avenue near the Pic-Pac grocery that fixed her bike one time, but somehow that was not an option when mine broke down. In an angry fit one afternoon when I could not get it to work, I threw my bicycle down on the sidewalk and told my friend Catherine:

"You take it! I don't want the damn thing anymore."

Already my quick temper was bringing on self-defeating behaviors. I never got another bicycle until I was married with a child of my own. I've been riding one ever since.

Rearing Saints

I'm not sure just when Mama began working outside the home, but she did for many years as a matter of economic necessity. Much of that work in the early years was in the office of

The Half Life of a Free Radical

the Fred P. Gattas Co., a wholesale mail-order and variety store at 387 South Main Street. The two-story building was a few blocks from Mulberry Street and the Lorraine Motel, and a block south of the old hotel where Dr. King's assassin was said to have taken aim.

In a "Ladies' Fare" column titled "Dual Role of Some Mothers," Mama reveals her own feelings as a working mother as reflected in the life of Zolie Martin, also a working mother of nine, whose child was St. Thérèse of the Child Jesus:

> *Her complete resignation to the will of God in the worries about her work, the physical tiredness, frustration and the high hopes that all mothers feel are a source of consolation and inspiration. Ask her help, seek her advice, in rearing your children to be saints, for that is surely what you want for them working as you do to provide them with a good Catholic education.*[69]

Over the years, Mr. Gattas offered us older Hanrahan teenagers our much-needed after-school and summer jobs. During many summers and through the Christmas rush my workspace was in the Watch Department, defined by four display cases arranged in a square. My supervisor, Frieda Riesman, was a strong and outspoken woman. She was a heavy smoker with a leathery face and shrewd manner and wore her eyeglasses on a chain. I liked her irreverent wit.

I also worked with the elfin, white-haired Mr. Lee in the Toy Department. During many Christmas seasons I patrolled the aisles to keep the shelves neat and to offer assistance to frantic customers. Dolls were Mr. Lee's fascination. He delighted in ordering life-like baby dolls with soft bodies and eyes that opened and closed. He especially disliked the new-fangled dolls the customers demanded—the ones that walked and talked and whose hard bodies encased large batteries and mechanical devices, like Mattel's Chatty Cathy, with a pull string and record of monotonous phrases, and Baby First Step, "the world's first walking doll."

I also helped in the Leather Goods Department. This was Uncle John Gattas' domain. He was good humored and fun and kept a silver flask on a back shelf in the narrow stock room behind the counter. He would slip back for a taste now and again throughout the day. All

Our Enterprising Mama

the Gattas children spent most of their summer days working at the family business which closed operations at the South Main street store in 1975.

Saint Jude & Danny Thomas

It was a cold morning on November 2, 1958, when Mama took some of us with her for the groundbreaking ceremony for St. Jude Hospital. Smoke was still rising from the smoldering debris of some nearby buildings in what had been a "colored" neighborhood near Lauderdale and North Parkway.

I learned later that Danny Thomas had used his cigar lighter to set the fire to clear the seventeen-acre site. Today the ever-expanding hospital complex has swallowed even more of the neighborhood, including St. Joseph's Hospital where six of my siblings were born.

During our teenage years Mama worked as a regional fundraiser with St. Jude. We participated in the Teenagers March against Leukemia, going door-to-door collecting funds. The hospital was named for St. Jude Thaddeus, the patron of hopeless causes. In a time of personal difficulty, the story goes, Danny Thomas petitioned the saint: "Help me find my way in life, and I will build you a shrine."

St. Jude Hospital opened in 1962 in a star-shaped building dedicated to the treatment of childhood leukemia, "without regard to race, religion, creed or ability to pay." This was at a time when most other Memphis hospitals remained segregated. In fact, every major private hospital in Memphis, all with church affiliations, excluded black doctors and patients, and the one public hospital that did admit blacks still refused to allow black doctors in active practice on staff.[70]

Both Mama and our brother Danny had their photo taken with Danny Thomas when the star of *Make Room for Daddy* made one of his frequent Memphis visits. One summer when I volunteered at the hospital, Mama and I rode an elevator with him. I looked on, tongue tied, as he and Mama talked about the progress of the Teenager's March. Mama seemed like such an important person then, and we were all very proud to have helped with the venture.

In 1960 the National Auto Show held an annual fund-raiser for St. Jude Hospital at the still-segregated civic arena, Ellis Auditorium.[71] This resulted in an NAACP-initiated boycott of Memphis auto dealers

The Half Life of a Free Radical

and an increase in local activism pushing for complete desegregation of public facilities. Change was incremental in Memphis and such situations were commonplace in our divided city.

Mr. Gattas was on the Memphis Steering Committee for St. Jude Children's Research Hospital and a leader in the American Lebanese Syrian Associated Charities (ALSAC).

"Daddy reached out to help any Arabs who moved to Memphis," his daughter Catherine remembered. He certainly helped out our Irish family as well.

Throughout our childhood we gathered each year to celebrate the Fourth of July on the grounds of the St. Peter Orphanage. It was a century-old tradition. The Fred P. Gattas Co. always had a large tent set up for games where many prizes could be won. Proceeds supported the orphanage. Every politician in town made an appearance at the St. Peter Fourth of July Picnic.

The large campus, at Poplar and McLean, over time grew to include Memphis Catholic High School, where my brothers Tommy, Danny and Robert graduated, and where Robert's wife Vernua taught Religion. All of Robert & Vernua's children and grandchildren have been, or are still being educated at Memphis Catholic High School.

Mama lived her last twenty-five years at the St. Peter Manor Apartments and Villa on the same oak-shaded campus. Target House is there now in place of the old orphanage building, and provides accommodations for families of children receiving cancer treatment at St. Jude. Robert's daughter Katrina still helps raise funds for St. Jude Hospital in the tradition of her Grandmother Alice.

7

A Culture of Racism

Oh, Jim Crow's come to town As you all must know,
An' he wheel about, he turn about, He do jis so,
An' ebery time he wheel about He jump Jim Crow.

The extent of the institutional racism used to shape and sustain the oppressive treatment of people of color in Memphis is startling to discover. The antidote for such pervasive poison was the continual dose of respect for the dignity of all that our parents taught by example throughout our childhood.

The Commercial Appeal ran a daily cartoon called Hambone's Meditations penned by J. P. Alley and later his son Cal Alley. Hambone was "a caricature of a Negro, balding, wearing baggy pants, and sometimes a defeated-looking hat. ..always engaged in some menial activity, such as bringing in an armload of wood or sweeping and dusting."[72]

In one 1954 cartoon, Hambone is walking along with a bundle tied on a stick and slung over his shoulder. The caption is written to mimic the dialect and cadence of Hambone's speech:

Folks sayes trouble ketch up wid you but it's out in front waitin' fuh me—tain' nevuh taihed fum runnin' w'en it grab me!![73]

Censoring Social Equality

In movies and television, "Negro" characters were depicted in subservient roles: cooks, maids, butlers and, at best, taxi-drivers like Amos in the *Amos and Andy* show. I didn't realize then that Memphis had an official censor, Loyd T. Binford, who ruled the Memphis Censor Board from 1928 until 1956. Any films with "Negro actors performing in roles not depicting the ordinary roles played by Negro citizens," were banned from the screen for white or mixed audiences. Censorship of films, plays and other public exhibitions as a means of social control persisted in Memphis until 1965.[74]

In 1947, Binford censored Curley, a Little Rascals-type comedy, simply because it included one scene that showed black and white children in a classroom together. In his official letter to the United Artists distributors, Binford explained:

> *The Memphis Censor Board ... is unable to approve your picture with the little Negroes, as the South does not permit Negroes in white schools nor recognize social equality between the races, even in children.*[75]

We Catholics had our own censors, in the form of the Legion of Decency with its weekly rating of current movies. Before we were allowed to see a movie we had to check the list in the *Tennessee Register*. If the movie was listed as A-1, we might be allowed to see it. On many summer Saturdays, we "big kids" were given a dime or a quarter and warned to "stay together" as we walked to the neighborhood Suzore or Rialto theaters or the Rosemary at Jackson and Watkins. The cowboy and Indian movies we watched, despite all the violence against native Americans, always had an A-1 rating.

"A Very Worthy Negro"

The only park I knew in Memphis that didn't honor a Confederate general or veteran of some war or another was Tom Lee Park, a narrow, mile-long strip of green along the river. Mama always pointed out the monument when we went to the park, and she made sure we knew the story.

Tom Lee was a laborer who worked on the Mississippi levees. In 1925 he was out on the river in a skiff when he saw the large steamboat M.E. Norman capsize and spill all seventy two white

A Culture of Racism

passengers into the swirling river. Even though he could not swim, Lee turned his open boat downstream and began to collect the drowning passengers who were struggling to keep afloat in the main channel of the Mississippi. Lee managed to pull four boatloads of people from the water, rescuing thirty two persons. The City of Memphis renamed a park at the foot of Beale Street in his honor. The inscription on the memorial obelisk described Tom Lee as "a very worthy Negro," as if such bravery was the exception for people of color.

The memorial was blown over in 2003 by the storm known locally as "Hurricane Elvis," that produced straight-line winds in excess of 100 mph. Mama's apartment faced toward the river and the storm was so intense it soaked her ninth-floor apartment.

Tom Lee's monument has since been repaired and now sits near a dramatic new statue depicting Lee reaching from his boat to save a drowning man.

In early May 2011 Regina and I were passing through Memphis after a visit in Dallas with Jessica and my two grands, Jaxson and Josieanne. The Mississippi was in flood again, cresting at nearly forty-eight feet, just short of the 1937 record. The water was so high that it lapped around the new Tom Lee memorial. His boat seemed to be afloat again as he reached into the swirling waters to rescue the drowning white folk.

People from all over the mid-south region gathered along Front Street as the river continued to rise, flooding Riverside Drive. The rising river "flushed tributaries so far backward that the Loosahatchie River became a mile-wide lake," joining with the Wolf River in a single outpouring more than three miles wide.[76]

Fair to Middling

Memphis before the Civil War was a major slave-trading market. The sale of human beings, hardwood lumber, cotton, and the mules for working the fields, was a significant part of the commerce of the city.

One summer afternoon on a family outing to the Mississippi near Jefferson Davis Park, Mama pointed out the cobblestones that paved the river bank. She told us about the enslaved Africans made to unload huge bales of cotton from the river barges and then heft them onto mule carts to take to the markets on Front Street. I don't remember ever hearing about the part the Irish immigrants played in this enterprise.

In researching this period of Memphis history, I came across this passage from the 1862 book, *The Cotton Kingdom*, by Frederick Law Olmsted: Irish manned the most dangerous lower galleys of a steamboat being loaded with cotton:

> *Negro hands were sent to the top of the bank, to roll the bales to the side, and Irishmen were kept below to remove them, and stow them. On asking the mate(with some surmising) the reason of this arrangement, he said—'The niggers are worth too much to be risked here; if the Paddies are knocked overboard, or get their backs broke, nobody loses anything!*[87]

The cotton businesses on Front Street, known as Cotton Row, kept their doors wide open to the river breeze throughout the summer. When I walked past on my way to the Cossitt Library I could see the workers standing at long tables grading cotton samples. Tufts of the "white gold" floated on the breeze. Fair and Middling were among the nine different grades of cotton. There also were seven different cotton colors, and seventeen staples of cotton.

Hundred pound bales of cotton, wrapped in burlap and bound with metal bands, stood here and there along Front street, much as they had in the days prior to emancipation when the African men, women and children who worked the fields were displayed for sale on a flat-topped boulder still standing on Auction Street just blocks from the river.

The phrase "fair to middling" became a common response we Southerners made to a friendly "How are you doing?" And we were taught by example always to greet people we passed on the streets with some pleasantry or another, even our "colored" neighbors, whose response would often be, "all right!" and a nod as they continued on their way, averting their gaze.

And always, our family addressed all adults, regardless of race, with a respectful Mr. or Mrs. and never, ever, by their given name alone.

A Culture of Racism

"Yes sir or Yes ma'am" was the required response in any interaction with an adult. It was a courtesy that I seldom witnessed other whites offering to our colored neighbors.

"King Cotton's Bale of Fun"

Mama received the $100 prize for her winning theme for the 1960 Cotton Carnival: "King Cotton's Bale of Fun." She had her picture in the paper along with an article about the carnival events. I didn't know then of the racist history of the carnival, which had since 1931 provided a week of free festivities celebrating the cotton culture.

In 1936, prominent Memphis "Negroes" organized a parallel event, "The Beale Street Cotton Makers Fiesta," later named "The Cotton Makers' Jubilee," with Grand Marshall W. C. Handy. The Jubilee was a protest against the Memphis Cotton Carnival celebration in which Negroes were seen "pulling floats, picking banjoes… and eating watermelon atop bales of cotton," according to historians.

Prior to 1946, when Memphis Cotton Carnival parade floats were motorized, floats carrying the white elite were pulled by a team of black men wearing white tunics. As a further indignity, heavy-set black women were hired at $1.50 a day to sit on the street corners dressed as Aunt Jemimas. I cringe now at the thought of such blatant disrespect and abuse of the dignity of darker-skinned Memphians in those Jim Crow days.

Racist apartheid was embedded into every aspect of public life. I never did see The Cotton Makers' Jubilee on Beale Street. It wasn't until 1962, when I was fourteen, that the City of Memphis permitted the Cotton Makers' Jubilee Grand Parade to march down Main Street. As the Civil Rights Movement continued to push for integration, the Memphis Cotton Carnival and its cruelly sentimental depiction of the ante-bellum era fell out of favor.

We kids always sat curbside on Main Street to watch the Cotton Carnival Parade. Memphis' cotton merchant families, dressed in the elaborate costume and masks of their Grand Krewes, tossed out candies and trinkets. Our neighbor, Jeff Calhoun, on his huge Palomino, tipped his hat to us as he strutted by on his horse. The main event of carnival festivities was the arrival of the King and Queen of Cotton and their royal court, seated on an elaborately-decorated barge docked on the river's edge. Crowds gathered at dusk on the cobblestones to await the fireworks that accompanied the royal arrival. We brought large pieces of cardboard to sit on and to slide down the steep grassy embankment. We pushed off from the high bluff at the railroad tracks and skidded to a halt on Riverside Drive near Beale Street. There was a carnival midway on Riverside Drive. Its sideshows included a fat lady, Siamese twins, and a sword swallower. Vendors sold cones of spun-sugar "cotton candy," barkers hyped games, and a high Ferris Wheel lit up the night sky along the river. The carnival has evolved over the years into the Memphis in May celebration.

"The Land of Cotton"

On one rare Sunday afternoon family excursion into rural Arkansas when we were quite small, Mama pointed out the field workers moving among the long rows of cotton. They carried huge burlap bags over one shoulder and dragged them through the fields filling them with the fluffy bolls. Mules followed nearby pulling old wagons piled high with the seedy cotton. Gray wooden plank shacks were clustered here and there in the hot, flat and treeless fields. The poverty was everywhere visible.

I have very early memories of the old school bus that passed our house at dusk loaded with workers returning from the fields. Mama used it as an opportunity to talk with us about the people who had to leave home before dawn to work in the cotton fields in Arkansas.

I recently came upon a 1942 children's book, *The Bobbsey Twins In The Land of Cotton*. One passage is indicative of how children's texts perpetuated the prevailing racist attitudes, shaping the minds of people for generations:

> Colonel Percy was waiting for the children. He drove them in a car to watch the wagons and trucks being loaded with cotton pickers. The Negroes, both men and women, were gaily dressed in bright-colored shirts, or sunbonnets and aprons. Most of them were singing.
> "They must like their work," said Nan. "They seem so happy."
> "Cotton picking is healthful exercise," smiled the plantation owner.[77]

A Culture of Racism

One summer I spent several weeks visiting with my school friend Catherine at her grandmother's home in the rural community of Crumrod, near Elaine, Arkansas. We children took long walks down dusty country roads that seemed to stretch on forever through the wide-open fields of cotton and soybeans.

Catherine's Aunt Ruth and Uncle Jimmy also lived at Grandmother Wood's home. I was particularly fascinated with the huge deer head with big glassy eyes mounted over Uncle Jimmy's bed. Aunt Mary and her husband and ten children lived across the road. We had quite a gang of kids to run with when we visited. I remember the day Aunt Ruth, a school teacher, tried to shield us from the common country scene of copulating dogs. "Shoo, Shoo, go on dog, go on..." she yelled, shaking a stick as we stared in fascination.

Catherine's mother, Holly Eugenia, had been Mama's classmate at Siena College. She was a social worker before she married into the Lebanese Gattas family from Clarksdale, Mississippi, a Delta community just across the river.

Elaine has had quite a racial history, but I knew nothing of this when I visited as a child. Elaine was the site of a 1919 riot when tensions between white landholders and black sharecroppers erupted into violence. Attempts by the Farmers and Household Union of America to organize workers were upsetting the economic status quo. The emancipation of slaves had destroyed the plantations' source of free labor and replaced it with the sharecropper system. Historians studying social relations in the Delta note: "whenever the black under classes seriously challenged the economic structures and social hierarchy of the plantation world, the planters and the local white leaders and elites allied with them could quickly cease to be protectors and instead became perpetrators of violence and repression."[78]

Before she married, Mama taught literacy to sharecropper families in the Delta. By the time I visited Elaine, forty years had passed since the so-called "Elaine Massacre." Even so, the social hierarchy was still evident.

Mozelle and Henry lived just outside the back door of Grandmother Wood's two-story farmhouse in a small wooden shack. I never knew the couple's last name. Catherine recalls that Henry could no longer work as he had been crippled in an accident and lost a leg. Mozelle helped out with domestic chores in the Wood

The Half Life of a Free Radical

household. Another household helper named Tilde, perhaps for Matilda, lived by the cotton gin in one of the row houses across the railroad tracks.

One Saturday afternoon I watched Mozelle chase down a chicken. She took it by its neck and swung it around and around until it snapped, and then chopped off the chicken's head and hung the body upside down on a high clothesline to let the blood drip out. I was horrified. This scene gave new meaning to Mama's oft-repeated warning when she was especially frustrated with us kids:

"I've told you for the umpteenth time, stop that now or I'll wring your neck!"

That same dead chicken was served up for Sunday dinner the very next day. I refused to eat the meal. It was the first time I had seen the brutal truth of killing animals for food. This was perhaps the earliest stirring of conscience toward my later commitment to a vegetarian diet.

Recently I was walking along a rural highway in Georgia on a peace pilgrimage when truck after truck loaded with caged chickens passed on the road. The cages were stacked the length and height of the large truck and the young chickens were clearly in distress, feathers flying. The stench of death filled the air as the trucks sped to the slaughterhouse. By comparison, wringing the chicken's neck in that Arkansas backyard so long ago seems a much more honest way to provide meat for the Sunday dinner table.

Catherine's cousin Ann was the oldest daughter of her Aunt Mary's ten children. We all enjoyed roaming about the back roads of Elaine or circling around the Dairy Queen in the tiny downtown, flirting with the local teenagers. Sometimes Ann would visit Memphis and we would show her the back alleys of our urban stomping grounds. We thought life would go on forever. But we soon found out, it doesn't. Ann was killed in a car accident near her home just after her high school graduation. She and a friend had been returning from "Blue Hole," a favorite local swimming spot. The car she was riding in hit a tractor backing onto the highway. Ann's death was the first of many that shocked us with the reality of our mortality. I never returned to Elaine after that, but will always remember the gift of those seemingly-endless country summers.

A Culture of Racism

Neighborhood Changes

During the 1960's our neighborhood and our city went through many changes. The whole South was in turmoil. Color lines were challenged and crossed everywhere. Many families moved out of the inner city as others, of darker skin, moved in.

There was much talk then of prejudice and discrimination, of racists and "nigger lovers," but I don't remember much being said about the structures that held it all in place.

Martin Luther King, Jr. had stirred the nation with his "I Have a Dream" speech, and he later shook hands with Malcolm X in a promise for more coordinated direct action to gain passage of civil rights legislation. I didn't realize then what all this would mean on the national scene, but in our North Memphis neighborhood we witnessed the "white flight" and felt the rising militancy as black youth gained courage.

People had started calling North Memphis a "bad neighborhood." Many of our friends had moved and were wary of traveling back to the old neighborhood at night. My teenage siblings and I did not have ready access to a car. The neighborhood theaters had either closed or were showing only old films, and there was little else to occupy our after-school, after-work hours.

Speculative "block-busting" real-estate agents tried to frighten our neighbors into selling with alarming stories about what would happen when the "niggers" moved next door. Mama suspected that it was those same white real-estate agents who hired black youth to prowl the streets and break windows in the homes of slow-to-sell elderly white widows. Mama tried to quell the fears of our neighbors and adamantly declined the realtor's offers to sell. It was around that time that the Methodist minister next door moved and Tommy Joe and his family from across the street also sold their home.

After the preacher moved, there was a succession of renters in the old parsonage. Once I arrived home to see our neighbor's furniture set out on the curb. When I asked Mama about it, she said flatly. "They didn't pay the rent." Economic hardship was becoming the lot of most in our neighborhood then.

"But where will they go?" I wanted to know.

The Half Life of a Free Radical

No one had the answer. Our family stayed on through it all, unwilling and unable to take part in the "white flight," yet not immune from the violence as entrenched privilege was challenged and two very distinct southern cultures clashed.

Michael and John, like their older brothers, also managed newspaper routes during those times. When the interstate highway cut through our neighborhood in 1967, many houses were seized by eminent domain. As Michael recalls, the families resisted until the very end. They were eventually forced to move and their homes were demolished.

"Most of the houses were on Johnny's paper route. It went from 160 customers to only sixteen." The loss left Johnny without his much-needed income and destroyed the heart of the neighborhood we had roamed as children.

Johnny died before I had the opportunity to reminisce with him about our childhood days as I have with some of my other siblings. His stories would have been rich in detail and humor.

"We knew most of the kids," Michael later recalled. "And then they all were gone. They just disappeared."

Michael kept rocks in his newspaper bag when he went out at dawn to deliver papers. He said he kept them handy so he could throw them at the "creepy men" that cruised the neighborhood, and there were plenty. Also during this time the "pimp mobiles," as we called them, started showing up here and there in the neighborhood, blaring the so-called "race music" and asserting a strong presence.

There were even chartered buses that drove slowly through our streets bringing white liberals from the North on a tour of inner-city Memphis. Mama and I were working in the front yard one summer afternoon when one such chartered bus passed. Mama wasn't pleased being "gaped at" from the bus windows, nor did she ever accept that ours was a bad neighborhood, despite the changes that sometimes left us all feeling unsafe walking home after dark.

One night during those days of social chaos Daddy limped home from the corner bus stop. He was shaken and agitated. He said he had been set upon by a group of angry blacks after he got off the bus. His attitude toward our neighbors of color changed after that encounter.

Racial tensions were high and in the summer of 1967 rumors of race riots were in the air. The anger from centuries of injustice was

A Culture of Racism

spilling over onto everyone. Soon our whole world would erupt. The simmering seething racism of some and the growing militancy and determination of the oppressed clashed. The racial inequities of our Southern way of life were under continued challenge.

By 2010 there were nearly 60,000 abandoned buildings in Memphis, most in the deteriorating urban core. Some attribute this inner-city decay to the tax-advantaged suburban development and racial disharmony that accelerated after the assassination of Dr. King.

I visited Memphis again in October 2013 for the tenth annual Gandhi-King Conference, held close to the downtown riverfront near the neighborhood where my grand and great-grandparents once lived. The encroachment of upscale development on one end contrasts on the other with the small and deteriorating homes of the mostly black residents, interspersed with vacant and boarded houses.

During my brief visit, *The Commercial Appeal* Sunday headline boldly proclaimed what Memphis' oldest neighborhoods starkly reveal: "Memphis named poorest metro area."[79]

Poverty in Memphis continues to divide on racial lines, with the poverty rate for blacks at 33.6 percent, three times that of the white population. People with the means to do so are still fleeing the inner city. The outward migration of the white population is hastening decay of the urban core. On Faxon Avenue where Robert and his family still live, numerous houses sit vacant and boarded, abandoned by owners and boarded up by the city. Many of the homes I once knew have been razed, leaving vacant lots and wasteland in the neighborhood of my childhood.

8

Crossing the Color Lines

Racism is a disease of white people — Albert Einstein

When Daddy was a student at Fordham, he subscribed to *The Catholic Worker*, a newspaper edited by the Catholic convert and pacifist anarchist Dorothy Day and the itinerant philosopher Peter Maurin. The tabloid advocated justice for laborers and the homeless. Daddy told me he first purchased a copy for one penny from a street vendor in Union Square.

The Catholic Worker landed in our Memphis home each month among the stacks of bills and other correspondence that dropped through the mail slot by the front door. Ada Bethune's masthead graphic of two workers, one black and one white, holding hands in front of the figure of Jesus at the cross, was distinctive enough to catch my eye.

It was through this connection that Helen Caldwell Day came into our lives. Helen was raised in Holly Springs, Mississippi, the same town where Ida B. Wells was born. She went to nursing school in New York City. While there, Helen became friends with Dorothy Day who was providing advocacy and hospitality to the city's destitute.

When Helen returned south she contacted my parents and other sympathetic Catholics from a list of local subscribers to *The Catholic Worker* newspaper. She had an idea for a Catholic Action group. Helen was a convert to Catholicism and a single mother. She was also

Crossing The Color Lines

a nurse, a journalist and an author. In her 1952 book, *Not Without Tears*, Helen wrote:

"It is hard to go back to the South if you have ever lived away from it, when you are a Negro. ...As soon as the 'White Only,' 'Colored Only' signs begin to appear, something inside me shrinks and I feel choked and hurt. But I still come back."[80]

Blessed Martin Catholic Worker House

My parents and many of their friends joined with Helen in an interracial study group called the "Outer Circle." The group provided support for the Blessed Martin House, a day care and community center for families that Helen founded. It was named after Martin de Porres, the patron saint of mixed-race people and all those seeking interracial harmony.

Blessed Martin House was in a small building at 299 S. Fourth Street, near Beale, around the corner from St. Patrick's Catholic Church and adjacent to the Clayborn Temple at the corner of Hernando Street and Pontotoc Avenue. Clayborn Temple is where the civil rights marches started and ended during the Sanitation Workers' Strike.

I stood at Mama's knee when Josephite Priest, Father John J. Coyne, gave the ritual blessing to Memphis' first Catholic Worker House on January 13, 1952. I was three. Eileen sat on our mother's lap. Mama was pregnant with Michael at the time. Our Daddy had a hand on the shoulder of each of the twins, Danny and Tommy. Our family friend, *Memphis Press Scimitar* reporter Clark Porteous, took a photograph for the record.

Helen was the first woman of color to come into our home, not as a domestic worker, but as a friend and colleague of our parents. Sometimes she brought her six-year-old son, Butch, who was recovering from polio. I remember especially the summer day we gathered in our back yard for his birthday party. In apartheid Memphis we were breaking a social taboo with this "mixing the races" in a social setting. Helen and Mama were friends and she became our sister Regina's Godmother.

When Mama and Helen rode the city bus together, they made a point to sit side by side in a center seat, just in front of that painted white line that marked the back of the bus. It was a quiet challenge

The Half Life of a Free Radical

to Jim Crow laws. And together they approached then Catholic Bishop William Adrian for his approval of the Blessed Martin House. They met with him on the campus of the old St. Peter's Orphanage, as Mama recalled, "letting their presence together speak to the interracial nature of the work."[81]

Dorothy Day visited Blessed Martin House in 1952. She later wrote in her "On Pilgrimage" column in *The Catholic Worker* that Helen had warned her before she came to Memphis:

"You'll be breaking the law by staying overnight in the same house with a Negro."[82]

Mama remembered meeting Dorothy Day, who spoke at LeMoyne Owen, Siena and Christian Brothers College, and in several other venues.

Father James W. Murphy, who was named as the "spiritual advisor" for the work at Blessed Martin House, was later named in court documents and depositions alleging his sexual abuse of young boys.[83]

I met with Murphy on several occasions in Memphis in the 1980's when I was researching that early inter-racial effort. We were trained early to view priests as "elevated individuals," and I never would have suspected him of being the sexual abuser he is alleged to have been. Who knew?

Catholic clergy in Memphis had good words for the work of Blessed Martin House until Helen and other supporters began to raise the issue of economic justice and labor rights. Clergy of all faiths were counseling gradualism with regard to race relations, and labor issues have always been a hot button. In Memphis, unionism brought with it a fear that race mixing in the labor struggle might be another step toward the forbidden social equality.

In the early 1980's, when I again lived in Memphis, I encountered some other Catholic Workers, Betty and Charlye Gifford. The couple managed the St. Rose House of Hospitality in mid-town Memphis, and the Joseph Leppert House "up in old Pinch." Over the years they provided housing and offered friendship to many, many homeless women and men, often taking overflow into their own small home where they raised their six children. Betty's account of those times, *Catholic Worker Daze*, was published in her 80th year.[84]

It was Betty who first showed me Helen's book, *Not Without Tears*. Like Mama, Helen Day was a journalist. She wrote a regular

Crossing The Color Lines

column called "Looking Things Over" for the *Memphis World*, "The South's oldest and leading Colored semi-weekly newspaper." Helen's articles challenged racism, the Korean War and the injustice faced by returning black veterans. Helen mentioned Mama in her book, and wrote of the support The Outer Circle gave to Blessed Martin House. I interviewed many of the people who participated in the early inter-racial Catholic Action group, and published it in a booklet, *Looking Things Over—Again, Memphis Catholic Workers in the 1950's & the Blessed Martin House of Hospitality*.[85]

From the Bus Window

Our home faced Breedlove where it dead-ends at Faxon Avenue. As many as eight times a day the number 19 Vollintine bus would drive straight down Breedlove and make its turn in front of our house. The acrid smell of the hot tar from the summer streets, mixed with the exhaust of the passing bus.

I could catch a glimpse of life on the other side of the color line from the bus windows. The injustice was everywhere evident. Weary looking women, with several children in tow, and young and old men alike, were all crowded to the back of the bus behind the cruel line that divided passengers by the color of our skin. I always felt uneasy taking my place in a front seat; I knew something was very wrong.

The 19 Vollintine, 52 Jackson, and 53 Summer routes still operate in the city, though the scene from the windows has changed. During my childhood, the buses passed through separate but clearly unequal neighborhoods, past the Chinese corner grocery shops and small Free Will and Missionary Baptist, Holiness Tabernacle, Colored Methodist Episcopal (CME) and African Methodist Episcopal (AME) churches. They were situated here and there among dilapidated wooden houses with Victorian trim and the small segregated city parks.

As the bus passed, I watched the pedestrians along the sidewalk. Many were bent over or limping, struggling with bags of groceries and other parcels, even on the coldest of days. There were more people out and about on foot during those years. I keenly felt their plight, and would send them a prayer, wishing with all my might that they would not have such a hard life. This was a spiritual practice I kept to myself. My compassion for my "colored" neighbors seemed

The Half Life of a Free Radical

too tender an emotion to safely share in the prevailing culture of 1950's Memphis.

When the 52 Jackson bus turned onto North Main Street, close to where the North End bus terminal now stands, I looked out for the old man who often sat out on the stoop of his small clapboard house on a tiny corner lot. His mule was tied to a nearby cottonwood tree and a small garden of collard and mustard greens flourished in the back. Well into the 1940's and 50's mules were in use at the cobblestone riverfront where the cotton bales were unloaded. Memphis was known as the world's largest mule market until after WWII.

This scene provided a rare glimpse of a remnant way of life on the edge of our busy downtown. To my young eyes, the old man looked like the kindly old Uncle Remus in the classic African folktale *Uncle Remus and Br'er Rabbit*. But I doubt that he was singing *Zip a dee doo dah, zip a dee a, My oh my, what a wonderful day*, like the character in the controversial 1946 Disney movie Song of the South.

I was eight when the movie was re-released in 1956. I really loved the animation and joyous singing, but I knew nothing of the earlier criticism of the film by the NAACP for depicting an "idyllic master-slave relationship." The racist stereotypes were lost on me then.

So-called urban renewal of the 1960's and 1970's swept away many of the homes and businesses in Memphis' oldest neighborhoods, and the old man's humble home was among those lost. A replica of an Egyptian pyramid, a 1991 Memphis boondoggle, now stands in its place.

I don't know if my inherent sense of the injustice of what I witnessed would have been sufficient to withstand the dominant racist culture had it not been for the validation of our parent's guidance and example. Their wise recognition of the dignity of all persons helped to equip me and my siblings with the courage and confidence to challenge the attitudes of our peers. But it also set us apart. We endured the taunt of "nigger lover" from neighborhood playmates, and the rebuke of grownups who, in less crass words, clearly conveyed their disapproval.

We all learned to navigate in the real world by riding the city bus. Mama would sometimes sit in a middle seat beside her friend Helen, long before Rosa Parks set off the revolution in Birmingham. The

Crossing The Color Lines

white riders looked at us with mean expressions. But we learned from Mama about integration and the simple acts of everyday solidarity. Mama would take us to the so-called "colored" parks to play during segregation, and to the public swimming pool after de-segregation, when most of the neighborhood whites had moved out of the inner city to places like the suburb "Whitehaven" where they swam in private pools.

Desegregation & "Race Mixing"

I was ten or twelve when I noticed the social order in Memphis begin to shift. I rode the city bus to and from school most days and watched the drama unfold on the 52 Jackson route.

"Negro" ladies (as we were taught to say) began to assert their hard-won right. Many would sit, silent and determined, one to each double seat in the front of the bus. Many white riders were too hardened and proud to sit next to a person they knew only as a "nigger" (a word our parents forbade us to use). They stood through the journey, mumbling indignantly as they were jostled about along the route.

I often shared a conspirator's smile with the "Negro" ladies and sometimes I would boldly take my seat beside them on the bus. These were women like Stella Mae, Bertha and Martha, who wore the white-trimmed gray uniform dress of maids and worked for sometimes as little as $5 weekly in the homes of neighbors and, on very rare occasions, in our own home. I knew very early that I was on their side in this battle.

Sometimes the women who worked as maids in our friend's homes would bring their children with them. They would join us in whatever games we had going on in the back yards. Eileen remembers one of the girls showing her how to fasten safety pins to turn her dress into pants so she could climb a tree without the boys seeing her panties.

Memphis city buses, the public library, swimming pools, parks, and other city facilities were desegregated in 1960. These visible changes were coming fast. But discriminatory ballot restrictions and intimidation of people of color continued.

It would take until 1963 before all of Memphis' public facilities were desegregated. The Memphis NAACP applied legal pressure and

The Half Life of a Free Radical

persisted in a campaign of weekly marches, picketing and selective boycotts of downtown businesses. There were sit-ins at lunch counters, libraries, and the Mid-South Fairgrounds. Bumper stickers reading "Don't buy gas where you can't use the restroom" and signs asking "Communists can eat here. Why can't we?" helped make the discontent visible. Racist placards prominent in the Delta region bluntly expressed the fearful thinking of the times: "Race Mixing is Communism."

In the mid-1960's a roadside billboard with a large photograph of Dr. Martin Luther King and others seated in a classroom at the Highlander Center was seen throughout the south. The caption read: "Martin Luther King at Communist Training School." King was circled among the photographed participants. The Highlander Center, whose work continues today, has a long history of inter-racial and labor organizing and of serving as a catalyst for grassroots social change.

When I lived in St. Petersburg, Florida, in the early 1980's I met the tall and lanky West Virginia poet, Don West, a co-founder with Myles Horton of The Highlander Center. Don and his wife Connie were part of an activist group meeting at the home of my friend Ruth Uphaus whose husband Rev. Willard Uphaus had taught Don West at Vanderbilt University.

I later learned that Don West was suspended from his Georgia high school for leading a protest against a screening of the film *The Birth of a Nation*. My New York grandfather, Daniel F. Hanrahan, a chemist, worked on film coloration for that 1915 racist epic. Color tinting enhanced such scenes as "The Burning of Atlanta" and "The Ride of the Ku Klux Klan" at the climax of the movie. I had no idea then what *The Birth of a Nation* represented, nor do I recall Daddy ever mentioning the racist views in the film.

Kneeling In

In the 1950's Catholics were only ten percent of Memphis' church-going people. Our Jewish neighbors comprised about two percent, while the mostly-fundamentalist Protestant sects dominated, making up eighty-eight percent of church-going Memphians.

Crossing The Color Lines

Every Saturday morning, solemn men in black suits and long beards walked past our house, nodding and tipping their hats. They were on the way to the synagogue at the corner of Bellevue and North Parkway.

There were more churches than gas stations in Memphis in what was known then as the Baptist Bible Belt. Within four blocks of our home there was a Methodist, a Baptist and a Greek Orthodox church and a Synagogue. Episcopal, Presbyterian, Lutheran, and Congregational churches also had a place in Memphis, but all were "off-limits" to we Catholic children.

Throughout my childhood only once did I venture into a non-Catholic church. Mama had to get a "special dispensation" from the Bishop to attend the wedding of her first cousin, Peggy Gardner. Peggy and her sister Mary Ann lived on Baltic Avenue with their parents, Mama's Uncle Mayger and Aunt Cora. I can remember visiting with them there on several occasions. I wondered then what could be so dangerous inside a Protestant church that we had to get a "special dispensation" to attend cousin Peggy's wedding.

Most white churches in Memphis participated in and upheld the structural racism of Jim Crow, as the post-Civil War period of legally-enforced segregation was commonly known. Jim Crow was a popular caricature of southern blacks that appeared in minstrel shows as early as 1828.

Among Catholics in Memphis, racial discrimination was sustained with separate churches and schools and even a separate order of priests, the Josephites, whose mission was to serve the "Negro" parishes.

Many times during those apartheid days Mama would lead us on the two-mile walk up Breedlove toward Vollintine Avenue to the now-demolished St. Anthony Catholic Church where we helped to integrate Sunday Mass. It was our own "kneel in" in reverse, and another way Mama found to teach by action and example. The institutional church, with its "gradualist" approach, was way behind our Mama, who once told me, "I was raised on Catholic Action." When we complained about the long walk, she repeated her familiar refrain: "Offer it up."

The original black parish of St. Anthony, located at Hill and Concord, had been closed to accommodate the building of St. Jude Hospital. The congregation then built the smaller church on

The Half Life of a Free Radical

Vollintine Avenue. Eventually it too was shut down when then Bishop William Adrian decided that the parish was too small to employ a full-time priest. St. Anthony was the "colored" parish where all "Negroes" living North of Madison Avenue were encouraged to attend. The other black Catholic church was St. Augustine, near LeMoyne-Owen College.

Sunday's Blue Laws remained in effect in Memphis until 1970, but Eileen remembers there was a little corner store where we could still buy a cold drink for the long walk home.

The first official "kneel-in" happened in Memphis in August 1960, when small groups of African-Americans visited services at various churches. I remember there was a mixed reaction at Little Flower parish when it came to integrating the church. Father Leppert had always maintained an open door, but it did cause a stir in the pews when black Catholics attended Mass.

According to priest-historian Milton Guthrie, after the African-Americans took a seat, some white parishioners got up from their pews and moved to seats in front of them, reasoning that "No black person is going to be in front of me."[86]

Integration of the white Baptist churches was not well received either. According to news reports, when the "kneel in" activists tried to integrate nearby Bellevue Baptist Church, one of the largest Southern Baptist churches in the country, they were arrested on complaint before they made it inside.

Gradualism

The 1954 Supreme Court ruling in *Brown vs. Board of Education* mandated that schools be integrated with "all deliberate speed." In Memphis and the Deep South, "all deliberate speed" was marked by delay and inaction.

In 1961, thirteen first-graders chosen by leaders of the NAACP desegregated the Memphis City Schools, one grade at a time. My younger siblings, who attended public high schools in their later years, had more opportunity than I to form classroom friendships across the color divide.

It wasn't until the fall of 1963 that black children were admitted to Catholic schools in Memphis, and then only in the first four grades. Many of the city's priests were opposed to desegregation. Gradualism was the doctrine of the day. According to one Catholic historian, then Bishop William Adrian "was not an advocate of swift change."[90]

Little Flower parish became the first Catholic school in the diocese to desegregate. Father Leppert, later a monsignor, was more progressive than most. During the Sanitation Workers' Strike he was among the Memphis clergy who appealed to Mayor Loeb to listen to the workers concerns.

In 1966, my last year at Sacred Heart, there was only one black student desegregating our senior class. I remember her name was Gail. She was sophisticated and brave, but I didn't know her well and our paths never crossed outside the classroom. By that time, the Memphis City Schools faculty had been integrated and all twelve grades were technically desegregated.

I don't remember any classroom discussion of the racial turbulence swirling all about us. Times then, as they are now, were fraught with dangers and marked by bravery.

That summer, civil rights activist James Meredith began his solo "March Against Fear" to encourage voting rights actions. He was shot by a white racist on Highway 51 near Hernando, Mississippi, not far from Memphis.

Nearly fifty years later, I read a 2014 news report that the statue of James Meredith erected in his honor at Mississippi State University in Jackson, had been desecrated with a noose.[91]

"Segregation now; segregation tomorrow; segregation forever!" George Wallace had promised in his inaugural address as Governor of Alabama on January 14, 1963. He seemed to embody the racism that permeated the Delta throughout my childhood, seeping into the crevices and settling about the city like poison gas.

Like the deadly currents in the Mississippi River, racism still lurks about even when much of the surface seems calm. Today, its poisons are rising again like a deadly fog off the surface of deep and troubled waters.

9

The Secret Vote

The will of the people ...shall be expressed in periodic and genuine elections which ...shall be held by secret vote or by equivalent free voting procedures.
— *International Declaration of Human Rights*

The first presidential campaign I remember was the 1956 Eisenhower-Stevenson race. There were a lot of the old "I like Ike" buttons around town then. Eisenhower won Tennessee and the Presidential election. He picked Richard Nixon for his Vice-President.

Mama didn't trust Nixon. She called him "Tricky Dick," as many people did in those days. But whenever we asked her who she voted for, Mama would always answer: "It's a secret vote."

The convention was televised and Mama invited our neighbor, Mrs. Fisk, to watch with her. We kids would wander in and out of the room as they discussed the candidates.

In a 1958 election, Daddy supported Senator Albert Gore, Sr. Daddy enlisted us kids to stand at a regulated distance from the polling place at the neighborhood firehouse to distribute Gore campaign literature. We hauled the cards to the polls in our red wagon. We had so many campaign cards left over that I used them to build a cardboard tower that reached at least four-feet high. I amused myself for an entire afternoon with Gore's excess campaign cards until someone else needed the corner space and the tower came tumbling down.

When John F. Kennedy ran for office in 1960, Mama didn't keep her choice a secret. There was a lot of talk around town about this

The Secret Vote

Catholic candidate. People were afraid that if he was elected that the Catholic church and the Pope would take over the country. We all crowded around the TV to watch the Presidential debates.

I thought that John F. Kennedy would save us all from the communists who were plotting our destruction in the "secret cells" we learned about from the TV series *I Led Three Lives*.

In September, 1960, Kennedy campaigned in Memphis. Mama took us to Madison Avenue near McLean where we found a spot along a low concrete wall to watch as the caravan from the airport passed. Kennedy waved and smiled from the top of the back seat of a Chevy Impala convertible, just like a Cotton Carnival beauty queen. Mayor Henry Loeb, in his first term of office, sat in the back seat. Kennedy's sister Eunice was up front with the driver. We jumped and cheered from the sidewalk as Kennedy's car, with American flags on the bumpers, drove slowly past.

The Tennessee poll tax had been repealed in 1953, but for black sharecroppers in nearby Fayette and Haywood counties, voting for the next President was still costly. Many were threatened, kicked out of their homes and blacklisted by merchants because they had registered or tried to register to vote. Forced out with no home, money or food, they gathered together in a rural encampment. The "Tent City" eventually drew national media coverage, and resulted in the first federal lawsuit brought under the 1957 Civil Rights Act.[88]

Communists Coming Down the River

Every Saturday at noon the air-raid siren atop Fire Station No. 15 at the corner of Faxon and Decatur sounded its shrill alarm. Mama's Uncle Mayger had been the Captain there. Though he had retired long before, I always felt proud every time I walked past. When the siren blared I would try and imagine what would become of our family in case of a nuclear war. This was the era of "duck and cover," when many school children throughout the country practiced weekly drills taking cover beneath school desks, as if this could be of any help in a nuclear attack.

Making light of the matter, the *Beany and Cecil* cartoon show parodied the nuclear hysteria. One segment I remember mapped the way to "No Bikini Atoll." Bikini Atoll in the Marshall Islands had been the site of twenty-three U.S. atomic weapons tests that made

The Half Life of a Free Radical

the island uninhabitable for generations. Times were particularly tense during the Cuban Missile crisis of 1961 and the disastrous Bay of Pigs CIA invasion of Cuba. I remember coming home from school in a panic one afternoon insisting that we prepare a fallout shelter in our hallway, the only room in the house without a window. I took cans of green beans, hominy, spinach and mixed vegetables from the kitchen pantry, filled Mason jars with tap water and emptied the linen closet to make room for our survival stores. Then I tried to envision how we could all find a place to sleep in that small hallway. I was thirteen then and in seventh grade and quite sure the world would soon be consumed in a nuclear blast.

Reminiscing with Regina during a Thanksgiving weekend in her Lexington, Tennessee, home in 2000, we talked about those days.

"You had me terrified," she recalled. "I thought we were going to be attacked at any time."

Regina had helped me stack the food from the kitchen pantry into the hall closet for our in-house bomb shelter.

"Tommy told me that the communists were on boats coming down the river to invade," Regina remembered. "Then Mama called out, 'Bedtime,' and I couldn't understand how we could just go to bed with the communists on the way."

At least one Memphis priest contributed to the Communist fear mongering. He served a parish in the white-flight suburb aptly named Whitehaven. In 1964 he was quoted in a local paper:

"There can be no co-existence... even if the alternative be nuclear war and total annihilation of the human race."[89]

Lyndon Johnson's presidential campaign broadcast the so-called "Daisy Ad," portraying a little girl standing alone in a field picking petals from a daisy, counting up to ten. Then a male voice could be heard counting down from ten to zero. A close-up of the pupil of the little girl's eye reflected the explosion of a nuclear bomb. Times were scary then, and annihilation seemed close.

I never could figure out what people meant when they talked about the Iron Curtain, but I came to understand that anyone who lived behind it didn't believe in God, was probably a Communist, and was somehow a danger to our way of life.

During that time too, Mama took us to see a demonstration model of an underground fallout shelter. We had lots of schoolyard conversations then about the ethics of survival. Would we let somebody else in our own safe place after the air-raid siren had sounded and the door was closed? That was, of course, a moot point. The fallout shelters advertised in the magazines and the models we visited on Saturday outings were priced beyond reach of folks like us. I knew that if the bomb fell on Memphis, we would be on our own, with only a narrow hallway between us and oblivion.

Despite those early fears of nuclear war, the more immediate threat to Memphis then was in the growing tensions of unresolved racial inequities that would make our streets a battleground for many years to come.

Murder in Dallas

The silence was heavy in my ninth-grade classroom when the principal announced over the intercom the shocking news of President Kennedy's assassination. It was one week after my fifteenth birthday. Classes were dismissed and we all assembled in the gym for prayer. There was fear and sadness in the air. Mama came to pick us up in the old Chevy station wagon. She seemed very anxious to get us all home as soon as possible. We crowded around the TV in the living room corner, its rabbit ears topped with balls of aluminum foil to improve reception.

President Kennedy was dead. How could this be? What was happening?

The following Sunday, while most everyone else was away at Mass, I watched on live TV as the accused assassin, Lee Harvey Oswald, was murdered. A fat man in a dark suit and hat rushed forward out of the crowd, thrust the gun into Oswald's belly, and shot him dead.

It was all happening so fast. The world seemed to be turning upside down. We heard rumors that public school classrooms around the country had erupted in cheers when the students were told of Kennedy's death.

The assassination pulled me out of my small world of home and school and neighborhood. It caused me to think about the larger outside world of politics and of good and evil.

Many years later, when Jessica and I were living in St. Petersburg, Florida, we attended the Quaker meeting. One of the members, Ruth Hyde Paine, had been the landlady of Lee Harvey and Marina Oswald.

The Half Life of a Free Radical

I didn't realize then the cloud of suspicion that she has lived with regarding her relationship with the Oswald family. She seemed, like many Quakers I knew then, to be a gentle, kind person with deep concerns for peace and justice. We never talked about her life in Dallas or of the death of the President who had meant so much to me as a Catholic child in Memphis.

10

Teen-Age Turmoil

I could feel changes comin' on People started singin' different songs Searchin' for the place where they belong I could feel changes comin' on.
— Alabama, Mountain Music Album

An important rite of passage for us adolescent girls was when we first wore a bra. Most of my classmates were already wearing them by eighth grade. Boys would run up behind a girl and snap the tell-tale strap.

Teen-age boys were obsessed with breasts in a much different way than we girls were. *Playboy* magazine provided them with a forbidden opportunity to have a look. My breasts had not really developed enough to need a bra, and I could not bring myself to ask Mama for one. I feared her ridicule. Eventually I saved enough money to buy a cotton bra at Kent's Dollar Store that had recently opened in a small shopping area about a mile from home.

When the bra-burning days of the 1960's arrived, I was happy for the excuse to quit wearing the uncomfortable, and for me unnecessary, bra. It wasn't until my six-month prison sentence in 2001 that I put one on again.

The ill-fitting, prison-issue bras were part of our uniform, worn beneath the khaki military-style shirts. They were required, we were told, so that women prisoners would not be a cause of temptation to the mostly-male guards. Some of the male guards in our women's prison behaved with a similar prurient curiosity during routine bed checks as my adolescent brothers had when poring over the *Playboy* centerfold.

Danny hid his copies of the illicit magazines under his mattress. Sometimes he would bring them down into the many-chambered tunnels we dug in the backyard. He would show me the pictures of half-naked women with huge breasts. The images were shocking. I knew Mama would kill us if she found out we were looking at these pictures. It had to be a Mortal sin.

"When your titties get big, we can make a lot of money," Danny promised.

I knew that wasn't likely as I was a full-fledged member of the eighth-grade "Itty Bitty Titty Club," and had to stuff my new bra with Kleenex to fill out the cups.

I had my own ideas about sex then, largely gleaned from the paper-back books Danny also kept under his mattress. I would sneak one out and read furtively, trying to understand. One time I was so shocked at the descriptions of how men treated women when having sex that I tore up the paperback and flushed it down the toilet, page by page. When Daddy bellowed from the bedroom for me to quit flushing the toilet, I stuffed the remaining soggy mess behind the dining room radiator. Guilt and shame and confusion swirled about in my head.

During high school picnics to Maywood Beach, just over the Tennessee line in Mississippi, most of the girls wore the new two-piece swimming suits. The boxer-style pants covered the belly button and the ample top revealed no cleavage, even if there had been any. Maywood was a spring-fed lake with imported sand beaches. It was a favorite destination for class trips.

I saved up to buy a Madras plaid two-piece swim suit. My middle section was pasty white so I laid out in the back-yard for hours to get a tan, then borrowed Daddy's Gillette single-edged razor and aerosol shaving cream to shave my legs. I never owned up to the crime when he found his dull razor the next morning. When Mama saw me showing off in my new swimsuit she laughed out loud.

"You look like a plucked chicken," she said. My confidence plummeted. Her ridicule stung.

Teen Age Turmoil

My First Kiss

Frankie held me up against the damp concrete wall, pressed himself close, and kissed me. I was taken by surprise. Then, just as quickly as he had come upon me, he ran off. I was fifteen. This was my first kiss. We were just inside one of the dark tunnels under the city streets where rainwater runoff is directed to the sewers. I had taken a detour through the tunnel to smoke a cigarette.

I walked home in a bit of a daze. Someone had kissed me! Finally I felt like I was a real teenager. I sat alone for a while on our front porch, leaning back in the rusting metal chair with my feet up on the banister. The traffic light at the corner of Jackson and Breedlove turned red, then green, then red again, going on for several more cycles as dusk gathered. I savored that first kiss until Mama's call to supper. I saw little more of Frankie after that, but it was no less a sweet experience because it was short-lived.

We girls weren't allowed to go out on a date until we were sixteen, and Mama had a rule against us calling a boy on the telephone. I had to wait until someone I'd met at a school dance asked for my number and called me. My date was expected to come to the front door and meet Mama or Daddy before I could go out. Honking the horn at the curb was not acceptable.

I worried about what would be going on in the house when my date arrived. I was embarrassed by the perpetual clutter, and especially horrified if the roaches were on the prowl. I worried too about who would be home, as I didn't want my date to have to endure the curious scrutiny of my younger siblings or the inevitable harassment from my older brothers.

Midnight was the absolute deadline to be home on week-ends, and 10 p.m. on school nights. Usually we went to a football game or a movie. Sometimes we found a dark street to park and make out. A goodnight kiss at the front porch was risky. There seemed always to be some sibling or another around, or a neighbor ready to report our goings and comings.

Sometimes my girlfriends and I would load up in someone's parents' car and drive round and round in the parking lot of Shoney's Big Boy on Summer Avenue where we mingled with the boys from the nearby public schools, usually after a night at a football game.

The Half Life of a Free Radical

Gladys' handsome older brothers, Bernard and Stephen, were both star football players for Memphis Catholic High. I loved those fall evenings in Crump stadium. The playing field was daylight bright, the air crisp, and excitement everywhere. What we Catholic girls really enjoyed was roaming about looking at all the boys from the rival teams. I also remember some early events at Russwood Park before it burned to the ground in a spectacular five-alarm fire in 1960.

In my junior year I dated one of Gladys' friends, a Catholic High graduate just a few years older than me. We had barely started to go out when he wanted me all to himself. He began to shower me with jewelry and other gifts. One evening he parked the car a few blocks from my house, near the Crosstown movie theater. He had something he needed to show me, he said. Then, to my surprise and shock, he took out his false teeth and revealed his bare gums. It was a brave act on his part, but I was aghast. Not long after that I broke off the relationship.

I wasn't much practiced then in how to let someone down gently, and may have seemed abrupt and cruel. For weeks after, he parked outside my house and watched all my goings and comings until Mama intervened. I recently learned of his death. He had lived and worked in Memphis all his life, steady and good, I am sure. What a different life that would have been.

"And When She Was Bad..."

In the summer of my sixteenth year my period began to flow. I was on the back porch in the middle of a *Monopoly* game with a neighborhood boy. I began feeling cramps and strange sensations. I excused myself to the bathroom and discovered my underpants were a bloody mess. Mama had shown me where she kept the Kotex pads in the big blue box at the bottom of her cedar chest. She had already given me an elastic belt to wear around my hips to hold the pad in place, so I was all set. I excused myself from the game with some excuse and went to bed.

I didn't tell anyone about my moment of passage into life as a young woman. Mama was not comfortable talking about such things. I didn't share my news with my three sisters either. It was just not a subject for discussion. The only conversation I remember having with Mama about menstruation took place a year earlier when she

Teen Age Turmoil

asked me to walk with her to the corner grocery store. Along the way she asked if I had started my period. I had not. But I had already learned all I thought I needed to know from my girlfriends who had been dealing with their periods for years. I was skinny, undernourished, weighing little more than ninety pounds, and by then addicted to cigarettes. This might have played a role in the delayed onset of my period.

The most difficult part of having my period was when I had to go to the drugstore to buy a giant blue box of Kotex sanitary pads. They were kept behind the pharmacy counter, as they were considered too personal an item to display on an open shelf. I had a crush on the boy who worked the counter in the afternoons so I always tried to wait until I was sure he was off work before making the purchase.

The premenstrual rage that would rise in me every month seemed to take on a life of its own. My dramatic mood changes were never identified as hormonal then, nor was there any relief offered. Mama would notice the change in my countenance:

"Get that black look off your face," she would command, catching me in the midst of an inner storm that had to run its course. These premenstrual torments plagued me throughout my fertile years.

I was particularly at odds with Mama in my teenage years. I had neither understanding nor compassion for the extreme difficulties she faced in raising nine children almost single handedly. I decided early on that the life of domestic drudgery would not be my life.

Daddy always seemed more approachable, and would counter my "black looks" with a poem:

There once was a girl, who had a little curl,
Right in the middle of her forehead.
And when she was good,
She was very, very good.
And when she was bad,
She was horrid.

And horrid I was when the anger swept over me like a venomous wave. We developed a ritual, Mama and I. I would unleash my furor on Mama, set off by any number of frustrations and disappointments— no money for a movie, or to buy a new dress, or even if my hair wouldn't flip in the current style. Sooner or later I would calm down and try to win her forgiveness. It was hard to walk into her quiet, darkened bedroom where she had retreated seeking the peace and quiet that eluded us all in that intense household. I would walk up to her bed where she lay flat on her back perfectly still. Her countenance was stony. *To thee I come, before thee I stand sinful and sorrowful.* The prayer droned on in my head.

"I'm sorry, Mama," I confessed. Then, after a long moment of silence she would nod, accepting my apology and then dismiss me with few words, if any, but never a hug.

"We Are Daughters True"

I was not quite fourteen in 1962 when I started high school at Sacred Heart High School in the same Catholic parish where my parents had been married. There were about 500 girls in grades 9 through 12 taught by the Sisters of Charity. The school was a yellow-brick, two-story building adjacent to the convent and across from the church and rectory.

We were way out of step with the fashion of the day in the uniforms that marked us as Catholic school girls. During the fall and winter months we wore a navy-blue wool blazer over a white blouse with a blue-and-gray-plaid pleated skirt that fell well below the knee. We had to keep our black-and-white saddle oxfords polished and wear white bobbie socks. In the spring we wore pastel cotton shirtwaist dresses and a lace doily to cover our heads in church.

After school we rolled up the waistband of our skirts until the length was mid knee in keeping with the current style. Sometimes we would gather at the corner of Madison and Cleveland in hopes of meeting up with boys from the nearby Memphis Catholic High who transferred buses there. We did a lot of furtive flirting and smoking as we waited on the corner.

Monsignor Shea, the stern and gaunt parish patriarch, soon got wind of our bus-stop gatherings. He called an assembly at the church and from his perch in the high pulpit he admonished us as "brazen hussies" and forbade us from talking with the boys at the bus stop, or altering the length of our skirts. We all had a good laugh about it, and for a while were a little less "brazen" out in public.

Teen Age Turmoil

I didn't like the old man, especially the way he talked to us. He made a sin out of anything we did beyond the orderly lines of prudish behavior. He never spoke to us of the greater social sins of poverty, war and racist apartheid practiced by both church and state.

I was not docile. I squared off against the nuns, and anyone else in authority whose opinions I did not respect, hurling invective with what one teacher called my "thousand dollar vocabulary."

Early in my first year at Sacred Heart, one of the tougher girls in the school, Irma Jean, announced that she had arranged an afternoon fist fight between me and another unpopular classmate who rode the bus in from the rural community of Bartlett. I was to meet Barbara behind the corner convenience store after class and have it out with her. In the hierarchy of our school the kids that came in on the Bartlett bus were on the bottom rung of the social ladder. Somehow the nuns got wind of this planned stand-off and intervened, much to my relief. I don't recall any conflict I had with this classmate, and I really didn't want to fight with her, and I'm sure she did not want to fight with me. But as long as she was on the bottom rung, I wasn't considered the least popular girl at school.

During my junior and senior years I was at war with our music teacher, Sister Frederick Maria, a tall and thin female version of Monsignor. Shea. She was out of her mind. In the classroom she would fling her arms out from her body holding them outstretched, as if suspended on the cross, while we students were expected to continue with our voice exercises. "e e e e ah ah ah ah ah" we intoned, with our index and middle fingers between our teeth to create the proper shape.

Sister reminded us often how much we were persecuting her. I was one of the worst, laughing out loud whenever she went into her martyr routine. As punishment, for the rest of the year I was banished to a lone chair on the stage at the other end of the auditorium with my back to the rest of the class. Sister was especially distraught about the theological changes in the church, collectively known as the Second Vatican Council (1962-1965). The Mass would soon be celebrated in the vernacular English. The Latin Mass she loved, with all the ancient Gregorian chants and call and response Latin prayers, would be no more. As a parting gift the last day of class, she gave us each a copy of the old Latin hymnals.

"You'll be glad to have these later when it's all gone," she said.

The Half Life of a Free Radical

I loved to sing the Latin hymns, but I discarded my hymnal, as I discarded so many things from those days at Sacred Heart High.

"We are daughters true, and we're all for you," as the school song promised, did not ring true for me.

Sometimes after school I hung out at the Southern Bowling Lanes on Cleveland. Other times I would take the bus downtown and go to the women's lounge on the second floor of Goldsmiths Department Store. There I could smoke, do my homework and gossip with my girlfriends in air-conditioned comfort until the saleslady got wind of our hideout.

My senior year, I wasn't too worried when I didn't have a date for the Prom. But I was relieved when Mary Alice asked a friend of hers to escort me. The prom was held in the Skyway ballroom of the famous Peabody Hotel, the same place Elvis had attended his prom a decade earlier. My date was from a Greek Orthodox family in the neighborhood. Mama helped me pick out a prom dress at the old Lerner's dress shop on Main Street across from Walgreens. It was a modest light pink, ankle length dress with a high collar. I felt elegant.

Vanity and Charm

Throughout my adolescence, my self esteem plummeted, distorting my appreciation of my own beauty. I can still hear Mama's admonition whenever she caught me lingering at the tall mirror in the center hallway.

"Why do you keep looking at yourself? It's vain."

Vanity was yet another sin in a growing list of forbidden behaviors. I couldn't understand why Mama thought I was being vain. A compliment of some sort might have been a kinder and more helpful way to ease my acute insecurity. Perhaps Mama was echoing the stern approbation of the nuns in her Catholic boarding school days where modesty and humility were stressed.

At Little Flower School, in the second-floor bathroom where we 7th and 8th grade girls hung out after lunch, I could find a place at the long mirror mounted sideways on the wall. In the narrow space, on tiptoe, between the toilet stalls and the mirror, I could check out the new bouffant-style hairdo that framed my face like a helmet. To achieve this stylish look I endured a night of torture with brush rollers, back-combed my hair into a nest of tangles, and smoothed

Teen Age Turmoil

strands of hair over the tangle, then held it all in place with copious amounts of Spray Net, for me a hard-to-come by aerosol hair spray that cost one dollar a can.

One summer Mama enrolled me in a week of "Charm School" at Goldsmith Department Store. It was a teen class in poise and manners. I was not the white glove, ladylike type, but I endured several sessions, including one where we practiced walking across the room with a book balanced on our head. I didn't pick up much charm. I was more interested in going down to the river where I could roam along the cobblestones and watch the great swirling waters flow past, around the bend and far, far away.

Sometimes my anger at the unfairness I felt in our circumstances would erupt with a fury that took me by surprise. I remember a screaming fight I had with Daddy one night when I was about fourteen. I wanted to get a Toni permanent wave.

"If God wanted you to have curly hair, you would have been born with it," Daddy said, and refused to provide the money I needed to buy the kit. Later, Mama tried to give both Mary and me a permanent wave from one package, but she ran out of the curling solution before she could do the back of my hair. I endured some stinging ridicule from classmates who laughed at my frizzy side curls and the straight hair in the back.

Grounded in Shame

On my sixteenth birthday my friends Catherine and Sharon made a surprise visit. I was suffering the consequences of another angry and defiant outburst. My punishment that day was to scrub the linoleum tile on the kitchen floor on my hands and knees. I was in that position when my girlfriends arrived, and still feeling angry with Mama and now very ashamed. Even though I had been grounded for cursing and smoking, Mama relented and let me go to the surprise birthday party.

I couldn't easily explain to my friends why I had such a tumultuous relationship with Mama. Rebellion and defiance were ways I could feel my strength and hold my own in situations where I felt diminished and devalued.

My adolescent bouts with *herpes simplex*, what was then called shingles, a persistent eye tick, and a complexion blemished with pimples, took a heavy toll on my self-esteem. When active, the virus would turn my lips into a horrible mass of oozing, stinging blisters that would grow more inflamed each day, lasting sometimes for several weeks. I had to go to school with that visible affliction and felt like a leper.

"Who have you been kissing?" Mama wanted to know. But I hadn't been kissing anyone. Then she warned me,

"Don't put your lips on the metal when you drink out of a water fountain."

But my affliction persisted. Maybe it came from one of the discarded cigarette "shorts" I picked up from a public ashtray when I had no money to feed my nicotine habit.

By the time I wanted to date, I was in a desperate mood. I walked up to Jackson Avenue to the small doctor's office where I remembered occasionally going as a child. I asked for help with my affliction. I had no idea what such a visit might cost, nor any money to pay, but I simply could not face another day of hiding my face. The doctor looked at my lips and then offered to give me a shot of something to help. I have no idea what it was, but within the week the blisters had all dried up. Weeks later the bill arrived. Mama wasn't pleased. I have no idea how the bill was paid, but I was incredibly relieved that the blisters were gone.

Today during stressful times, or when I get too much sun, the tell-tale tingle will begin—but never with the intensity it once did—at least not until my sixty-fifth year when I was encouraged by a doctor to get a shingles vaccination. My body reacted dramatically. Once again I had the inflamed, blistered and oozing lips from fifty years before, and along with the blisters, the old feelings of overwhelming shame.

"Pimple face, pimple face!" was another taunt. The child in me still winces.

"They fill every inch of your face," my sister Mary once charged. Indeed, it seemed they did, despite all my efforts with Noxzema, Clearasil and Stridex pads, or any other remedy in current fashion that I could scrounge the money to buy.

Once a sample bar of Neutrogena, a new soap on the market, arrived in the mail box. I gave it a try, lathering it up in a thick paste that I left on like mud mask. My face soon became inflamed with an allergic reaction that lasted for days. I kept my head down a lot after that.

Others would taunt me when I wandered over to the nearby North Parkway neighborhood to join up with the gang of kids running through the alleys and playing ball at the water works. I was greeted with a chorus of "Here comes Cooties!"

"Sticks and stones can break my bones, but names can never hurt me," I countered in sing-song fashion, repeating the rhyme Mama taught me. But the names did hurt. They always hurt. Though in truth, I was dishing them out as fast as they were being hurled at me.

"You're Crazy"

Everyone has a role to play in every family. In ours, where alcoholism took an insidious toll, it's hard to know just who among we nine took on which persona to keep the tenuous balance.

Mary, the eldest, was perhaps our hero. She won big prizes in The Pillsbury Bake-Off then went off to Europe after high school and stayed. All reports were of her high accomplishments. Danny and Tommy also took on heroic roles with their willingness to put their life on the line in the military. But they were so wounded by the experience, I'm not sure they ever found their way back home again. I was the "crazy" one, always challenging authority with my contrary opinions and stridently speaking my mind. Eileen was quiet, studious and helpful, maybe lost in the shuffle? Michael and John, both caught in the middle, had to fend off their older brothers, stay out of the way of their sisters, and somehow find their own place. Regina was off and running the neighborhood as soon as she could, at a far more dangerous time and with less opportunities than her older sisters. Then came Robert, kind and sure. Mama's last child, perhaps the closest to her, who stayed by her side, faithful and true all the days of her life.

"You're crazy." Mama would accuse me when I expressed a contrary opinion. My siblings picked up on her assessment. "You're crazy." It was meant to take me down a notch, keep me in my place, wherever that was. Even today nephews sometimes still call me "Crazy Aunt Clare."

The Half Life of a Free Radical

I wasn't crazy. Contrary? Yes. Strident? Certainly. But not crazy. Though sometimes along this wild and impulsive journey that has been my life I have wondered now and again if it would have been easier. I imagined that really being crazy might offer a kind of oblivion. I became instead reactive, guarded and armored against a world in which it never felt really safe to reveal my deepest, most sincere self. I'm only now finding the cracks in the armor.

Had our family had the means or opportunity to seek help, we might have come away with a variety of diagnoses. Over the years different family members have been beset with addiction, depression, panic attacks, anxiety, and more perhaps. We were all a bit crazy in the crowded cauldron of our household. It might be how we were able to survive, those of us who did, and thrive, those of us who have. There was a heavy energy within our home that sometimes seemed to close in on me—a concentrated sadness with an explosive edge.

There is yet so much I don't remember about those Memphis years. The grief of loss. The shame of alcoholism. The judgment of the church. Those feelings are clear. Other feelings emerge in my dreams:

> *I'm careening downhill in a car. Suddenly I'm blind, and trying to stay clear of the ditches, hands on the wheel, foot tapping the brakes, slowing down, and finally, finally coming to a safe stop.*

Where is the value of all this recounting? With so many gaps in memory am I still flying blind?

Public School Detour

Family finances were especially tight during my senior year of high school. Mama could no longer afford the ever-rising tuition to keep us in Catholic schools. In a bold move she removed me and all my siblings from parochial schools. I had to enroll in Central High, a co-ed public school with about five times as many students as the all-girl Sacred Heart. Uniforms were not required, and I had few other suitable clothes. Some of the classes were a full academic year behind. I was even more bored than I had been at Sacred Heart.

Teen Age Turmoil

After a few months I had accumulated multiple detentions for violations of school rules, such as moving about the school without a hall pass, smoking on premises, and other minor infractions of institutional order. I was required to stay after school for an hour-long study hall. I had to walk the long distance home at dusk through neighborhoods where predators surely lurked.

I was a defiant, stubborn and angry teen. I steeled myself against feeling the hurt and confusion, and didn't let anyone know how much it bothered me.

My boyfriend at the time realized my distress. He offered to pay the tuition at Sacred Heart High so I could finish my senior year When I told Mama, she wisely declined his generous offer. It would have indebted me to him in ways I didn't realize. Somehow she found a way for me to return to finish my senior year. When I walked back into the second-floor classroom after a few months absence, I was surprised when everyone clapped. I honestly didn't think they had missed me.

Mary Alice was by then traveling in Europe where she met her Canadian husband, Neal. She eventually found work in Geneva with the United Nations. She left Memphis when she was denied the scholarship help she needed to continue at Siena College. As I remember the situation, Daddy didn't want to disclose his income, or lack thereof. Whatever the reason, it must have been a painful disappointment.

Mary first traveled in Europe as a buyer for the Fred P. Gattas Co. where she had worked throughout high school. Before she left, she had organized employees there to send care packages to soldiers in Viet Nam.

Tommy was in Viet Nam then, and Danny was at Memphis State, but would soon follow his twin into the Marines.

Our younger siblings first attended Snowden, across from the zoo, then Eileen and John enrolled in Central High School. Michael and Regina went to Memphis Technical on Poplar near Crosstown. Robert attended Snowden, then because of complications with his epilepsy, Mama home-schooled him for one year. He finished high school at Memphis Catholic. They were all caught in the turmoil of the times as integration and school busing heightened tensions in the city. Eileen says now that she "hated Snowden and could not wait to get out." And Regina, Eileen says, may not have felt safe at Memphis Technical High School. She dropped out, and later earned her GED.

"The Gift of Understanding"

Robert went on to graduate from Christian Brothers College where he met his Arkansas-born wife-to-be Vernua, who also graduated from the private Catholic college. Robert and Vernua's marriage in 1977 "brought us the gift of understanding," Mama once said. She and Vernua became best of friends.

I was living out of Memphis at the time and didn't meet Vernua until after their daughter, Katrina Allison was born.

Michael remembers his hesitation when he learned of his brother's planned inter-racial marriage.

"Don't, man," he recalls saying. "This world is not right for it."

But Vernua and Robert were right for one another, and together they were strong enough to counter any concerns about what they might face in the racist climate of Memphis. When they married, It had only been ten years since state laws prohibiting inter-racial marriage were declared unconstitutional by the United States Supreme Court in the case of *Loving v. Virginia*.

Times were changing and so were we.

Vernua and Robert's marriage is strong and has endured all these many years. I was in Memphis recently for my fiftieth high-school reunion and had the opportunity to celebrate with Robert and Vernua on their thirty-ninth wedding anniversary.

Their children and grandchildren, raised in the same house where we were, look out on a very different neighborhood in a very different city. Robert and Vernua's eldest, Katrina Allison, recently posted on her *Facebook* account a Maya Angelou quote:

"It's wise to know where you come from, who called your name."
She then added her own thoughts:

> *I come from a very mixed heritage that I am very lucky to know. Cherokee, Black, and Irish. I do not claim one over the other. I am an "other," a mixture, blended.*
>
> *For years I hated filling out forms and watching people erase my answers to put something that satisfies them. I would go behind them and clearly mark that 'other' circle.*

Teen Age Turmoil

The whole concept of race and its many insidious uses to exploit and oppress is persistent. Today, the restrictions against same-sex marriage are being challenged. My nephew John and his husband Ben had to leave Tennessee and travel to California to marry. There is a fierce strength in those who have survived those oppressions, the "others" who can bring to us all "the gift of understanding."

Do not Fold, Spindle or Mutilate

Sometime during my last year of high school Mama encouraged me to go on a retreat at the Mother house of the Sisters of Charity in Nazareth, Kentucky. All I remember of the trip is walking alone along a beautiful wooded path beside a wide lake. Though I had a contemplative bent, the dogma of the church did not resonate with me, and I certainly did not want to be a nun. The trip provided a rare opportunity to get out of the inner city, so I went. But clearly, being a "Bride of Christ" was not my path.

My communion has long been found in quiet moments along woodland trails, in the mountains, along the riverside, and with the persistent weeds in wayside places breaking through the pavement cracks to claim the sunlight. I felt no resonance with the church where I had been compelled to spend so much of my youth.

I graduated from Sacred Heart High School in 1966 with ninety nine other, mostly chaste, Catholic school girls. I wasn't to see most of them again until our fortieth reunion in 2006 when we again walked together through the two-story, yellow-brick building remembering our years together. Our alma mater had since combined with Memphis Catholic High School. It is time again for a reunion, our fiftieth. Fewer of our classmates will make the journey back to Memphis. Many of us are grandmothers, even great grandmothers now. Some of us have died.

After high school, I enrolled at Memphis State University, one year behind my brother Danny. My high school friend and neighbor Madeline Montesi and her sister, Regina, were also students there and I was able to share the early-morning ride to campus with them. Years later, when Regina worked as a nurse, she was murdered as she returned to her mid-town apartment. Another young life lost to violence.

The Half Life of a Free Radical

I spent the time between classes at the Newman Center, a Catholic campus organization. I didn't know where else to go. After classes I had to catch the first bus out to my job and work until 9 p.m. I had it in mind to get a journalism degree, but I still lived at home where it was crowded with siblings and seldom quiet enough for focused study. I dropped out after my first year.

At Mama's strong urging, I enrolled in the Memphis Area Vocational Technical School. I learned *Gregg* shorthand, honed my skill on the manual typewriter to over 100 wpm, and became an expert operator of the IBM punch card machine, carefully keying in data on cards inscribed with the warning: "Do not fold, spindle, or mutilate." But if truth were told, it was my own creative soul that was being mutilated by being tethered to those office machines.

Secretarial school provided me with marketable "back pocket" skills, as Mama called them. But it also led to my imprisonment in the fluorescent-lit, windowless offices of the soulless business world where my fettered fingers sped across the keyboard to the cadence of another's words. Though these skills have served me in good stead for livelihood throughout the years, in many ways they stifled and narrowed my possibilities. I really wanted to work as a journalist as Mama had, but I felt little encouragement in that direction from her and settled for the more accessible career field of secretarial work.

I was hired at the Anderson-Clayton Cotton Company on Front Street just across from the main post office. My job involved tracing lost bales of cotton from warehouse to warehouse throughout the South via invoices and shipping orders. My monthly salary was $325. My immediate supervisor, who had been with the company nearly thirty years, was looking forward to retirement. A new manager fired him less than a year before he was due to receive full retirement benefits. He was crushed. So much for career loyalty. That lesson stayed with me a long time. I was beginning to see a pattern of church, state, and corporate betrayals. Things were not what they had seemed.

"Lie back and Enjoy it?"

One afternoon as I waited at the bus stop after school, a man pulled up to the curb in a boat-like old Chevy. He called me over. As I approached his car, I realized he was masturbating. I quickly stepped away and turned my back. With dusk coming on, I

Teen Age Turmoil

had little choice but to wait a frightening fifteen minutes more until my bus arrived. The creep also waited, then followed the bus. When I got off at my stop, there he was again, waiting. I ran at top speed down North Parkway against the flow of traffic and through a neighbor's backyard to scale the fence into our yard. I must have given Mama quite a fright when I burst in through the unlocked back door screaming that a pervert was after me. Daddy expressed some concern and said that he would have his friends at the police station look into it, but nothing came of that.

Daddy and my older brothers were then fond of repeating the old misogynist saw, "If rape is inevitable, lie back and enjoy it." I wasn't sure just how to counter that attitude, which left me feeling very confused.

In grade school the nuns told us the story of the Italian saint Maria Goretti who was just twelve when a neighbor boy tried to sexually assault her. Maria Goretti didn't just "lie back and enjoy it." To do that, she knew, would have been "a Mortal sin." Instead, she resisted and was stabbed to death. We were told that outcome wasn't all bad because she forgave her attacker as she lay bleeding to death. Maria Goretti was canonized in 1950, and she is now considered the Catholic Church's patron saint of youth, young women, and rape victims. So, what is the message in that? Submitting is a mortal sin resulting in the eternal fires of hell. Resisting is sure death, with the promise of heaven only if you forgive the rapist before you die.

11

Next Stop Is Viet Nam

Now come on mothers throughout the land, pack your boys off to Viet Nam,
Come on fathers don't hesitate, send your sons off before its too late,
Be the first one on your block, to have your boy come home in a box
— Country Joe & the Fish

By the end of 1965, the year Danny and Tommy graduated from high school, more than 180,000 American soldiers were in Viet Nam and preparations were underway to send another 160,000 men. The war was sucking the life out of our generation. More and more of our childhood friends were headed off to Southeast Asia.

The summer of 1966 was to be our last together. We danced through the sultry nights, the air pungent with the scent of the Mississippi, as the city heated up with racial tensions. We had a lot of parties that summer, meeting up at one house or another to dance the "Dirty Dog" or the "Cool Jerk."

Our neighborhood friends, Joe and Jerome Russo, set up their drums and electric guitars in the front room for their Rock 'N' Roll band. Other times we tuned the radio to the top hits on WHBQ or WMPS, like the Gentry's "Keep on Dancing," or The Young Rascals' "Good Loving." We tuned to WDIA for Wilson Pickett's "Mustang

Next Stop is Viet Nam

Sally", the Supremes' "Can't Hurry Love," or the Temptations' "My Girl," and more of the good music of the day.

Danny and Tommy were both very handsome, with coal black hair, deep brown eyes and a keen intellect and quick wit. They had no trouble winning the hearts of my classmates. I was especially welcome at the teen parties if I invited my girlfriends, and they were especially eager to come. We closed out each dance with a waltz. Sometimes it was the Righteous Brothers' "Soul and Inspiration," but more often than not it was our favorite oldie from the Lettermen, "Theme from A Summer Place."

Without the watchful presence of the chaperons that were always lurking at the Memphis Catholic High School dances, we could move together close enough to rouse those first stirrings of sexuality and experience a hint of the forbidden pleasures. Between dances we sat out on the porch banisters to catch what breeze might blow through the tall oaks in the front yard and shared the illicit alcohol and cigarettes that somehow always were available.

At one party, somewhere across town, there was a lot of drinking going on. I wanted to show off how well I could hold my liquor. I picked up a bottle of gin from the table and gulped it down before anyone noticed. The next thing I knew I was waking up in the back seat of a taxicab headed home. I must have passed out. I was very sick for the next several days. From then on I was careful to limit my intake of alcohol, a lesson in moderation that I am glad came early for me.

"Back Our Boys in Viet Nam"

Tommy was in Viet Nam by the fall of 1966. Rather than wait on the draft, he had joined the Marines. We really could not have known then how this decision would shatter us all. I wrote him regularly, with poems lauding his "heroic" stand:

> *Brother dear, since you're away*
> *I seem to think more of you every day*
> *The simple thoughts that bring a tear,*
> *I try to hold back but fail, I fear.*
> *Now you're a soldier, not a boy but a man*
> *Defending our country as best you can*

The Half Life of a Free Radical

You stand tall and proud,
A twinkle in your eye
This is what you wanted;
You've said your goodbyes.

At the time, I wasn't in touch with any organized anti-war movement in Memphis. The few hippies that crossed my path were disparaged as unpatriotic, and I don't remember any critical discussions about the war in our classrooms and few at home. Our chief concern was getting our brother and friends home safely. The only bumper sticker I ever saw on our family car was "Back our boys in Viet Nam."

In my high school writing class, I read aloud my naive patriotic poem. A classmate also read a poem about the war, but hers was strongly anti-war. It was the beginning of a time of great confusion for me and for many of us whose brothers were already far away in the jungles of Southeast Asia.

My classmate and friend Gladys' brother Stephen was among the many who was forever changed. Like my brothers he joined the military rather than wait on the draft, and like my brothers, on his return he tried to chase the pain with drinking. Some years after his return from Viet Nam, Stephen crashed his car into a tree and died.

The Catholic church has a doctrine about what constitutes a "Just War," but even if that concept were ever valid, the Viet Nam bloodbath, and all the subsequent U.S. wars of aggression, would never qualify. How many other alumni of Memphis Catholic High School were sacrificed in that criminal war? Why did the clergy not intervene? Did they ever speak against the war?

Mama and Daddy must have been beside themselves with worry. I went with Mama a few times to the Marine Corps Mother's Club where mothers of other teen soldiers gathered for mutual support. Mama never talked with me about how frightened she must have been during those times, but the television images from the battlefield provided us all with ample reason for concern.

In the year 2000, long after we buried our war-broken brothers, Mama sent me by mail a bulletin from the Catholic parish she attended. It was an argument about the so-called "Just War" teaching. By that time I had been an outspoken war-tax resister for nearly twenty years. In a one-line email follow up Mama asked:

Next Stop is Viet Nam

"Did you get what I sent?"

I wasn't prepared emotionally then to take on that discussion with Mama. I wish I had, as she bore the greater pain of the loss of two sons in the aftermath of that unjust, immoral, and illegal war. I wonder what my Marine brothers would say about "Just War."

I recently came across a 1939 commentary our Mama wrote as editor-in-chief of her Siena College newspaper, *The Flame*. She wrote:

"I will fight with words, in behalf of truth, as long as words suffice and then I'll take up my gun!"

I wonder now if her views changed after the war in Viet Nam.

Marine at the Door

The uniformed Marine parked his black car at the curb and came knocking at the front door one early December day in 1966. Eileen, Regina, and me were home with Mama.

"Don't open that door!" Mama sternly ordered Eileen. The Marine waited awhile on the porch and then left to get our then next-door neighbor, Mrs. Wiseman. He knocked again. The two stood and waited on the porch until Mama finally gathered her courage to hear what he had come to say.

"Your son has been wounded. He was on patrol near Phu Bai, Viet Nam," the Marine reported. "He will be transferred to the hospital in Millington by Christmas."

Regina remembers: "When Mama heard the news, she just crumpled." After the shock, we felt relief to know that our brother Tommy was alive and would be coming home.

Tommy was only nineteen and one of twenty-one other volunteers in the 3rd Reconnaissance Battalion, C Company, 2nd Platoon, 3rd Marine Division. We later learned that the soldier beside him that day was killed, and the man behind him lost an arm from what was later called "friendly fire."

It was a few days before Christmas when Tommy returned. Mama gathered her children, and we all crowded into the car and went to the VA hospital at Millington to welcome our brother home. The authorities didn't want to let us all into the ward, but Mama held her ground. Defying orders, we walked in together. There was Tommy lying on his bed in a large open room. He was surrounded

The Half Life of a Free Radical

by many other wounded men from the Mid-South area, including his friend and patrol radio operator, Charlie Cuzzort, a fine singer and musician from Nashville.

In my naivete I rushed to my brother's bedside to embrace him. I may even have called him "my hero" as I approached, expecting a hug. Lightning fast his good arm flailed out knocking me across the room and onto the floor.

"Wake up!" he said. "Wake up you stupid bitch."

I can still hear those harsh words. Dazed and confused I picked myself up and backed away. This was not the brother I had sent away with a patriotic poem, proudly recited before my senior class, as he suffered in the field of terror in Southeast Asia.

It was December 5, 1966, when the bullets sprayed across Tommy's chest, hitting the Zippo in his breast pocket and blowing the ring and middle fingers off his right hand. He later discovered the bullet dents in the cigarette lighter. It had saved his life. Danny later said that he had felt excruciating pain in his own right hand around the time his twin was shot down in Viet Nam.

Our family friend Clark Porteous interviewed Tommy and wrote a feature story in the *Memphis Press Scimitar*.[92]

"If I am going to live in this country, I've got to pay the rent," Tommy was quoted in the article. Little then did he realize how high the rent would be and how long he would have to keep paying.

Years later, when I tried to encourage Tommy to write about his time in Viet Nam he looked at me for a very long time before he responded:

"If I tell the truth about what we did, they will come and kill me," he said. But they didn't have to come for Tommy. The Agent Orange poisons that finished him off were already coursing through his system.

After Viet Nam, Tommy found it very hard to let anyone close. He kept me at a distance with his all-too-frequent use of the word "bitch," a term he applied to all women, and one he used often in addressing his sisters:

"Bitch, get me a cigarette. Bitch, buy me a beer. Bitch, loan me some money."

Much later I read about the systematic misogyny of the Marine drill instructors who shout obscenities at the recruits to undermine any respectful relationship they may have had with women, be they mother, sister, or girlfriend. Feminist writer Mary Daly nailed it:

> The bonding of trained killers requires the perpetual semantic degradation of women in an effort to kill male weakness, misnamed 'the woman' in them.[93]

After Tommy returned from the war, Danny dropped out of Memphis State University and enlisted in the Marines under a 120-day plan. He was scheduled to leave in March, 1967.

Daddy and Tommy both tried vainly to keep Danny from going to war, but like his brother before him, he was undeterred. Daddy even went so far as to bring Tommy to the recruiter's office and try to pass him off as Danny, showing the recruiter Tommy's wounded hand with the two missing fingers.

"I cut them off to keep him from going to Viet Nam," our Daddy lied. But the ruse did not work. Danny went anyway into that dark and deadly war, never, ever, to fully recover. Mama and I went with him to the Federal Building Plaza overlooking the Mississippi river in the summer of 1967 to see him off to basic training. It was a sad goodbye.

Danny's life would have taken a far different course, perhaps had he been able to stay with Up With People, an international singing group founded in 1965 on the principle of using music as a means of communicating with and inspiring people. Danny had really enjoyed his part in those musical productions. Instead of traveling the world singing, he joined the Marines and went to war.

"I could not have stopped them," Mama lamented years later. "There was nothing I could do."

"The Change is Forever"

With church and state both conspiring to depict the military as a righteous profession, and neither questioning the war, nor offering an alternative, it's no wonder that there was little our Mama could do to keep her sons from the military.

My brothers returned from Marine boot camp, and later from the Viet Nam battlefields, utterly changed. Especially hard were the hurtful and objectifying words they spewed when speaking of women.

The Half Life of a Free Radical

On one Memphis visit, long after that war, Jessica and I stopped by Tommy's home to say hello. He seemed glad to see us. But when he addressed Jessica with the same disrespectful words he had so often used with me, "Bitch, get me a beer," or some such demand, I stopped him short.

"If you ever again speak to either of us in that way, Tommy, it will be the last time we visit." Setting such boundaries and holding my ground was not easy for me. Tommy backed off from his insults, at least when we were around.

A dream image of Tommy has haunted me for years.

> *We are standing face to face. Tommy is dressed in combat fatigues. He is young–so very, very young. He looks me straight in the eye then slowly, without a word, he takes off his combat helmet. His expression is profoundly sad.*

Today as I write this, I have in hand the Purple Heart medal that the U. S. Marine Corps awarded to Tommy. Later, they awarded another to Danny. I wear Tommy's medal now and again at Memorial Day services to honor my long-dead brothers and all the soldiers and civilians lost to the criminal enterprise of these endless wars.

In the months after Tommy's return from Viet Nam he brought home many wounded soldiers he'd met during his stay at the naval hospital. Most lived too far from their own homes for a weekend journey, so Mama welcomed them all. Michael remembers the time:

> *Our home became an open house to all the survivors. Our family's front porch had more crips and combat vets per square foot than anywhere in the U.S. I was in my teens, long haired and asking , seeking answers from kids only a couple of years older than me. They had no answers. I do not think they have any answers today.*

The Fall of Our Twin Towers

Over a year after the September 11 attack on the World Trade Center, and with the U.S. on the verge of yet another war, Michael emailed me a loving tribute to our older brothers:

Next Stop is Viet Nam

> *The events leading to the loss of the Twin Towers begins with the loss of my own twin towers—my older twin brothers Dan and Tom Hanrahan.*
>
> *In the sixties they both dropped out of college to join the Marines. Super achievers and true believers they went off to war. That was what boys with a good Catholic education and a belief in their country felt compelled to do. No chicken hawks in my family. Tom returned maimed by the Third Marine Force Recon. The Memphis papers put him on the front page. Six months later his classmates in body bags barely got a mention in the obits.*
>
> *Dan fared better as an Air Traffic Controller in DaNang. Yet he could not stand to bring in men on the end of a Huey string day after day. To relieve his stress he volunteered for missions as a gunner in that doorway to hell on a Huey. Dan was shot down, finding his way back from a job he did not have to do.*
>
> *My twin towers died in their forties. Combat vets. Their dreams and lives shattered by my country's lust for war.*

At a homecoming party for Tommy on his release from the naval hospital, our house was filled with well-wishers. We were not sure just what to say to our brother with his bandaged hand and very changed temperament. Johnny, who must have been about fifteen when Tommy returned from Viet Nam, introduced some of his characteristic black humor to break the tension. He approached Tommy with a small box held firmly in his palm. We all gathered around in excitement.

"Look inside," he said. Tommy lifted the lid of the box. To our horror two bloody fingers wiggled in the bottom. There was a moment of shocked silence. Then we all roared with laughter as Johnny withdrew his own catsup-covered fingers from the holes in the box and wisely backed away to avoid any repercussion from our volatile older brother.

Any sudden noise, such as an automobile backfire, would startle Tommy out of sleep and he would tear down the attic stairs and through the house in an attack mode.

Danny also had trouble fitting back in to civilian life. At one party we attended, I noticed how nervous his old friends seemed when he tried to talk about his experiences in Viet Nam. They were in vastly different worlds by then and just could not understand. How could we? Danny soon re-enlisted and worked as a Marine recruiter in the Memphis office. Michael says his heart wasn't in it. Danny would tolerate none of my criticism of the war. We grew even further apart.

After he returned from war, Danny's appetite for pornography seemed to grow. I visited his home once, shortly after his second divorce, and quickly backed out after seeing the revolving rack of pornography prominently displayed in his living room. Tommy seemed drawn to *True Detective* and other pulp magazines with covers depicting barely-clothed women, the victims of gruesome murders. I recoil even now with the memory of those images.

Despite their disrespectful ways of speaking of women, I tried to maintain a relationship with both my brothers, but it became too painful. To their credit, both were able to return to college and graduate, and both tried repeatedly to recover from their addictions.

Tommy received a Master's degree in Political Science and traveled a lot.

"If you really want to learn about war, read C. Wright Mills," Tommy once told me. I haven't yet, though his book, *The Power Elite*, has been on my shelf for years.

Danny stayed closer to home. After his discharge from the Marines, he finished college at Rhodes College, then worked with the non-profit community development corporation, CoDe North, initiated by the Parish Council of Holy Names Church. The project restored many of the old Victorian homes up in old Pinch, the neighborhood near where Mama was raised. Our sister-in-law Vernua had been president of the board of directors.

I find it nearly impossible even now to read about the Viet Nam war. But for years I have stood with the Veterans for Peace in public vigils, feeling the spirit of my war-wounded brothers on either side of me as I go into battle as a warrior for peace.

As the American war on Viet Nam continued, many young Memphis men were among the wounded and dead, too many for anyone to keep up with. And too many more whose deaths came later, as our brothers' did, from the Agent Orange poison that lingered and later killed them. These names were not etched on the Viet Nam War memorial wall in Washington, DC, nor on the memorial wall later erected in Overton Park in Memphis near the World War I Doughboy statue.

Next Stop is Viet Nam

On my last Memphis visit I wrote my brothers' names on slips of paper and pasted them on the memorial wall in Overton Park. Still, I couldn't release the full force of the rage and grief held in my own body. A gust of wind blew the paper away.

"All we are is dust in the wind," my daughter's graduation song expressed the sentiment of the day. "Dust in the wind."

Rogue Romance

Tommy's Marine friends spent a lot of time visiting our home, and often stayed overnight when they had no other place to go. One was a rather rough-looking twenty year old named Gus who had seen some horrible combat in Viet Nam. He had three Purple Hearts, though none of his injuries were visible to me.

He flirted with both Eileen and I, then he asked me on a date. We were soon engaging in passionate kisses in the back hallway or in the back seat at the drive-in movie. But kissing this Marine was not the same as kissing my high-school dates. He was unrelenting in his efforts to seduce me. He even bought me a small diamond ring and we became officially engaged. I was so terribly naïve, even at nineteen, and had no clear sense of myself or my direction in life.

Gus invited me to Washington, D.C. for the annual Marine Corps Ball. I had been to the Nation's Capitol once before, traveling by train for my high-school class trip. This time we would fly into D.C. for the weekend gala. Mama agreed to let me go only if she came along as a chaperon. I think she was well aware of the danger to my virginity. Mama's escort was another of the wounded soldiers who had spent many weekends at our house on leave from the hospital. They paid our way and put us up in a hotel room. The ballroom was elegant. All the Marines wore their dress blues. It was all pageantry and pomp. Mama danced with grace and elegance, floating across the floor. I stumbled about without the slightest idea how to waltz. We had a grand time.

Back in Memphis, Gus borrowed a car and we took a day-long drive into the Arkansas countryside. He drove down a dirt road and parked. We began to make out in the relatively chaste way that was my custom. Gus seemed more insistent than usual. Soon the situation felt out of my control. In the nick of time a farmer drove up beside the car.

The Half Life of a Free Radical

"What's going on here?" he demanded, and sent us away. My Guardian Angel must have been nearby that day. Rape may have seemed inevitable, had the farmer not come, but I was not at all inclined to "lie back and enjoy it!" in the front seat of of a borrowed car in an Arkansas soybean field.

Soon after that event Gus broke off our engagement. I came home one afternoon from secretarial school and found him waiting. Mama was at work and everyone else was out and about somewhere.

"I don't want to get married," he bluntly declared. I was stunned. My heart went cold. Without a word I took the ring off my finger, handed it to him, and then turned and walked out of the house. I walked and walked and walked. I found a corner spot way up under the concrete overpass where construction had begun on the new Interstate 40 that was cutting a swath through our neighborhood. I sat there for hours as the sun set, rocking back and forth as the feeling of abandonment washed over me.

Gus was living at our house then, sharing space in the attic with my brothers. I didn't want to go home and have to face him, but I didn't know where else to go. As night fell, I walked the several miles to my friend Hedy's home. She was Danny's fiancé at the time and was frequently a guest in our home while he was away in Viet Nam. Hedy took me in her car and we drove deep into rural Mississippi. Hedy was far more worldly wise than me and was a great support as I reeled from my first heartbreak. Later that evening she took me home.

"You had me worried sick," Mama said when I walked through the front door. I was still quite distraught and somewhat out of my mind with the hurt. Everything seemed to be happening in a blur.

Once inside, I collapsed on the floor. Daddy carried me into the back bedroom and brought me a cup of hot tea. I heard Mama say, "Hide all the razor blades!" It had never occurred to me to kill myself.

It took many months for me to recover from that emotional blow, especially since it took weeks before Gus moved out of the house. Some nights he would come down from the attic where he stayed with my brothers all dressed up and wearing cologne for a night out.

Finally, to my relief, Mama asked him to leave. It was then that she suggested to Eileen and me that we volunteer at the USO. Mama had been a USO volunteer during World War II and said it would be

Next Stop is Viet Nam

a way for us to help out in a meaningful way, and for me to take my mind off my heartbreak. Eileen and I joined, as did our friend Gladys, whose brothers were in the Navy. We went to the week-end USO dances at the YWCA on Monroe Avenue. Soon we were helping plan many activities at the center. We also volunteered at the VA hospital, this time to grieve the broken bodies and terrible losses suffered by these stunned and discarded men whose idealism was so horribly betrayed.

Murderers & Rapists At Large

The summer of 1969 was my last in Memphis. That was the year serial killer George Howard Putt strangled or stabbed to death five people, including one woman who lived on North Bellevue, just a few blocks from Sacred Heart High and just over one mile from our home.

Everyone was terrified, but there wasn't much we could do except keep a wary eye in our goings and comings and try to make it home before dark. I learned early to hone my senses and trust my instincts when I sensed danger on the streets of Memphis.

Eileen, who was eighteen then, worked at the Girls Club on North 7th Street. She had to walk the nearly two miles home every evening around dusk. She later told me of the dream she had in which she saw the face of the murderer. The next afternoon, the *Memphis Press Scimitar* reported that the killer, still covered in blood from his last assault, was chased through the neighborhood and apprehended. His home had been just two blocks from Eileen's workplace. The newspaper photo of the killer was the very same face she had seen in her dream. George Howard Putt died in a middle Tennessee prison in 2015.

Regina was about fourteen as the turmoil and change swirled about in the neighborhood. By this time, the new residents next door, in what had been the preacher's house, were running what seemed to us like a prostitution ring. Regina remembers that men were coming and going at all hours where the preacher once lived.

"I would hear a knock on our front door and open it to see a stranger standing there. His eyes would get wide with surprise to see a white girl answer," she said. "It happened a lot, especially on weekends. I would just point him to the house next door."

The Half Life of a Free Radical

On the other side, in what had been the Kernodle's home, a group of radical nuns had rented the house. Across the street, in Mrs. Fisk's old house, Michael remembers that the guru Ram Dass lived there for a time in a communal household.

Regina and Robert bore the brunt of the hardships as the neighborhood dynamics deteriorated and family economics worsened in the late 1960's and early 1970's. Regina's teenage years came after our brothers returned from Viet Nam. Their war experiences had made them mean. I wish I could have been there to stand up for her, but I was far away in Maine where I had fled out of that difficult and violent city and into a loveless marriage. Regina married young too, but hers ended with death, not with divorce, as mine would. In the dawning hours of Mother's Day, 1978, Regina's husband Carleton died when his car crashed into a cyclone fence just blocks from their home. My sister was left a widow. She was only twenty four with two very small children, Natasha and Jon.

12

Marching In Memphis

Three hundred years of humiliation, abuse and deprivation cannot be expected to find voice in a whisper.
—Martin Luther King Jr., *Why We Can't Wait*

The dangerous and dirty work of collecting garbage in Memphis was left to "Negro" men. Most were paid less than two dollars an hour. Despite years of local effort to improve conditions and organize workers, the injustice persisted.

It took a horrific accident to catalyze action. Sanitation workers Robert Walker and Echol Cole were "ground up like garbage," on a cold and rainy February 1, 1968.

According to the report in *The Commercial Appeal*, they had been hanging on just inside the back of the orange barrel-like garbage packing truck sheltering from the rain when the cut-off mechanism of the compression unit shorted out. One after the other the men were sucked into the truck and killed.

It wasn't until 2014 that a marker was dedicated in the East Memphis neighborhood at the site of their deaths.[94]

Civil rights organizers and national and international union organizers converged in Memphis. Mayor Henry Loeb was adamant that a strike by city workers was illegal and unacceptable. Even so, the 1,100 sanitation workers voted unanimously to strike.

The Half Life of a Free Radical

During this time I was a secretary at Anderson-Clayton Cotton Company. I often walked along Main Street on my lunch hour where striking workers and their allies paced single file, up and down the sidewalk in front of department stores and other businesses. Their sandwich-board placards read:

"I am a Man," and "Dignity and Decency for our Sanitation Workers."

Back at my desk, I overheard the racial slurs and the angry and fearful words of many of my employers and co-workers who were threatened by the changing times and hardened in their racist attitudes. On my bus rides to and from work, winding through the so-called "colored" neighborhoods, I saw the garbage piled outside houses, dumped in vacant lots or spilled in the middle of the street. The unusually cold winter minimized the stench and reduced the threat of river rats feasting on the refuse, but the strike was taking a toll on the city. Many North Memphis residents expressed solidarity with strikers by keeping their garbage cans off the curb. With a household as large as ours, the steel barrels quickly filled and overflowed in the backyard out by the old fig tree. In the neighborhoods to the east, where most affluent whites had moved, the city provided a limited schedule of curbside pickup. The few operating trucks with strike-breaking laborers were under police escort.

"Some Difficult Days Ahead"

Dr. Martin Luther King, Jr. Was persuaded by others in the Southern Christian Leadership Council to come to Memphis and lead a march in support of the sanitation workers. His was a name I heard in nightly newscasts and read about in our local paper, but I was too preoccupied with my own life to realize the importance of his presence and of the Civil Rights Movement that was re-shaping our city.

On the day of his scheduled arrival, March 22, 1968, a massive storm dropped nearly seventeen inches of snow and shut down the city. The blizzard forced the cancellation of Dr. King's Memphis march. But he came back, arriving late on March 28 to a large crowd assembled in the streets.

Marching in Memphis

As many as 22,000 students from the mostly-black Northside and Hamilton High schools left classes to join the march. Some wore jackets with the Black Power insignia of the Memphis Invaders on the back. They were a wild-card energy impatient with the slow progress of racial justice.

At one of the earlier mass meetings held at Clayborn Temple, reports say that a member of the Memphis Invaders had taken the microphone:

"We gotta do some fighting—not marching! Fighting!"

The group had been organizing in Memphis neighborhoods for at least a year. The speaker was definitely expressing the rising anger and impatience of youth with the "gradual" approach to justice.

The city was tense. I did not witness that march, though I had started to follow more closely the news reports. As the story goes—and there are various versions—police had been escorting the march along Main Street for about six blocks, with marchers walking the agreed-upon eight abreast. Some of the black youth began snaking through the marchers, using sticks to shatter store windows. Police moved in and ordered that marchers walk four abreast, using squad cars to herd the marchers into one lane.

One woman yelled when a police car rolled over her foot. Several young protesters began to rock the escort cars. Riot police began to club and mace marchers. The leaders turned the march around and Dr. King was escorted away. That day, reports show, 62 marchers were injured, 372 arrested. Later that day, a sixteen-year-old suspected looter, Larry Payne, was cornered and shot dead by Patrolman L.D. Jones.

The Governor ordered a 9 p.m. curfew and sent 3,800 armed Tennessee National Guard troops to Memphis. A judge issued an injunction against another march, but Dr. King would not be deterred. He was determined to lead a nonviolent march in Memphis prior to the scheduled Poor People's March on Washington just weeks away.

Martin Luther King, Jr. was giving voice to the connections between racism, poverty and the militarism so horribly played out in the Viet Nam War.

"The Great Society has been shot down on the battlefields of Viet Nam." he said at his famous Riverside church speech in 1967.

The Half Life of a Free Radical

I was coming to know of more and more young men whose lives were interrupted by the war, as my brothers' had been.

Back on Faxon, Mama and I watched the TV news on March 31, 1968, as President Lyndon B. Johnson announced he would not seek re-election.

> *With America's sons in the fields far away, with America's future under challenge right here at home, with our hopes and the world's hopes for peace in the balance every day, ... I shall not seek, and I will not accept, the nomination of my party for another term as your President.*

We cheered. It was the war in Viet Nam that concerned us most then. We didn't realize how close the violence would come.

Murder at the Lorraine

Michael, who was about sixteen then, remembers the stormy night of April 3, 1968, when Dr. King returned to Memphis. The Mason Temple, a large black congregation headquarters to the Church of God in Christ, was filling with people waiting to hear Dr. King speak, despite storm warnings.

"I met up with my friend Robert," Michael remembers. "He was in my World Geography class at Tech. We walked to the church, but there was standing room only inside. We could hear Dr. King speaking, but barely. It was so cold and wet; I went on home."

Late the next afternoon, Dr. Martin Luther King was murdered as he stood on the balcony of the Lorraine Hotel on Mulberry Street, April 4, 1968.

I arrived home at dusk and heard the news. I may have caught the last available bus from downtown that night. Mama worked on South Main at the Fred P. Gattas store, just blocks from the Lorraine Hotel where the shooter was said to have taken aim. She too would have been making her way home by bus that night, passing the hotel where James Earl Ray had waited, rifle in hand.

The alleged get-away car, a white Mustang, was said to be speeding east on Jackson Avenue, just blocks from our home. Our neighbors, Tommy and Gene Baker, had a short-wave radio. Michael remembers they listened to the police scanners reporting the pursuit of a white Mustang.

Marching in Memphis

Mama got off the bus at Jackson and Decatur that night. She later told Eileen that she had seen a white car with men inside who were acting in a suspicious manner. She reported this to the police, but never heard anything further. Tommy talked about the out-of-town military men he had seen having drinks at a VFW or some such veterans club on Jackson Avenue just days before the assassination.

Dr. King was pronounced dead at St. Joseph's Hospital at 6:01 p.m. The television news played the last few paragraphs of his Memphis speech, delivered the night before at Mason Temple. Over and over we heard his prophetic words:

> *And then I got into Memphis. And some began to say the threats, or talk about the threats that were out. What would happen to me from some of our sick white brothers? Well, I don't know what will happen now. We've got some difficult days ahead. But it really doesn't matter with me now, because I've been to the mountaintop.*
>
> *And I don't mind. Like anybody, I would like to live a long life. Longevity has its place. But I'm not concerned about that now. I just want to do God's will. And He's allowed me to go up to the mountain.*
>
> *And I've looked over. And I've seen the Promised Land. I may not get there with you. But I want you to know tonight, that we, as a people, will get to the Promised Land!* [95]

I listened as never before, riveted by the strength of his voice and the power of his words. National Guard soldiers swarmed the city, troop carriers prowled the neighborhood and huge helicopters hovered, their spotlights sweeping over our North Memphis streets. The smell of smoke was in the air. Sirens screamed through the night, and fires lit up the sky. Eileen remembers sitting at the living room window after the assassination and looking up Breedlove Avenue to see the troop transports passing along Jackson Avenue. Times were tense.

"How Long Will it Take?"

At my workplace at Anderson-Clayton there was tangible alarm as plans were announced for a memorial march. The managers dismissed us early on April 8 with a dire warning:

"Go home and get your guns. The niggers are marching again."

The Half Life of a Free Radical

I was surprised at the level of fear. Most of these executives lived at least ten miles east of downtown, well beyond the inner-city. Memphis Transit bus service was canceled so I walked the few miles home along North Parkway. I told Eileen what I had heard. I was determined to go back downtown and walk in the memorial march. I was glad she was willing to join me.

It was cloudy and cool that afternoon as we walked quickly down North Parkway to downtown. We arrived as the speakers were addressing mourners from the large scaffold platform set up in front of the new city hall at 100 North Main. Eileen and I stood near the back of the crowd. We heard Harry Belafonte introduce Coretta Scott King to the assembly. Many were tearful as Dr. King's widow addressed the mourners.

"How many more must die before we can really have a free and true and peaceful society? How long will it take?" Mrs. King asked.

Among the notable mourners were Senator Ted Kennedy, Dr. Benjamin Spock, and Mrs. Rosa Parks. I would meet Mrs. Parks many years later at a Highlander Center homecoming gathering in New Market, Tennessee. And in January 1987, I would be arrested with the same Dr. Spock and 126 others for crossing over the fence at Cape Canaveral Air Force Base protesting the test launch of the Trident D-2 first-strike nuclear missile. But that day, I was just a nineteen-year-old white girl standing with my sister and witnessing a most profound and sad event in Memphis history. It was a transforming experience.

Soon after the speakers concluded, the assembly linked arms to sing "We Shall Overcome." Then began the silent procession back down Main Street toward Beale, returning to Clayborn Temple.

Eileen and I were swept up in the silent, grieving mass. Eight abreast, arms linked, we walked down Main Street with a measured cadence between gauntlets of National Guard troops, bayonets affixed to rifles, who lined the entire route. Some soldiers perched in the turrets of M-48 tanks.

About the time we reached Main and Gayoso, near the Goldsmith's Department Store, I saw Daddy standing at the curb with Michael and John. He was snapping pictures with his small Kodak Instamatic with its blue cube flash bulbs. I don't think the photos survived over these many years, but the image of that day is burned on my mind. Daddy quickly dispatched a brother to us.

Marching in Memphis

"Daddy says it's okay to march, but meet us at the corner of Main and Beale. We can walk back home together."

Though the memorial march was somber and silent, Daddy was reasonably concerned about the potential for trouble. The earlier march, led by Dr. King and Rev. Jim Lawson, had been joined by scores of angry black youth, many who were said to identify as part of the local Memphis Invaders. They used the sticks from "I Am a Man" placards to break windows all along South Main and Beale Street. Police response with mace and clubs had been brutal.

Twelve days after Dr. King's assassination, and sixty-five days after the Sanitation Workers' Strike began, the city conceded, recognized the union, and granted dues check-off.

The assassination brought even more national attention to Memphis' racist policies. I was compelled to listen even more deeply to the call for racial and economic justice. Dr. King's words about the "triple evils of racism, extreme materialism and militarism," were a felt truth. I was beginning to see the cost of war in my own family. I knew first hand about poverty and its many insidious forms, and I had daily witnessed the entrenched structural racism that infected our city.

As I walked with the striking sanitation workers I experienced soul force played out, as Dr. King said, "on the high plane of dignity and discipline."

13

"For Better or Worse"

But all my ex's live in Texas And that's why I hang my hat in Tennessee.
—American country singer George Strait

As I packed up my few possessions and made ready to leave Faxon Avenue, Mama's warning was clear:
"Be sure you are ready to make it on your own."

It was November, 1968. I had just turned twenty, had a steady income from my secretarial job and was certain I was ready.

Eileen was next in line for the bedroom and I knew it would not be available to me again once I walked out the door. I didn't think I would ever have to come back.

Gladys and I shared a $125 a month, one-bedroom apartment on Jefferson Avenue, across from the new VA hospital where, years later, Daddy would take his last breath. We both worked at the Anderson-Clayton Cotton Company, volunteered at the USO, and had brothers in the military. Gladys, a fiery red-head, was determined and ambitious with a strong sense of her own worth; I was less sure of myself, yearning for adventure, and as my Daddy once told me, I was "much too opinionated."

It was great to have a place of our own, though we created some controversy when we invited a few of our new friends from the USO to swim at the pool. We didn't realize the backlash this would cause with the management, who were not at all happy with our integrated swimming party. The laws had changed but the attitudes of many in

"For Better of Worse"

Memphis had not. I don't remember all the repercussions, but signs were soon up at the pool limiting use to "Residents only."

Gladys and I stayed for the duration of our one-year lease, then we both found our way into marriage, hers an enduring one with our friend Donald, and I? Well, that's another story altogether.

I did end up spending a night or two back on Faxon after all, sharing the bed with Eileen. I had come home seeking a little sympathy after Daddy and I were in an auto accident. He slammed on the brakes to miss hitting another car. Instinctively, he flung his right arm across my chest in an effort to protect me. He was still wearing a cast from a few months earlier after he stepped off the curb and was hit by a mail truck.

I don't think Daddy's car even had seat belts. Despite his efforts to protect me, I lurched forward, smashing the windshield with my head, ripping out a plug of hair, twisting my ankle and tearing at the ligaments in my right leg. I was in a lot of pain.

Those few nights back on Faxon were difficult. Mama meant it when she told me that I had better be ready to make it on my own. She showed little sympathy as I moaned with the pain. Thankfully, in the next day or so, I was able to get some medication and a cast, and soon was back at my apartment, trying again to make it on my own.

"Miss USO"

In the Spring of 1969 I was encouraged by friends to enter the "Miss USO" contest. I wore my high-school prom dress and swept my long hair up into an elegant French knot.

As part of the competition I wrote a two-page essay. It reflected my ignorance of the causes and consequences of the Viet Nam war. I read my patriotic speech with its emphasis on the "responsibility to serve our country" before a large audience at the YWCA. It was my first try at public speaking.

Tommy, Eileen and our friend Catherine were in the audience. Tommy had coached me beforehand on how to pick out a sympathetic face or two in the crowd to lessen my panic.

I won the contest, though in retrospect, the brave woman who used her essay as an opportunity to question the war would have gotten my vote today.[96]

The Half Life of a Free Radical

In my role as "Miss USO" I had to welcome the King and Queen of the Cotton Carnival to the USO. These remnants of the old Plantation South came to show support for the men drafted into the military and awaiting orders to Viet Nam.

I was also sent to New York City to meet with other women working on programs throughout the country offered through the USO. It was an interesting trip and whetted my appetite for more travel. I had arranged with Daddy to meet me in New York after my responsibilities were over so that we could travel together to New Jersey and visit his family. His accident with the mail truck, just days before he was to meet me there, prevented him from making the trip.

I was at the USO on July 20, 1969, watching with a crowd of others as astronauts Neil Armstrong and Buzz Aldrin landed the Lunar Module on the moon. There was so much going on that year—so many huge changes.

I learned a lot about racism at the USO by listening to the black draftees who would recount the indignities and brutalities of the racism they had endured throughout their lifetimes. We met weekly for an interracial discussion group where we shared our points of view with young men who would soon be shipped off to fight, and for too many, to die in Viet Nam. Outside the USO, we continued our conversations about race relations, war, and peace, around the corner at the Bon-Ton Café.

These black soldiers were still unwelcome many places in Memphis. Despite legal restrictions being lifted, racist social conventions persisted. Even some churches turned away uniformed black soldiers from their still-segregated congregations.

Many years later at a gathering in Memphis I had a conversation with a black veteran who had been stationed at Millington in the late 1960's. He told me that just before he was to be shipped out to Viet Nam, he dressed in his Navy uniform and walked to the nearest church for Sunday service. He was turned away at the door. His story was not uncommon.

The black draftees from the northern states carried themselves differently than the southern black men I encountered growing up. Southern blacks had long lived with the perpetual threat of physical harm, even lynching, for showing any familiarity with a white woman. These northern blacks, on the other hand, looked me straight in the

"For Better of Worse"

eye. They were direct in their manner of speech, with none of the deferential attitude I experienced from Southern blacks.

At the USO we all danced together. This intimate social mixing was a new experience for me. The slow dancing I enjoyed with these northern black draftees would never have passed the ruler test used by chaperons at our Memphis Catholic High School dances.

In the South there were swift and brutal reprisals for any hint of sexual interest a black man might show to a white woman. Sometimes rape would be charged even when there was no threat or intent, as in 1951 in Yanceyville, North Carolina, when black tenant farmer Matt Ingrahm was charged with assault and attempted rape based solely on a young white woman's accusation of the farmer's "reckless eyeballing." That kind of virulent, savage racism was never far from the surface.

"It's Not What You Think"

One week past my twenty-first birthday, I took my wedding vows. It was November 22, 1969. I barely knew my husband-to-be. He was one of many new recruits who came to weekend events at the USO.

It was his intelligence that first interested me and I was flattered by the attentions of this smooth-talker. One evening as we walked from the USO to the Bon Ton Café, I was taken aback by one of those intuitive flashes with the ring of certainty. I had a strong feeling that I had met the father of my child.

We had only started to date when he received orders to report for duty at the Brunswick Naval Air Station in Maine. Before he left, he surprised me with a proposal. The promise of travel to a faraway place had more than a little influence on my hasty decision. I gave little thought to who this man was, what his values were, or how compatible we might be. I was ready for adventure and he was the ticket! Besides, I was more than ready to surrender my virginity. In my view then, marriage was the only sanctioned way.

Despite strong objections from Mama, and Daddy's warning, "I don't like his eyes," I stubbornly went forward with my plans, staging a traditional wedding at St. Mary's Catholic Church.

My husband-to-be was not a Catholic and this was yet another mark against him in my parents' view. Mama was convinced that such

The Half Life of a Free Radical

a marriage would endanger my faith. When she learned I had already mailed out engraved invitations to the list of guests supplied by my future mother-in-law, Mama threatened to put a notice in the Dallas paper that "Mr. & Mrs. Daniel G. Hanrahan" most certainly did not approve of this union.

I married anyway in a long, white, second-hand gown that I paid for myself. My friends Catherine and Gladys stood by me as maids of honor. Daddy walked me down the aisle and into the troubled and short-lived marriage of two young, ill-suited people. Danny, using Mama's Kodak Speed Graphic camera, offered to take photos. He developed them in his make-shift darkroom in the kitchen pantry on Faxon. Like his Mama, Danny had a good eye as a photographer.

At the last minute, Mama showed up at the wedding, stern and grim. Daddy had been more conciliatory and helped arrange a reception at the soon-to-close Hotel King Cotton, the same hotel where our family had stayed a decade earlier after the electrical short in the attic fan caught our house on fire. I soon learned the truth in Mama's dire warning:

"If you are marrying for sex, it's not what you think."

It certainly wasn't. Not with this man who seemed quite confused throughout about his sexual preferences. I was too naïve to realize the problem, and had no other sexual experience to compare ours with. I had made a very foolish mistake.

Our first home was a small apartment across from the Bath Iron Works, a large shipbuilding operation in the little town of Bath, Maine. I found work within walking distance in a small office of The Arthritis Foundation. Later I worked in Lewiston, Maine, at Bates Manufacturing Co., where I was eventually fired for agitating for a union. The company had hired an efficiency expert from New York City who lurked around our desks timing every keystroke. I was a highly-skilled typist and diligent, but this overseer annoyed me. His scrutiny made me feel like an automaton, valued only for the speed of production.

Liberated Betrayals

While we lived in Bath and later in Brunswick, Maine, I met weekly with a small circle of women involved in the so-called Women's Liberation Movement. We shared our life stories

"For Better of Worse"

and strategies about how to assert our independence and gain equal treatment at home and in the workplace.

One of the women in the group took an interest in my husband, perhaps realizing before I did that the bond was not strong between us. Soon they began an affair. Another woman called to ask me if she, too, could have sex with my husband. She was gay, she said, but hetero-curious and thought my husband might be the one to help her make up her mind.

It seemed everyone but me was challenging sexual mores. It was a time of deep hurt and confusion, and I felt isolated and alone. I had been raised in the monogamous, till-death-do-you-part value system of the Catholic Church, and could not accept these new ways of living in relationship.

On "Women's Liberation Day" April 17, 1971, I traveled to Boston to march from Copley Square Plaza to the Boston Commons with hundreds of others, demanding equality. I didn't know then that I was two-months pregnant. When this new life first quickened in my womb, I felt a lightness and joy unlike any feeling I had known before.

My husband's military unit had already been transferred for a brief tour of duty in Bermuda, and I had stayed behind, pregnant now and very alone. The early Maine winter brought the deepest snow I had ever experienced, reaching nearly to our second-story apartment windows. There were many long and lonely nights.

In one, I awakened from a night terror convinced that some sinister entity was climbing the stairs to my bedroom. In my fear, my first impulse was to make the Sign of the Cross, as I had so many years before when I feared an apparition of grandpa's ghost. But I steeled myself against invoking the protection of a creed I no longer embraced. I was determined to face down the fear without resorting to such a shield. After a few terrifying moments, the fear washed over me, passed through me, and was gone.

Around that time my school friend Catherine, who had just graduated nursing school in Memphis, came for a visit. This helped to ease my sense of isolation. My wayward husband returned from his deployment just in time for the birth of our daughter, Jessica Colleen, on November 26, 1971. She was the first granddaughter in both families.

The Half Life of a Free Radical

I had practiced the breathing techniques of the Lamaze Method, and after my initial panic subsided, childbirth was easy. Jessica was nearly a month premature, and weighed less than six pounds, no doubt due to my stubborn nicotine habit. I welcomed my daughter's arrival with deep joy, despite feeling so alone and unloved in my marriage. I needed to share my joy, so I flew home to Memphis to introduce Jessica to my family. I was breastfeeding then and must have broken a taboo by attempting to feed my infant daughter in the living room on Faxon where other family were gathered.

"You just want to show off your big titties," Danny accused. His hurtful quip sent me into hiding, and made profane what to me was a sacred time. I didn't have a name then for the misogyny of my older brothers that made me cringe inside.

I took another flight to Dallas to introduce Jessica to her father's family. They were gracious and kind, and perhaps a little confused as to why I had come without my husband. I could not share with them the truth of our failing relationship. I couldn't face it myself.

Jessica's father had stayed behind in Maine and during my absence he continued the affair with the woman I thought was a friend. On our return, they did little to hide their liaison. I felt doubly betrayed. Her unsolicited advice to me was especially disconcerting:

"You need to go out and have an affair of your own," she said. "You're practically a virgin." Perhaps she was right, but such a response was out of the question for me, even when I met a kind and interested man in a Yoga class on base. Having an affair was a hurdle I could not leap. I needed to get away, but I didn't have the courage, the resources, or any place to go.

Angelic Intervention

One cold February night in 1972, my Guardian Angel intervened to save Jessica from harm. She was just three-months old. We lived then in Wiscasset, Maine in a small two-story cottage. Outside the trees were laden with ice and the snow of many storms lay deep. I was awakened several times during that night with a nagging sense that I should move Jessica's crib from its place beneath the skylight. Each time, when I dismissed the feeling as needless worry and fell back into sleep, I was awakened again.

"For Better of Worse"

Finally an insistent voice called me out of sleep. I awakened again to find myself floating near the ceiling above Jessica's crib. Then, quite abruptly, I was back in my bed, certain now that the crib must be moved. I rousted my husband from sleep, and with some convincing, he got up to help move the crib. Only then was I able to sleep. At dawn we were both startled awake again, this time by a loud crash. A heavy limb had fallen during a windstorm and broken through the skylight, crashing to the floor where Jessica's crib had been. Shards of glass covered the carpet. The intervention of that unseen guardian had saved her from harm.

Many years later, while living in Limestone, Tennessee, I found time to write about the experience. My account, the first article I published for pay, appeared in *FATE* magazine.[97]

Back in Memphis, times were hard. That summer Mama sent both Michael and Regina, teenagers then, to visit me in Maine. I loved having them nearby. We had a grand time exploring the region from the mountains to the sea. We even climbed to the top of Katahdin, Maine's highest peak.

Regina was a capable and welcome helper with newborn Jessica Colleen at a time when her father was not. Because of financial pressures I had to wean Jessica early and return to work. One day, Regina ran the several blocks to my workplace with Jessica bundled in her arms so that I could offer my breast to quiet her crying. I remember then how much I wanted to stay home with my daughter, and to write about my powerful experience of natural childbirth. But my time at the typewriter was always taken up with the routine tasks of office work. At home I never seemed to find the quiet or the focus to write. My drawer began to fill up with unfinished essays and bits of poetry, buried— as my talents seemed to be— beneath the detritus of my life.

During this time, my husband and many of his friends from the naval base were experimenting with drugs such as LSD and hashish. I witnessed the bad trips of several who had taken LSD while visiting in our home. I did not want to risk a similar fate and decided to limit my drug experiments to the occasional high from cannabis. One time, the pipe that was passed to me had been laced with something far more potent. It felt as if my spirit was spiraling out the top of my head. I was in a hallucinatory haze for the next two days, and somehow muddled my way through work. It scared me. I didn't like feeling out of control, and I lost trust in my husband and his friends.

One bright spot in my time as a Navy wife was a six-month trip to Rota, Spain, where my husband was briefly stationed. Our Jessica was only six-months old, and I still held her close in a Snuggly infant carrier.

While in Europe we were able to visit Mary Alice who then lived near Geneva, Switzerland, where she worked at the United Nations. Also during that time, Catherine's brother Donald, who had been wandering around Europe on his own, found his way to our door and traveled with us to Barcelona and Geneva. It would be the last time I would see Donald alive. He was murdered in Memphis in 1976, not far from his father's store.

In the college town of Brunswick, where the Naval Air Station was located, I encountered many people who were openly challenging the Viet Nam war, particularly after the National Guard shot and killed four students at Kent State University. With others, my husband and I began producing a small monthly tabloid critical of the war. We distributed it on base for several months until a Naval officer warned my husband:

"You need to control your wife."

Control was not something I took to very well, but military orders were not to be lightly ignored by enlisted men. We ceased publication.

I encountered a similar prohibition of political speech on a military base decades later, in Fort Benning, Georgia, in the demonstrations against the U.S. Army School of Americas, more truthfully called the "School of Assassins." My peaceful protests there, in the company of tens of thousands of others, eventually led to my six-month incarceration in Alderson Federal Prison for "interfering with the mission of the base," a misdemeanor conviction punished to the full extent of the law.

All My Ex's Live in Texas

Throughout my marriage I longed to return to college. I found my opportunity at El Centro Junior College in Dallas. I earned tuition working part-time in the Social Services Department at the downtown Dallas campus.

"For Better of Worse"

I enrolled Jessica in day care near our apartment, transporting her there in a child seat mounted on the back of my bicycle. Then I caught a bus to school. Back in college I met many people who affirmed me in ways I had not before experienced, and my self-esteem and courage grew. I graduated with a 4.0 average and an Associate degree in Arts and Sciences on May 20, 1975.

My relationship was in steady decline. Jessica's father offered little support of my efforts to finish my education, and I carried most of the burden of after-hours childcare and housework. My consciousness had been raised by the Women's Movement, but putting women's liberation principles into practice with an uncooperative and unfaithful husband was quite another story.

I missed many school days staying home to care for Jessica when she was sick, and many nights of sleep sitting up with her, as mothers do. During one exam period, I asked her father if he would stay home one day and care for our daughter while I took my final exams. His refusal, after all the years of betrayal, was the proverbial last straw. His words went something like:

"My work will always take priority." He had finally articulated the inherent inequality of the relationship, and I had finally found the strength to act in my own best interest. The marriage was over.

During those difficult weeks following my decision to leave I had a dream of a red-brick, two-story apartment complex enclosing a wide expanse of lawn with large shade trees. I knew this was to be our new home. Several days later, on a drive with a friend, I happened to pass those very apartments on Northwest Highway. Sure enough, there was a "For Rent" sign on the lawn. Within a week Jessica and I had moved. I furnished the one-bedroom, second-floor apartment with a sofa bed I bought with my first credit card (and I had to fight to get it in my name), a small table and chairs, Jessica's bed, a few towels and sheets, a pot and pan and personal items for each of us. I was relieved beyond measure to be on my own.

Four months after the Decree of Divorce, granted on March 16, 1976, I petitioned the court for a change of name. Then came the difficult work of finishing college, supporting Jessica and myself, and finding my way in Dallas as a single mother. I paid off the joint debts from the marriage, though most of it had been incurred by my ex-husband, whose idea of necessity was quite different than mine. I wanted to be free and clear.

The Half Life of a Free Radical

Divorce was an ugly word and the reality even more so. I had no preparation for this change in status. Despite all my efforts to "save the marriage" I knew I would find no solace or support from the Catholic Church and little sympathy from my "you make your bed, you lie in it," family, whose warnings I had ignored. It was many months before I even called Memphis to tell anyone of my changed status. I was a divorcee, and if I were to die then, in the custom of the day, that would be the first descriptor after my name in any obituary. I felt cast adrift in the patriarchal system, and doubly oppressed by poverty and gender. Where was the Women's Liberation Movement now?

As my loneliness deepened, the moral proscriptions against extra-marital sex that guided my behavior before marriage seemed no longer relevant or realistic. I cast them aside, attempting to find my own way and to develop my own moral compass.

14

Magna Cum Laude

I only want to write. And there's no college for that except life.
— Dodie Smith, *I Capture the Castle*

Poverty was a familiar but unwelcome companion. We lived ever on the edge, young Jessica and I, singing our way through the disappointments and the challenges as we faced into the next moment. I was too busy with the demands at hand to worry far into the future. Jessica's father seldom paid the agreed-upon child support, and the court system, already backed up with un-enforced orders, was unresponsive.

I chose not to apply for food stamps or other welfare benefits that might have been available to me then. To do so would require that I sign a document empowering the state to use whatever means necessary to enforce child support. I really didn't think it through. I toughed it out rather than unleash the full force of the state on my ex-husband, and subject myself to what I perceived as a denigrating state welfare system offering scant help at a high cost to personal dignity.

We Ain' t Got a Barrel of Money

With a stubborn pride I turned my back on the state, as I had the church. I didn't feel that either respected my value as an individual, nor the worth of my own truth. I would go it alone using whatever child support came to pay for the day-care costs while I worked to meet all other expenses. This obdurate pride kept me from seeking the help that might have made those years less difficult. It was a trait Mama had. She was ever on the side of helping others, and never sought public assistance, even in our most dire circumstances.

"God provides," was her mantra, and truth be told, somehow the universe and its mysterious benevolence seemed always to come through, though more often than not at the last possible moment. I learned to trust the unfolding and deny anxiety the upper hand. Each day brought its blessings and its challenges.

Single mothers were particularly vulnerable in the 1970's, with few social supports. After my divorce, I had already felt the shift in attitude when I revealed to people that I no longer had a husband. Men would approach me with an assumption that I was fair game for easy sex. Sometimes I was.

During those busy years I met many women in similar circumstance— struggling for basic economic survival, alienated from the institutional church and caught up in a time of changing sexual mores. I needed the intimacy and warmth of relationship but I was too emotionally wounded to consider another marriage. In fact, if anyone I was dating began to get too close emotionally, I would quickly move on, guarding my heart from the possibility of pain.

My B. S. Degree

I found part-time work in the law office of a Southern Methodist University (SMU) professor. We shared the suite in the Hartford Building with an insurance company, and I shared the job with a much older woman nearing retirement.

It was commonplace for the male agents to make sexually-suggestive comments to me and other women in the office We were particularly vulnerable in the elevator or when they passed by behind us at our desks. I tried to ignore them. I didn't feel empowered to complain or strong enough to confront them. I needed my job. All the women tried to laugh off the harassment, but it wasn't funny.

One afternoon I arrived at my desk to find a poster of a bikini-clad woman in a suggestive pose hanging on the wall directly in my line of sight. A wave of dark disappointment washed over me at the thought that this might be the kind of place I would have to spend my working life.

Magna Cum Laude

But help came, a reprieve. The same El Centro instructor who had steered me to this job, suggested I apply for a scholarship at SMU. I took the bus to the admissions office with the transcript of my perfect grades from El Centro in hand. Before the meeting was over I had a full scholarship to complete my college degree.

The campus was conveniently located just across the street from the day-care center where Jessica was enrolled, and on a bus-line to our apartment. Now it was my turn to sing, *Zip a dee doo dah, zip a dee ay, My oh my, what a wonderful day!*

Life as a single mother and an older returning student among the sons and daughters of Dallas' wealthy families had its own challenges. But I persisted.

During my last year at SMU I was feeling acutely the stress of my circumstances. I was having a hard time balancing my need to study for final exams with the responsibilities I had to Jessica and my workplace. I asked her father for help and he declined, as did his parents, who seemed to be walking a careful middle ground, attempting to stay out of our conflict.

I called Memphis and talked to Mama. I had not been home in quite some time and was unaware of the deteriorating circumstances there. Daddy and Tommy were both living at home, deep in their alcoholism, while Mama worked to keep the bills paid. With a long bus ride to her clerical job in East Memphis, she left early in the morning and didn't return until well after dark. I was desperate for help. I simply had to have time to study if I were to graduate.

"Send her on," Mama said. So I put my sweet daughter on a plane for Memphis for a two-week visit and hunkered down with my books.

With Mama at work, Jessica was home much of the time in the care of Daddy and Tommy, and probably somewhat fending for herself. Sometimes she rode the bus with Daddy to his office downtown. My high school friend Gladys, who also worked downtown, called to tell me she had seen Jessica with my father at the restaurant where they sometimes had lunch. Apparently she was dressed like a ragamuffin. Daddy's eyesight was failing, and in his later years he had taken on a bit of the Mr. Bojangles look, disheveled in his old suits with the cigar burns on the lapels, and holding on to his last threads of dignity as the alcoholism took its toll.

With my final exams behind me, Jessica rejoined me in Dallas. Whatever the circumstances she had weathered in Memphis, I was relieved to see that she seemed to be in her usual cheerful mood, no worse for the wear.

I graduated *magna cum laude* from Southern Methodist University with a Bachelor of Science degree on May 22, 1977.

Mama and Daddy made the trip from Memphis to celebrate my graduation and stayed a few days on the pull-out couch in our small inner-city apartment. Johnny came from Austin where he was studying film making and videography.

As my name was called to the stage to accept my diploma, Jessica, a precocious five year old then, walked right up behind me, shaking hands with the professors as I had done, to the delight of all. It was another happy day. I hardly looked back.

In fact, the next time I saw Southern Methodist University was to join in the protest at the opening of the George W. Bush Library in 2013. My friend Kit who graduated from El Centro and SMU the year after I did, joined me in Dallas as we projected "Arrest Bush" in studio lights on the blank side of a downtown Dallas business while all the living former presidents gathered on campus to honor the man who had lied this nation into yet another bloody war.

Down, Down in Memphis Town

The advantages that my college degree promised did not materialize. I really had no idea how to market my B. S. degree. I had turned down my employer's suggestion that I apply to SMU Law School and was in dire need of a full-time job. I was weary. Weary. Weary.

Jessica's father had quickly remarried and was living in a fine new home with his second wife and her young daughter. Jessica's half-brother was born soon after. With her father busy with a new family, his visits with Jessica became less frequent. My stress trying to find full-time work increased.

In a sudden decision, as has been my style, I called up Michael for a rescue. He came with his truck and moved Jessica and me and our few possessions from Dallas back to Memphis. It was a harrowing journey at high speeds down back roads as Jessica and I followed in our Toyota Corolla, my on-credit graduation present to myself.

Michael, a good humored brother most of the time, has always been willing to help. He worked as a carpenter and general contractor,

Magna Cum Laude

with much flexibility in how his day unfolded. I didn't yet know how to go about being self-employed, but I was attracted to the freedom such a lifestyle could offer.

Jessica and I stayed with Michael in his mid-town home until I found employment. I enrolled Jessica in a so-called Magnet School, considered one of the better choices in the public system. Michael provided a comfortable interim place to live, but his cupboards were always bare. He ate most of his meals at nearby restaurants, a luxury we could not afford. I had no income and my meager savings were going to pay the monthly note on the car. To keep afloat, I even sold the little bit of silver plate I had received as a wedding present. I had my degree now, and I was determined not to be a secretary, though it seemed those skills were the ones on my resume that most interested potential employers.

Tommy was a social worker then and suggested I apply for food stamps. I went into the office and waited what seemed like hours before I was called for an interview. I felt the scrutiny and judgment of the intake worker as I approached the desk. She looked me over, up and down, in a well-practiced assessment. I felt ashamed. That, mixed with my pride, resulted in my walking out before completing the process. Mama was a great help during those months of unemployment. Jessica and I shared meals with her on Faxon Avenue most evenings, and she paid the first month of daycare costs when I finally found work.

I eventually found a well-paying position as a psychiatric social worker in a day program called Lowenstein House, located in a Victorian house on Adams Street with the same name. The mission of the non-profit was to assist persons recently released from mental hospitals to reintegrate into the community through supported work opportunities. With a blend of my clerical skills and psychology degree, I took the position of Clerical Unit Leader. I had responsibility for as many as forty adults with varied psychiatric diagnoses. I trained them in different skills, including bulk-mail preparations and operating simple office machines.

The work was stressful and demanding and a full immersion into the world of the mentally ill. Many lived in the mid-town area in crowded and dirty boarding homes, some suffered the ill-effects of the psychiatric medications dispensed through the Community Mental Health Centers. They taught me much as they shared about

The Half Life of a Free Radical

their lives and struggles. Sometimes I could identify more with program participants than the professionals who were paid to assist them.

Still, I found it difficult to make ends meet and felt I was running in place, tired all of the time, and without a network of supportive friends. Many of our meals were from fast-food restaurants picked up on the way home.

We found an apartment in mid-town and tried to settle in. Mama worked long hours too, and offered what help she could. I just did not trust my father or brothers with Jessica's care when they were entertaining their dark and deadly companion, alcohol. My sisters, by then, were married and living away from Memphis.

"Is this it?" I asked myself. On my deepest levels I was not willing to settle for what I had, though I had no clarity yet about what I wanted. I was having trouble sleeping nights; plagued with intrusive thoughts about the workplace and the difficult personalities I dealt with there. My case load was overwhelming. I was headed for a nervous breakdown. Besides, the woman who was directing the program, a brash New York City transplant, was dating my brothers, Danny, Tommy and Michael, in turn. I felt my own privacy compromised.

A Great American Smoke-Out

On my thirtieth birthday, in another impulsive decision, I quit smoking. Cold turkey. I realized that I could not attempt to teach others to take hold of their lives and accept responsibility for their health until I was willing to do the same. Giving up nicotine was my first step.

I began by holding a clear mental image of myself as a non-smoker. This daily affirmation helped to quell the nearly-incessant cravings of those first several weeks, but it did little to relieve the physical discomforts. All the stress that I seemed to hold in check with the nicotine came to a head.

One day on my late lunch break, as I drove to Jessica's school to pick her up and transfer her to after-school care, I broke down and began to cry. I cried and cried and cried. I could not stop.

I made it back to my apartment and called my sister-in-law Vernua.

Magna Cum Laude

"Please, come get Jessica, I can't stop crying," I pleaded. And Vernua came, taking care of Jessica at a moment's notice for the several days until I could find my way back to emotional balance. I took a leave of absence from work, pulled my blinds, and slept, and slept, and slept.

When I returned to work after two weeks, the atmosphere was dramatically different. The women and men I had worked with as clients in the day program seemed wary, as did my co-workers. I felt as if I had fallen from grace. I knew I could not continue as I had been. I gave a month's notice, trained my replacement, and left. I had little to no savings, monthly car payments, a six-year-old child and no child support forthcoming from her dead-beat Dad.

"What's a Mother to do?"

"When In Doubt, Love"

I was in the midst of my own crisis when Daddy went into the VA hospital for cancer surgery.

After being overwhelmed by stress and quitting my job, I had sold everything that couldn't fit in the back of my Toyota Corolla and made ready to hit the road. I wanted to link up with my college friend, Kit. She was headed to Key West.

Daddy wasn't one to frequent doctors, and his health had been in slow decline for years. He suffered with cirrhosis and colon cancer. He returned from the hospital thin as a rail and very weak. During one visit, I walked into the living room on Faxon to find Daddy asleep in a chair, looking very nearly dead. Mama must have noticed the horrified look on my face as I gasped at the sight.

"When in doubt, love." she said.

There was no doubt that I loved my Daddy, even though he wasn't there for me in ways I wanted, or needed. It was terribly painful to see him in such a state. When Daddy heard I was going to Florida, he asked if he could come with me so he could visit his sister, Regina, in St. Petersburg. Aunt Regina was much younger than Daddy, and they had seen little of one another in the past thirty years. I wish now that I had said yes. Instead, I listened to Mama's dire prediction:

"If you let him go with you, he might die in the back seat."

He well could have. I left Memphis without him and never saw my Daddy alive again.

The Half Life of a Free Radical

Jessica and I hit the road. I was in flight again. We stayed for a time with Eileen and Eddie in Limestone, Tennessee, in the small farmhouse they rented close to a rural highway and across from a cow pasture. They had two children then, Alice and Joshua, and lived a quiet life compared to the hectic one we had left behind in Memphis.

We rested and relaxed, taking long country walks and eating the wholesome food they shared. Eileen had a large assortment of *Prevention* and *Organic Gardening* magazines. I began to read in earnest, learning about the basics of nutrition. I had been free of cigarettes for nearly six months then and felt my whole life turning around.

Jessica and I headed to Mobile, Alabama, for a visit with her Aunt Pam, husband John and their three children. I was determined that divorce would not sever her from her father's family. Jessica was especially fond of her cousin Johnny, just a year older, and it is good to know that they are still in touch today. Long after that trip, when Jessica was a young mother herself, I had a dream:

> *I am riding down an airport escalator. Jessica is coming toward me, pushing a wheelchair. She had been living away from my home place for many years. As we come closer to one another it becomes clear that it is her infirm father who she pushes in the chair. She is tending to his needs as he has never tended to hers.*
>
> *Anger wells up in me as they approach. I want to tip over the chair, unseating this villain who had abandoned us so long ago. Jessica, sensing my intent, cuts me a look. In her eyes is an appeal for mercy.*

"When in doubt, love."

Mama's words echo now as I look back on that dream, and on my father, and Jessica's father, and on all the disappointments and betrayals that life brings.

"Love in action is a harsh and dreadful thing compared to love in dreams." Fyodor Dostoyevsky wrote in *The Brothers Karamazov*. It was one of the books on our Mama's shelf.

15

Off the Grid

I chose the solitude of the fields; in the trees of the mountains I find society, the clear waters of the brooks are my mirrors, and to the trees and waters I make known my thoughts and charms.
—Miguel de Cervantes Saavedra, Don Quixote

I caught up with Kit in Vero Beach as she was packing all her belongings into a large Cadillac, heading to Key West. I followed in my overloaded Toyota, credit cards in hand. Kit made connections easily. Soon we were house-sitting an old conch-style house, the residence of some of the adventurers involved with the world-renowned treasure hunter Mel Fischer of Treasure Salvors, Inc. They were out diving the Gulf waters searching for the Spanish Galleon, *Nuestra Señora de Atocha*, that sank off the Florida coast in 1622.

To my amazement, many times the divers brought back piles of ancient treasure and gold they had found scattered on the seabed. They gleefully spread it out for all to see on the dining-room table. It would take another decade, and the death of a son, before Mel and the crews of Treasure Salvors discovered the fabled ship.

An Island Paradise

I felt like I had found paradise in Key West. Flowers seemed to bloom on every tree, their sweetness scenting the air. Walking around the island, sipping cocktails in the bars, listening to

The Half Life of a Free Radical

the live music, sitting under huge porch fans in old wooden rockers on sultry summer afternoons, watching as artists set up easels to capture the scene. It was a heady time. It seemed that everyone we met in Key West had escaped the traps of conventional livelihood and mundane obligations and were at a turning point in their lives.

My women's liberation group back in Maine would have applauded the "anything goes" atmosphere. The sexual revolution of the 1960's was still being played out in late 1970's Key West. But, all told, it was really too much for me.

As my cash savings depleted, I began to feel quite vulnerable. When I found myself about to charge the next week's groceries, I knew it was time for a change. On impulse, or intuition, I offered my resume at *The Key West Citizen*. The island newspaper was within walking distance of where we stayed. I was surprised at how casual the process was. I was hired to typeset news stories and lay out want ads. I had always wanted to be around writers and reporters. Now here I was, on a tropical island living out a dream.

One sunset, at Key West's Mallory Square, I met Paul. He was playing the flute within a small circle of drummers and other musicians. I was enchanted. In typical devil-may-care fashion I accepted his invitation to paddle out to his small sailboat anchored off shore. He said he needed to re-set the anchor. I ended up staying until dawn, getting back to shore barely in time for work at the newspaper. I spent the next day nodding out on the job. But I was head over heels and open to whatever unfolded with this adventuresome spirit.

Paul was a most unusual and resourceful person. Though he told me he had a disability from his time in the military, I had seen too much during my employment as a psychiatric social worker to give much credence to psychiatric labels. I judged Paul based on his day-to-day interactions with me, not by any diagnosis he had been given in the military.

He said he had been discharged from the Army after serving a difficult tour of duty in some secret underground compound called NORAD Mountain. There he had been subjected to strip searches each workday before he entered the installation. After his strenuous objection to the daily indignity, he said, he was committed to a mental hospital, restrained with high doses of medication, and then

Off the Grid

discharged with a psychiatric disability. He received a small monthly check as recompense.

His story played on my sympathies and heightened my disdain for the coercive ways of the military. Many years later, when I was imprisoned for peaceful protest, I also had to endure the indignity of invasive strip searches, almost every time I received a prison visitor. It was never easy.[98]

As we settled into the life of the island that summer, Jessica especially enjoyed cruises on the glass-bottomed boat. We took long walks brightened with mimosa, frangipani, bougainvillea, and other tropical blossoms. The stress that had almost overwhelmed me in Memphis fell away with each passing day.

One evening, while the jasmine blossoms scented the evening breeze and moonlight danced on the Gulf waters, Paul asked:

"How would you like to sail around the world?"

The derring-do of my childhood days still with me, without hesitation I replied, "Sure. When do we go?"

Before I could give much more thought to such an impetuous, fool-hardy adventure, Hurricane Frederick intervened. There was a mass exodus from the region, larger than any other evacuation in the past. Paul postponed his plans, sold his boat, and joined Jessica and me as we packed up my Toyota and headed back to Tennessee. We had seen an ad in *The Mother Earth News* for cheap Tennessee farm land, and we were off to try our hand as homesteaders.

Clinch Mountain Tipi

It was a bleak December day in 1979 when we first arrived in Hawkins County, Tennessee. The contour of the land, with its steep and rocky hills, deep ravines, and secluded hollows was visible through the barren trees. Roadside sumac bushes still held their scarlet clusters. Weathered wooden farm houses covered in tangled vines stood alongside abandoned country grocery stores with rusted signs for R.C. Cola and Wonder Bread.

Parcels of land in Lee valley sold for as little as $200 per acre. This chance at country living felt wholesome and right. Jessica was seven, and a rural home place would give her the freedom to roam safely out-of-doors. We bought six acres in a quiet hollow facing the sloping backyard of the previous owner, Barney Gloomer. Most of

The Half Life of a Free Radical

the land was steep hillside, richly forested with shagbark hickory, tulip poplar, locust, oak, sassafras, and many other trees whose names and qualities we would later come to know.

We found rent-free space in a small cabin that had been used for years as a storage shed. As the warmth from our make-shift wood stove chased out the cold, the cabin seemed to come alive. Insects and rodents, birds and bees, snakes and bats began to stir about. We were the intruders and did not have the heart to chase out our wild cabin mates. We kept a wary eye at night for crawling, creeping things as we looked for another place to spend the winter.

With the deep snow squeaking beneath our boots, the freezing air in our nostrils and a sharp wind biting at our cheeks, we moved again. The road was impassable by car so we pulled our possessions the few miles over the snow on Jessica's red sled. Paul rigged a makeshift tump line and I braced the thick strap across my forehead and carried the lighter loads in the sling of rope at the small of my back.

We sang as we walked, making up songs as we went. Jessica's clear and lovely voice carried through the winter air as the snow glistened and the icy creek flowed with a soothing mantra.

Rumor had it the cabin would flood each Spring "about the time Emily's cabbage was big enough for makin' krout." The ankle-high watermarks on the interior walls were proof enough. As the snows melted the creek began to rise, as promised. But it was a dry, dry spring and summer in Lee Valley and the feared flood never came to inundate our home.

Paul was inventive and resourceful and I trusted him to find a way to solve most any problem we encountered, and there were plenty in our day-to-day efforts at living lightly on the Earth. I had few skills for country life and was eager to learn.

While we waited for warm weather, and for the mail-order delivery of our twenty-two foot, Plains-Indian type tipi, we culled poles from a stand of tall pines in need of thinning and prepared a home site on our land.

In the waning days of winter we kept a fire blazing in an open pit as we worked, fueled by the dry locust trees that lay dead on the hillside. In the fullness of spring we moved on to our land. The tipi provided ample room for the three of us and our few possessions.

Off the Grid

Jessica attended the old Clinch School, built long before by local families and just up the road. Sometimes she came home with stories about the soap operas her teacher watched during class time. The lives of many of the people in the valley were themselves the stuff of a soap opera, ours included, as we had become quite a curiosity since our arrival.

On the week-ends we walked the back roads to see who lived where among the hidden hollows. One dirt road close to the base of Clinch Mountain led to an old cabin as rustic as any I had seen, with only three rooms and a small back porch. Little of the modern world had reached Nealie and her brother Ralph who lived there. Their front yard was fenced with what once had been a neat white picket and carpeted with clover. The front door was open to the summer breeze.

Nealie stepped out on the porch to greet us. She was the picture of an Appalachian mountain woman, nearing seventy and dressed in colorful layers, her several skirts and blouses covered by a large apron. Her skin was weathered and rough, like her sturdy shoes. Her eyes were clear and her direct gaze lit up with a ready laugh.

Every time we visited Nealie offered shortbread cookies. She rolled the dough out on the large expanse of a rough wooden-plank table, and baked them in a wood-fired oven that always had a kettle of tea water simmering on top. Her brother Ralph spent his days at the local store where other long-time residents gathered. He played guitar and sang old mountain songs. Nealie told us tales of her childhood in the valley, pausing to spit tobacco juice into the small coal fireplace as she reminisced. Our neighbors were wise and rich in the ways we were only beginning to understand, and Jessica and I never tired of our visits.

One sunny day a lone black man, strong and proud, walked down the path leading into our meadow. With a feedbag slung over his shoulder, he ambled our way whistling to announce his presence. We walked out to say hello, delighted to have a visitor.

Will had lived in the valley most all his life, he said, and now stayed just down the road in a long-neglected house "the white folk" used to own. As we talked Will pulled some strips of paw paw bark out of his sack and showed us how to weave a seat on a discarded wooden chair we had retrieved from the roadside. Before long, he invited us to his home to meet his wife.

The Half Life of a Free Radical

"She's a white woman," he said, "and some folks around here don't take too well to our living together."

When we visited their home, Paul and Will would sit for hours playing checkers and talking about how it used to be in the valley. Jessica and I would wander the fields with his wife picking catnip and horehound for tea. Both remembered when there used to be wheat and corn and other food crops grown all over the place and mills to take the grain for grinding. Now the fields were thick with the one cash crop: 'bacco.

About a mile down the main road Jeannie lived with her five children. We would see them out in the tobacco fields walking the rows and picking off the lovely yellow blossoms. Jeannie was a large woman who moved slowly at the task. One afternoon, the story goes, she just straightened up and fell down backwards in the field. Her children helped her to the car.

"She's just 'bacco sick," they figured. But it was a heart attack that took Jeannie. Too much bending and stooping in the hot sun, too much white bread and too much work. Jeannie's husband sobered up long enough to feel the shock of her passing. He set up folding chairs borrowed from the church on their sloping wooden front porch and the neighbors came by to sit and remember Jeannie. The children were back in the fields in a few days finishing the work that had finished their mother.

Paul soon made connections with the local church-going community. They loved him for his friendly charm and helpful attitude. One Sunday afternoon he came back to the house with a sad story. He had engaged in conversation in the class about the existence of hell and who was destined to go there. When he shared his opinion that non-church-going folks, such as I, might not necessarily burn in hell, he had crossed the theological line. He had to go. They could not fit him in with their beliefs, no matter how much they liked him.

On Easter Sunday Paul brought home a large and docile mule he had traded for with one of the neighbors. Jessica and I named her Lilly. Lilly was supposed to help plow the field for our garden, but she was stubborn and not at all interested in following orders from Paul, no matter how many "gee" "haw" commands he gave. We resorted to hand tools to turn the soil and plant our crops. We traded the mule for two Nubian goats and a family of ducks that fed happily on the iridescent Japanese beetles that swarmed over our okra crop.

At harvest time I was delighted with the smell of the damp earth and the heft of the shovel full of fat potatoes, my first such crop.

The work evoked ancient memory. One night as I fell into exhausted sleep after a day of harvesting, I had a strong dream:

> *I am sheltering inside a sod-roofed, thick-walled dwelling, huddled close with others around a peat fire. It is dark and musty inside and I am hungry, very hungry.*

It was just a glimpse from the past. I was overcome with a deep, pervasive sadness that lingered long after I awakened.

Puget Sound Awakenings

Paul's creative approach to life on the economic edge was one of his greatest gifts. He found joy in life at its most simple and taught us valuable skills of self-reliance and new ways of perceiving our frugal circumstances. My hunger for adventure was well satisfied in his company. But Paul missed the water and the sailing life.

As the cold weather approached, we began talking of another life. Paul had friends in Washington State and they invited us to come.

"If you think it is beautiful here," he told me, "Wait until I show you a place with snow-capped mountains and ancient forests that reach down to meet the sea."

In the early fall of 1980 we packed up our worldly goods again, including the tipi poles that were the bones of our mountain home. Resembling a scene out of *The Grapes of Wrath*, we set out on the road in a merry mood headed to Puget Sound.

I traded my car for a pick-up truck to carry our possessions. Along the way we stopped in Memphis and stayed with Tommy on Overton Park Avenue. His vacant second-floor apartment provided a comfortable way-station.

Back on Faxon Robert and Vernua and their children, Katrina and James, had moved in with Mama. I brought them a bushel of freshly-dug potatoes, proud of my first harvest. Mama was in her early sixties and on the waiting list then for an apartment at St. Peter

The Half Life of a Free Radical

Manor. She had quite a garden in the back yard, where in earlier days we had built forts, dug tunnels, and played hide-and-go-seek, softball, and chase. She grew lovely roses of many varieties, much like those in her Grandmother Amanda's garden, and lots of vegetables and herbs in the rich soil from her long-ago worm ranch.

I can't remember now how long that Memphis visit was, but I was glad to move on, my daughter in tow. In retrospect I cringe at the cavalier way I embraced such a nomadic lifestyle, and how little consideration I gave to the impact such instability might have on Jessica, however resilient she seemed. I was convinced that an experiential education was far better for her than being confined in a school building day in and day out.

Before too long we were on the road to Port Townsend, Washington, with a detour to explore the Grand Canyon. In Port Townsend, Paul soon found a derelict Catamaran in need of repairs and purchased it for $7,000, using the pick-up truck as a down payment.

We set up our tipi in the boat yard. Paul began work on the 42-foot plywood vessel that would become our floating home. I turned to the tasks of clearing a garden from the brambles that surrounded our tipi. We cooked outside using heavy iron pots nestled on a ring of large rocks that enclosed the fire. I set about identifying and learning about wild edibles and medicinal herbs in this new and diverse bio region. Jessica usually joined me on the foraging explorations.

The madrona trees with their smooth, reddish bark and shiny leaves were a lovely contrast to the deep green of the majestic firs and cedar trees that towered above the salal and fern and the rambling vines of blackberry. Alongside familiar yellow daffodil and deep purple hyacinth were the bright pink of salmon berry and bear currant.

I felt deep gratitude to be able to walk freely in these rich woodlands. I was at home with the Earth there and tender and protective of the fragile life that emerged.

By midsummer, our boat was sea worthy. We called her Freight Train, an apt name given her size and girth. We spent nearly a year sailing the inland waterways from anchorage to anchorage, home

Off the Grid

schooling Jessica and picking up work here and there, as we enjoyed the companionship of other cruising families.

Withdrawing Consent

During these years, I was always putting pen to paper or clacking away at my old manual typewriter set up in a cubby in the starboard hull. It was my own "Little Room" for writing, like Mama's back on Faxon.

The idyllic beauty of our new home place was shattered by the constant intrusion of the military. Nuclear submarines prowled on maneuver. Massive aircraft carriers with helicopters buzzing about them anchored next to whole islands given over to storage of weapons. Wild deer grazed grassy earthen bunkers where the weapons were buried, enclosed with miles and miles of chain-link fence. Overhead the thundering drone of troop helicopters violated the peace of the deep forest.

In ways I had never before had to consider, I felt the pain of the Earth and the dread of its destruction. The threat of a nuclear disaster was no longer just an abstract concept. In Puget Sound, I felt visceral fear and a rising grief for the planet. The dread I experienced went much deeper than concern for my own personal survival, or even that of my immediate family. It seemed to extend to the very core of my being. I recoiled in horror at the real danger these weapons posed to all life. I knew that I could not remain silent.

During one afternoon sail along Hood Canal we passed by a naval base on the opposite shore, a home port for the Trident Nuclear Submarine. It was ironic that as we passed, I had the Seattle newspaper in hand telling of the recent witness of Archbishop Raymond Hunthausen, who called that very base the "Auschwitz of Puget Sound." This Bishop had decided to withhold part of his income tax as a means of protest. I was deeply impressed by this courageous act.

On September 28, 1981, I wrote to Henry M. Jackson, the Senator from Washington State, declaring my intent to withdraw my taxes that supported the weapons. I have the faded carbon copy of my hand-written testimony in my files. It read, in part:

The Half Life of a Free Radical

> *I cannot, in conscience, deny my complicity with the evils of nuclear escalation if another penny of my money goes toward weapons of war, in whatever form they take. As I will not compromise my sense of right action, I have decided to stop payment of federal taxes. In order to effect this I have chosen to forgo the salaries, the lifestyle and the concomitant taxes for which my education and training have equipped me.*
>
> *The greatest freedom of any individual is the right to say No. I must call on this freedom now for it has become a responsibility.*

The Ground Zero peace community in Paulsboro, Washington, was not far from our anchorage near Port Townsend. Though I never visited there, I learned about their witness at the local Quaker bookstore. There were many books and magazines available on loan that spoke to my deep concerns, first awakened in my Memphis childhood and deepened when I walked arm-in-arm with Memphis sanitation workers in Dr. King's Memorial march.

Reading Mohandas Gandhi's *My Experiments With Truth*, and the Christian anarchism of Leo Tolstoy in *The Kingdom of God is Within*, found even more resonance when I read the life of Dorothy Day. Her autobiography, *The Long Loneliness* and other writings affirmed feelings that had been rising in me for some time.

Winds of Change

One afternoon we were caught in a fierce storm in the Straits of Jaun de Fuca on a passage from the San Juan Islands back to Port Townsend. Jessica was down below reading. I was topsides, trying to hold the boat on course while Paul went forward to put the storm jib in place. He all but disappeared into the swirling clouds of spray, while I was swept from side to side, barely able to hold on to the helm. I experienced a moment of sheer panic.

What if Paul were to be swept overboard? The boat was far too large for me to handle alone. Thankfully he returned from the bow and was able to steer our craft to safety in a nearby cove. It was a close call. I would not risk another storm on such a vessel. So we agreed to sell the boat and find another, more suitable craft.

During our time aboard the sail boat, I came to appreciate that change as a way of life can be a most exhilarating and soul inspiring journey. We enjoyed the kinship that we experienced among other sailing families. Like the water itself, we moved from place to place meeting and then passing, then meeting again. We shared in the joys and challenges of life paced to the rhythms of nature.

In the protected waters of Mystery Bay we dropped anchor for the last time as the winter storms were beginning to blow. We shared the sanctuary with Bonaparte Gulls, Grebes and Merganser. We saw Buffle Head, Golden Eye, Scaup, Old Squaw, Surf Scoter and Mallard ducks. Sea Gulls playfully chased Eagles against a backdrop of the long reaches of the Olympic range whose snow-draped majesty was visible on clear days.

Our mornings would begin with the rising sun and the cheerful early calls of our feathered friends. Occasionally we would catch sight of the seals who also made a home in the bay or a Great Blue Heron laboriously taking flight. The many gray and rainy days were relieved by just enough of the clear, bright and glorious ones that lift the spirits.

Around this time, Mary Alice and her husband Neal visited. Jessica and I returned with them to their home in Calgary, crossing through the mountains near Banff in a snow storm. After a good visit, we took a Greyhound for the long journey back to Memphis, my go-to place when my life was in upheaval. Paul joined us later.

Back in Memphis I felt really out of place. I had long been out of touch with my high school friends, was living a marginalized lifestyle, and still poor for reasons I didn't think they would understand. My deep stirrings of conscience that held me to the radical edge were such fragile feelings, cloaked with the familiar shame that is the dull companion of poverty. It weighted me like a sodden woolen overcoat. I never felt safe enough to speak of my own spirituality. It was so far removed from the dogma and rote ritual of the Catholic church.

Mississippi Backwater Shanty

We arrived back in Memphis debt-free but almost penniless. Tommy again offered us shelter until we could get our bearings and find our way.

For a time we engaged in "dumpster diving" from the back of the nearby Easy-Way produce store. We found ample fruit and vegetables, over-ripe and sometimes bruised, discarded each day

The Half Life of a Free Radical

behind the store. I felt that such waste had to be intercepted. We ate well throughout the summer. I also put seeds in a small garden plot in the backyard, but my gardening skills were not well-honed.

I found work in a downtown law office through Manpower, a temporary office service. I claimed "exempt" on my W-2 forms to keep the income tax from being deducted. It was an honest claim as I didn't expect to have to do the work for long. I had neither the patience nor the appetite for confinement in the fluorescent-lit, window-less rooms of the familiar downtown buildings. I had seen another side of life.

Paul was busy looking for alternatives. He found a news announcement of the dismantling of the old Memphis Yacht Club and the sale of the old boat houses there. After some negotiations Paul found a wooden structure for sale for just $150. It was far less than the price of a month's rent in my brother's apartment. We were homeowners of a sort, and we turned our attentions to scrounging for the scrap lumber we needed to make this boat house into our floating home. Jessica was ten, and still caught in my contrary lifestyle.

We called our shanty boat "Impecunious," reflecting the state of our finances, and moved her up harbor with the help of a Yacht Club work boat. We were pushed past Mud Island's new marina, past the barges loading at the Marquette Cement Co., under the new Memphis-Arkansas Bridge and past the old tugs and barges moored by the banks of Mud Island. We extended a line to a boulder on the island side, turning our backs to the multicolored mountain of flattened automobiles awaiting their turn in the monstrous steel-crunching machine on the opposite shore, and made fast our shanty home.

The willow branches moving gracefully in the afternoon breeze provided welcome relief from the desolation of the opposite shore. The scrap-metal machine spewed refuse over the river bank, covering it with the mangled ruins of upholstery foam and vinyl coverings, insulated wiring, broken glass, bits of tire, motor, chrome trim, and carpet. The debris choked all but the most tenacious plant life and spilled into a harbor no longer able to hide its burden of filth.

Our choice to live aboard a shanty boat on the edges of North Memphis was met with much resistance and dire warnings from family and acquaintances about the dangers of the neighborhood: a high crime rate and the likelihood of personal assault. Though we

Off the Grid

did not wish to court danger we were also disinclined to let fear dictate our lifestyle.

And what a life it was! Twenty-four hour sentry lights on the barges moored to the banks competed with the moonlight. Frequent tug and barge traffic at all hours created wakes that rocked our rickety boat house alarmingly and the tug captains' orders delivered over a loud-hailer kept us wakeful well into the night.

With names like *Little Helen* and *Betty Jean, Leta Jane* and *Margaret J*, they pushed tons of steel through the muddy waters moving barges loaded with oils, grain, soybeans, molasses, gravel, concrete and other items.

Besides the constant traffic in mid-harbor there was the clankety-screech, clackety-bang of the car-consuming monster on the opposite shore chewing and spewing cars with a sanity-threatening racket. It wasn't long before we moved.

Catching a favorable wind and using the house as a sail we made our way to the head of the harbor in the shadow of the huge grain elevators at Continental Grain and near the Illinois Central North Yard. We were anchored close to the old American Snuff Company where Grandpa Donnelly had worked for nearly half a century. There, just south of the Levy Road, sheltered beneath an ancient willow, we made our home.

Soaring gulls and diving night-hawks entertained us above and a playful pair of beaver could often be seen swimming and cavorting in the harbor. Occasionally white Egret visited, hitchhiking on north-bound barges.

With only three walls and just six of her forty feet floored, our home was little more than a floating shell. We gleaned lumber from a damaged dock that had broken loose in a storm. This provided much of the flooring material and some necessary flotation to go beneath. We also drew on our early summer gleanings of construction-demolition debris. We had old windows and doors, odd-sized plywood and shelving materials, lumber of various lengths and oak stair steps and railings. All of this we stored temporarily on the flat-surfaced barges half-submerged in the water at shore side.

During the first weeks we labored hard and slept soundly in a dome tent erected on the damaged dock tied beside our shanty. We cooked with a scrap-wood fire in a bucket of sand and hauled drinking water dawn from a spigot at Continental Grain. As veteran campers we were comfortable with the arrangement. We also had a measure of safety with a moat of muddy river water between our home and the city shore.

The sounds of the city were unceasing reminders of our urban environment. Sirens blared through the streets, adding an urgent note to the road noise from autos and gravel-filled dump trucks along the Levy Road. Trucks from all over the Mid-South parked on the edge of 2nd Street waiting turns as load after load of beans, corn, and wheat were sampled, tested and sucked up into the huge storage elevators at Continental Grain.

Helicopters, airplanes, gunshots and rumbling trains whose whistles cut into the early dawn were frequent intrusions. But mixed with these came other sounds: the bark of a fox calling from the sparse island woods, the cry of gulls, hooting owls hidden in the willows, cicada song from the trees that lined the island shore, and the slap of a beaver's tail diving into the turbid water. These were the welcome reminders of the little bit of wild left in the snug back harbor on the edge of Memphis.

Stuck in the Mire

Our sense of security receded with the low water. The brown moat of Mississippi backwaters that had kept us safely afloat and swinging at anchor steadily dropped leaving behind thick, black ooze. Within a few days our shanty home was stuck fast and vulnerable in the mud.

I won't soon forget the astonished look on Vernua's face when she ventured down during the early days of our adventure. Vernua had driven Mama to the river bank to have a look at where and how we were living.

When she hailed me from the shore I struck out across the mud flat. Soon I was calf-deep in the mire, my feet stuck so surely that to move I had to bend over and pull mightily to extract them, one at a time. This maneuver landed me flat on my butt in the none-too-fragrant slime. When I walked up the hill toward the car and my waiting mother I smelled like a bait shop and was caked with mud. Mama wasn't happy.

"This is what you got your college degree for?" she asked. Others spoke of my escapism, my lack of productivity, my copping out. I

Off the Grid

wasn't being a good mother; I wasn't providing a safe and stable environment. There was truth in all of these concerns, but I simply could not return to the prison of conventional work and the complicity with an unjust system that would entail.

Deeper currents were stirring in me and I was compelled to respond. I believed then, as I do now, that in being true to myself and attempting to live with integrity my daughter would learn how to do the same. It seemed the right recipe for an authentic life. Living on the edge honed an ever-deepening connection with the Universal Good.

"I am recovering a faith I paid only lip service to in times of plenty but one that is always reaffirmed in this time of lack," I wrote in my diary. Over three decades later, I recognize now, as I could not then, how such a precarious and contrarian lifestyle could be a detriment to Jessica's well-being.

The frequent moves, unconventional living arrangements, and my sense of impending doom took a toll on both of us. Poverty alone is an arduous journey fraught with pitfalls, but added to that was my unrelenting need to challenge every injustice. Even so, there were moments of great beauty and sheer joy.

Paul and I took advantage of the receding water to replace the damaged flotation foam and to put in place the additional flotation needed beneath the new floor. All the work was accomplished with a few hand tools and in full view of the local fisher folk—our home had settled into the mud blocking the only path to their favored fishing spots.

Folks walked within a foot of our back deck, which served as an open-air kitchen. Some fished from the barges where grain-fed catfish lingered in the deep waters of the channel. Other fishers chose the shore, sitting on over-turned milk cartons or five-gallon buckets patiently waiting for a bite on lines weighted with washers and strung from bamboo poles. Occasionally someone would arrive at the head of the bay and throw a net into the shallows, deftly hauling in a sizable catch of fish variously called "shiners" and "shad." Often the shores were littered with these hand-sized fish, many of which floated at water's edge belly up, victims of the backwater pollution.

It wasn't long before some passersby ventured a few questions as to how we came to be there and what we were about. Their concern for our needs and understanding of our ideas for simple and self-reliant living were heartening. These were country people displaced like so many into an urban environment with a harshness and expense that kept them in a cycle of dependence and struggle.

These families lived in the rented houses up the hill in the shadow of grain silos and factories, amidst scrap-yards and dumps, in neighborhoods pockmarked with vacant, boarded or partially-burned buildings. They shared generously with us from their backyard gardens. And we came to know them on those summer afternoons, serving them from the soup pot simmering on our newly-fashioned scrap-iron stove while we sat together and enjoyed easy conversation delighting in the beauty of the varied sunsets.

The homes of our friends across the road were small wooden structures that showed the wear of numerous tenants and many years of use. But the backyard gardens and well-tended flower beds distinguished them from the industrial wasteland that had grown up around them.

At Willie's house we were greeted by a Billy goat tethered in a yard piled high with accumulated treasures scavenged from discard piles around town. The flock of chickens feeding on grain gathered from truck spillage scattered as we approached, and the curious faces of his seven children peeked out at us from behind tattered plastic curtains. Willie and his family were always eager to lend a helping hand and they visited us many times. While Jessica and the kids paddled about in the canoe on the still backwater or played on a sandy shore, the grownups' conversations rambled on as the loading barges settled more deeply into the water and the pigeons flocked about the silos.

Lulu Mae came to visit too, chewing and spitting her plug of tobacco and always offering helpful advice. Her wiry frame and energetic spirit belied her sixty-odd years. She warned us to expect snakes when the water returned. She said they'd be "a crawlin' all over the barges." Though I never saw them in quite the abundance she described, we did encounter a few. One was twined up on a piece of foam beneath the floor boards of our home. Another took shelter from the sun under a bit of flotsam littering the shore, and yet another tried to board our home as Paul floated her down-harbor to the shade of some trees.

During July and August our work was hot and dirty. Thankfully, breezes off the water moved through our open-backed home and

Off the Grid

brought some relief from the unrelenting sun. We welcomed the southerly winds because they carried the sweet smell of molasses being filled into barges at Cargill. The Northerly breezes were not always a pleasure though. They often brought a heavy ammonia odor from the waste-treatment facility across Wolf River. During the hottest part of the day we did the interior work shaded from the sun. Our newly-floored home was welcome shelter from the heat and our dome tents, fashioned as mosquito netting over our beds, protected us from the hungry pests that plagued us after dark.

Sometimes after a day's work the grime on our skin was unbearable. The cool water all around us seemed so inviting that several times we succumbed to the temptation for a swim. If we stayed in too long though, rashes would follow. We limited our exposure to what the locals called "bad" water. If the grime of a workday was too great to be handled with a basin of hauled water, we compromised by taking a quick dive into the bay followed by a good rinse with clean water.

Once the longing for a shower overcame our pride. We canoed into town for a shower at the Salvation Army. We would have gladly paid a reasonable price for a weekly cleansing. After our shower, they suggested we arrange for an interview with a social worker if we wished to use their facilities again. The complexities of the bureaucratic charity were too much; we resigned ourselves to sponging off with water warmed on our wood stove rather than submitting to the required application and interview.

At times the construction work before us seemed an awesome task, and the lack of a steady income punctuated the precarious nature of our existence. The market for Paul's knife and tool-sharpening business was slim in our new neighborhood and he was so busy with the flooring and roofing work that he had little time to peddle his skills elsewhere.

Though I had opportunity for work in various downtown offices, that was increasingly out of the question for me. The world of high-rise Memphis was an alien camp and I no longer had the protective coloration to move within that world inconspicuously. The wood smoke from our open fire clung to my thrift-store clothing and the Mississippi mud to the soles of my boots. My transportation was a leaky canoe and my tolerance for fluorescent sunshine nil. Besides, writing was my vocation and I was no longer willing to hire out my fingers to stroke the keyboard in cadence to another's words, only to be left at day's end too tired to pursue my own ideas. I wanted the chance to uncover my long-stifled talents, to indulge in a closer communion with the little bit of wild left in the city of my youth.

Despite our cash-poor circumstance, our freedom was a great treasure. I spent day after day in the company of my curious and lovely daughter Jessica in those endless days of unstructured, unhindered being with one another and with the natural world that surrounded us.

Mud Island Wilds

On the water our time was our own. We awakened early to greet the sunrise and at dusk settled in for a quiet evening. We often read aloud and shared together the adventures in such books as *The Wind In The Willows, The Chronicles of Narnia, The Light Princess* and, of course, *Huckleberry Finn*.

Sometimes we canoed into town, paddling along easily with the wind or stroking with all our might if it blew against us. Once we fashioned a makeshift mast and boom and used an old sheet for a sail. We had such fun sailing downwind as a gentle breeze carried us on into town for our day at the library.

We had many visitors during our harbor stay. Some came out of curiosity— like the fellows from Continental Grain who watched our daily struggles from a vantage point high up on the grain elevators. Others came who seemed to understand the spirit of our venture and offered help in many ways.

One special friend who visited often, hailing us from shore and braving the crossing in our leaky canoe, was a local artist whose love for the river inspired her work. Her watercolors of Mississippi views graced our humble walls and reminded us of the strength of the mighty river whose call we could not yet answer. She shared many an afternoon with us, accepting our vision as a possibility and encouraging our efforts. Her thoughtfulness buoyed our spirits.

Once a week we set out on foot up Seventh Street to Chelsea Avenue and down to Faxon at Breedlove and my old home place. There we had a little patch of garden in a vacant lot beside Mama's yard. From there it was over to Overton Park Avenue to another bit

Off the Grid

of garden left in Tommy's backyard. Though the weeds were winning in these patches, we were able to glean enough to justify our journey.

On these occasions too we hauled our laundry in a duffel bag and made use of a washing machine. Hand washing in the muddy back waters would have been self-defeating and hauling enough fresh water for the job was out of the question.

By the time the water had risen high enough to float us again, Paul was prepared with an anchor. He had traded with a local welder. Together they had designed and built an anchor using scrap metal. Soon we were "on the hook" in the middle of the water at the head of the bay swinging in a wide arc that provided an ever-changing view. It felt good to be afloat again on our shanty home without the scrutiny of neighbors, the burden of rent or the inevitable complacency of too much comfort.

These were easier times. I was steadily working on my first attempt at carpentry and proudly completed a somewhat askew but adequate back wall. Paul began instructing us in some useful knots and set himself the task of knitting socks for the winter. Many days we took off to explore the north end of Mud Island where we found open fields where cottontail rabbits played, groves of scarlet sumac, woods of willow, cottonwood, sycamore and elm and acres and acres planted to corn, beans, okra and greens.

One delightful day while we rambled across the island we came upon a field of watermelons. We abandoned ourselves to the simple pleasure of eating the cool and juicy treat in the midst of an abundant patch. We exulted in our freedom to linger in the warm sunshine savoring each bite. We left a note for the farmer, and though we never caught up with the man who had planted that patch, we were thankful for his labors and would have gladly traded a day's work for the joy we experienced that summer day in a watermelon patch on Mud Island. Sometimes we walked across to the west shore of the island and sat on the edge of the great river feeling the awesome power of its presence.

On weekends the water skiers came up harbor, flying across the surface and sometimes spilling into the bay. They came in droves, their noisy motor boats cutting through the muddy waters leaving wakes that washed against the clay shore and cut into the banks. Sometimes they would circle us as we floated out in the middle, peering at us from a safe distance with binoculars or occasionally coming by close enough to chat. These energy-costly boats never really excited our longings for a craft. But the occasional sail-boat that moved with silent grace across the water held our attention like a swan in a mud hole and set our hearts a flutter.

Gleaning the Backwater Bounty

Always the day-to-day struggle for subsistence continued. As the garden produce diminished we needed more cash to buy food, and with nightfall earlier our costs to fuel our kerosene lamps increased. But the river brought us gifts that helped to sustain us: abundant driftwood that fueled our cook fires and later warmed us, a bounty of aluminum in cans that floated in from the mouth of the harbor. Once, a battered skiff known as a Jon boat, drifted our way, replacing our leaky canoe.

We collected the aluminum cans, skimming them off the surface or retrieving them from the littered shores. At twenty-eight cents per pound recycled, they were not meeting our cash needs though, so we were grateful for the tip from the maintenance man at the Missouri Portland Cement Company. He alerted us to the copper available for the picking from the debris-choked banks below the car-consuming machine at Samitized Steel. The bright blue, yellow, red and green of the insulating coating contrasted with the rusty brown offal of the processed cars. We picked out the copper wire by the bucketful, sometimes even discovering old coins among the rubble. Laden with our metallic treasures we hiked to the Southern Tin Compress Co on 7th Street where we sold the copper for fifty cents per pound.

Another source of bounty came from the soybeans, corn and wheat gleaned from diligent sweeping of the barges being filled at Continental Grain. We had noticed that after filling a barge the workmen routinely swept the surface clean, scattering pounds and pounds of whole food into the water.

We canoed alongside with bags and buckets and captured the otherwise wasted food, taking it home to winnow when the winds were strong. We ground the corn into a fine yellow meal with our hand-operated mill, a thoughtful gift from Mama, and the whole wheat was wonderful in breads, ground or sprouted. Soybeans, and occasionally the tiny grains of sorghum milo, were swept from the decks and we experimented with them in our newly built kitchen. Up the hill in a vacant lot we came across an old peach tree and freed it from choking vines as our thanks for its sweet fruit.

Throughout our six months in that busy backwater we often caught a favorable wind and moved our home to a different location along the three-and-one-half mile harbor. This helped to quell our yearning to be on the move. Jessica's favorite tie up was to a small sunken barge on the island side below APAC-Tennessee, Inc. There she played for hours in a mountain of white sand.

Sometimes if we took a notion to move in slack winds, Paul would tow us from the shore like a canal-barge mule while Jessica stood ready with a conch shell horn to blast a warning should we encounter any traffic. I would stand, pole in hand, ready to fend off from the barges moored along the bank and from the shore if we came in too close.

Sometimes we tied up to the island shore across from the Illinois Central North Yard. The cable-bound bundles of tree trunks called dolphins were sunk deeply into the bay providing a secure mooring for our shanty. While there we drew our drinking water from the outside spigot in the rail yard. The station employee shared many tales with us about the Irish squatters who decades before had drawn water from that same spigot when lifestyles such as ours were a common sight in river towns. They also showed a kind concern for our welfare, once sharing a bag full of freshly-picked greens which went well with our simmering pot of soybeans and our griddle hoe-cakes. We also were gifted with some surplus coal that helped keep our stove warm through the night as the chill of fall and early winter penetrated our wooden walls.

"People on the river are happy to give. Rollin', rollin', rollin' on the river," as the song goes.

Caught Red Handed

As we explored the neighborhood near the river on afternoon rambles, Paul soon discovered a large warehouse with a path beaten shiny into its open doors.

Inside were numerous items that looked like useful salvage: cases and cases of bottled water, and a ten-foot tall pile of vinyl panels used in making suitcases. This material had apparently been discarded long ago in this unlocked warehouse.

The Half Life of a Free Radical

With only a brief hesitation I joined Paul in this daylight theft. We walked in along the well-worn path, as others before us had done, and returned to our floating home with arm loads of bottled drinking water. Then we measured our leaking roof and discovered that a few dozen of the vinyl panels would serve us well as new roof shingles.

On one of these afternoon forays into the warehouse I looked up to see a young police officer strolling in through the open door.

"What are you doing here?" he asked.

Caught red-handed in the first theft of my life, with my dear daughter by my side, and my partner on top of the stack of vinyl handing down the next panel, there was nothing to do but tell the truth.

"We live on a houseboat on the river," I told him. "We were looking for a stand of cattails to harvest and found this open warehouse with all this bottled water and these piles of vinyl. We only needed a few to fix our leaking roof. It looks like no one cares about this stuff," I told him.

"It's all contaminated," he said. "It came from a train wreck.

When the officer asked "What's your name?" Jessica answered right away, using her father's last name. Paul offered his, and I gave my first name. I was thinking all the time how mortified Mama would be to see my name in the paper as a common thief.

"Put down what you have, get out of here, and don't come back," the officer said. We were relieved with the reprieve and didn't volunteer the fact that the new orange roof on our shanty home, by this time, was very nearly complete. We had not intended to return anyway.

Theft was not a survival skill I wanted to teach Jessica, and we talked a long time about what had happened and the ethics of dumpster diving and liberating discards. Sometimes the lines are blurred, and this time we were in a very gray area.

As the island trees gave up their brilliant leaves to reveal stark branches, and the migrating birds moved in waves of flight across the gray winter skies, the season of change was also upon us. It was apparent that our shanty home would never make it safely down river. We had no motor to maneuver her with and our encounters with the tugs and barges that moved in the harbor made us well aware of their awesome size.

Off the Grid

On many occasions Paul had talked with tug captains who told him frankly of what he might encounter on the lower Mississippi, cautioning him against the risk. Reluctantly we admitted that the time for our down river adventure had not yet arrived.

A Special Tribunal

One afternoon, on my way back to the river, I walked past St. Mary's Catholic Church on Market Street, the church where I had been married fifteen years before. On a sudden whim I went into the office and asked to speak to a priest. I'm sure I had a perceptible chip on my shoulder, evidenced in my tone.

In the eyes of the church I was "living in sin," and my relationship with Paul would not be seen as valid and true without an annulment of my first marriage. There was some part of me that wanted very much a blessing on our partnership. My divorce had been an act of bravery and self-care, but in the eyes of the church, I felt nothing but condemnation.

The Franciscan priest received me into his office. I asked him about the annulment process. He pulled out a sheath of papers from his file cabinet. I told him that I had been married there nearly fifteen years before, but was divorced now with a twelve-year-old daughter.

He explained that I would need to find witnesses to attest to the adultery of my husband and provide proof of any other grounds for annulment. Once the forms were complete he would send them to Rome where a decision would be made by a special tribunal.

"A special tribunal?" I could barely contain my disdain. I'm not sure now just what I was expecting, but the idea of tracking down anyone to attest to my ex-husband's marital infidelities and then sending that information to Rome was beyond the pale.

"I am to be judged by a tribunal of celibate men? Are you serious?" I asked. The brown-robed Franciscan listened quietly. He didn't attempt to counter my arguments. He told me I could come back and talk with him at any time. I left, having vented just a very small amount of a deep anger I feel with the patriarchal church. I never returned.

The Half Life of a Free Radical

I realized even more clearly then that the Catholic Church was not my spiritual home. I walked quickly away toward the Mississippi, whose ever-changing constancy is a source of power and strength.

Working for Peace & Justice

During our time on the river, Jessica and I volunteered many weekends at St. Rose House, a Catholic Worker ministry in mid-town Memphis founded by Betty and Charlye Gifford, parishioners of St. Patrick's Catholic Church near Beale. Betty was a Catholic convert, full of fervor and commitment to social justice.

St. Rose House offered shelter for up to five homeless women. On our weekend visits, Jessica and I cooked the evening meal and shared the table with residents in the homelike atmosphere. We also took advantage of the hot shower and laundry. It was a cooperative venture all around. The neighborhood was rough then, and gunshots and sirens were part of the background noise.

Just across the street a mother-daughter team delighted in making cloth dolls whose expressions and attire depicted many of the characters that frequented the neighborhood. They displayed these effigies of pimps and nuns, police and drug dealers on the porch for all to see.

When I learned that St. Patrick's was having an old-fashion revival that summer, I was amused and intrigued. And though I had not attended a Catholic service in many years, Jessica and I went. The changes were startling. The sanctuary had been cleared of most of the old wooden pews. People milled about talking, and one man was even smoking inside.

Betty welcomed me. She said she knew my mother and then asked if I had read the book, *Not Without Tears*, the story of the founding of the Blessed Martin House. I had not. Mama had long ago lost her only copy when she loaned it out. It was a great gift to read about my parents' connection with Blessed Martin House, I was amazed at their courage at a time when racial apartheid in Memphis was strong.

Throughout this time in Memphis, I wrote letters to the editor of various local and regional publications. Most often they were polemics against war and weapons manufacture, the death penalty,

Off the Grid

the use of toxic pesticides, and the environmental hazards of automobiles. I was challenging everyone then, quite certain that I had the right answers, and compelled to awaken others to what Martin Luther King, Jr. called "the fierce urgency of now."

I met others who shared my deep concerns. Among them Hubert and Lois Van Tol, and a dynamically radical nun, Sister Chris Dobrolowski, IHM, who volunteered at the St. Rose Catholic Worker House. They were among the founders of The Mid-South Peace & Justice Center which opened January 15, 1981, in an office near Memphis State University. I joined the effort, volunteering to keep up with filing the literature and periodicals from similar groups working on issues of disarmament and justice throughout the country. I was happy at last to have found my way into a community that understood my concerns about global issues and was prepared to act.

Soon, in addition to our weekend work at the shelter, Jessica and I spent each Wednesday at the Peace & Justice Center. I helped edit the newsletter, *Just Peace*. I was already deeply aware of the many injustices endured by the Memphis poor, and had been awakened early to the racism that persisted in our city. Now I was learning about my country's part in the horrible wars against the people of Central America, the ongoing apartheid in South Africa, and the imminent nuclear threat. The dedicated people we worked with and came to know there opened my eyes to the importance of a community of resistance as an organized response to injustice.

One afternoon Jessica and I joined another young mother, Lisa, on a mission into a nearby Arkansas community. There we connected with a family who introduced us to a man and woman from El Salvador. They were on the way to Canada seeking refuge from a military death threat. Our task was to deliver them to the next safe house, some hours away to the north. Lisa spoke fluent Spanish, and Jessica and I understood only a little, so we traveled mostly in silence. Their vulnerability and trust astonished and humbled me.

At one highway rest stop, the car stalled. It could have been disaster had our backseat guests been discovered. We let the car cool down for a while, prayed together about the circumstance, and then turned the key again. The engine started. With deep relief, we were back on the road to deliver our guests to the next way station.

This was a time, too, of widespread organizing for the Nuclear Weapons Freeze Campaign. Jessica and I joined others on a bus trip to Washington, D.C. for a FREEZE gathering. We marched with thousands in the nation's capital and visited the Congressional offices, pleading for a nuclear weapons freeze. Still home-schooled, Jessica was making history, not merely reading the sanitized and revised school-text version that I had experienced.

In August, 1983, we commemorated the atomic bombings of Hiroshima and Nagasaki, Japan, with a peace vigil outside a Titan II missile site near Conway, Arkansas. We held hands in a circle and sang the familiar songs, "Peace Is Flowing like a River" and "We Shall Overcome." A counter-demonstrator at the site carried the sign, "Catholics against the Nuclear Freeze." There was a great deal of difference between left-leaning Catholics and the more conservative ones who could not see the deep contradictions between Christianity and threatening others with nuclear annihilation.

With the help of friends we had met through Betty and Charlye Gifford, we left our shanty boat behind and found a live-in position care taking for an elderly man in his east Memphis home. Paul took on most of the day-to-day responsibilities of providing for his care. My volunteer commitments kept me busy out of the house. In my efforts to save the world I was giving little attention to the needs of my own family. The world was in peril. I felt compelled to act.

Though we were far from the river whose call we still heard, and from the island now threatened by an asphalt highway and an upscale housing development, we held on to our plans for a down-river journey. In his free time, Paul steadily worked building a sailing catamaran. Little by little he bought the materials and pieced together the small craft that would eventually carry us down the Mississippi, across Lake Pontchatrain, into the Gulf and on to safe anchor near St. Petersburg, Florida.

But Paul and I were growing apart. I seldom gave him or Jessica the courtesy of including them in my decisions. I was on an urgent mission, impassioned and fervent. *The Bulletin of Atomic Scientists* had set its symbolic Doomsday Clock at three minutes to midnight.

Three minutes until global nuclear catastrophe. There was no time to waste.

Off the Grid

My First Arrest

In 1984, I joined six others from the Mid-South Peace & Justice Center in a bold act of civil resistance against nuclear weapons. We stood together on the Memphis rail track where the so-called "White Train" with its deadly cargo of Trident I nuclear warheads crossed the Mississippi River from Arkansas. The train was coming from the Pantex weapons assembly plant near Amarillo, Texas, on its way to Charleston. South Carolina.

As we took our stand on the tracks, I fully expected that the railway officials would have us arrested and removed before the train arrived. Much to my surprise, they left us standing there.

"The most dramatic moment occurred as the train rolled across the Mississippi into Memphis at 30 mph," according to an account of the day in *People* magazine.[99]

As the train crossed the bridge, its whistle shrieked and its brakes screeched. We seven held our ground until the train came to a full stop. Then we were arrested and hauled away for a night in the city jail. It was my first arrest. Mama learned about it on the five o'clock news. Jessica watched with others from behind the fence.

In retrospect, I realize that I caused both my Mama and my daughter Jessica a great deal of anguish, acting as I did without full understanding of the trauma it would inflict. Jessica feels that I considered her needs as less important than taking action against nuclear weapons and war.

I'm sorry for the pain it has caused her. I believed I was acting on behalf of a world in imminent danger. Times then, as they do now, call for drastic action in defense of the Earth. I felt compelled to act, much in the same way, I suspect, that young men and women feel who are willing to step into harm's way as participants in U.S. military combat actions.

We engaged in this act of civil resistance with support of the Mid-South Peace & Justice Center to track the train along its route as part of a campaign initiated by Catholic activists Jim and Shelly Douglass of the Ground Zero Community near the Trident Nuclear submarine base in Poulsbo, Washington. I agreed with what this Catholic radical Jim Douglass said in the *People* magazine article:

The Half Life of a Free Radical

> *...the white train travels through the heart of the United States, through people's backyards and under their noses. It gives people a chance to accept responsibility for nuclear weapons, to say, 'They're ours— but we don't want them.'* [100]

Civil resistance takes a stand to uphold law, in this case, international laws prohibiting use of nuclear weapons; civil disobedience takes a stand in defiance of unjust laws, such as was the case with the Civil Rights Movement. I was moving into new territory with this action. I wrote about the experience in an article published in the *St. Petersburg Times*.[101]

> *I knew with that decision that I had crossed a line. My life would never be the same. ...With symbolic action our presence on the track sent a clear message that this nuclear train would never again pass unnoticed through our community.*

The $300 payment for the article came at a most critical time, when Jessica and I were adrift off the edge of St. Petersburg, Florida, in the somewhat derelict yawl we used as our floating home after our down river journey from Memphis and through the inter-coastal waterway to Florida.

Flowing With the River

We waded hip-deep into Memphis' McKellar lake the summer of 1984 to launch our home built sailboat, "Olympic Fire." Our journey began at dawn on a wing and a prayer borne by the vagrant winds and the river's steady flow.

We were exultant with the freedom of the moment and buoyed with the good wishes of friends and family as a fresh breeze carried us out the Tennessee Chute to the Mississippi river. There would be no turning back.

Our twenty-one foot plywood and fiberglass catamaran was designed as a week-end coastal cruiser. Her first journey would be a month-long adventure on the wide and wonderful Mississippi, our avenue to the sea.

A local artist using the name "Memphis T. Mississippi" traveled with us, sketchbook in hand, to Vicksburg; and "Jolly Roger," a black

Off the Grid

dachshund-terrier, came along too. His berth was a makeshift doggie cabin on the port bow. It was an intimate journey in close quarters.

From Memphis to Baton Rouge we had no motor. We relied instead on the wind in the sails, the swift current, and a pair of long wooden paddles. We had a lead-line for a depth sounder, a bucket for the "head" and a butane one-burner for a galley.

Time took on a different meaning on the river. The moments passed in a more natural rhythm. Our senses were keener and our concerns immediate. The world beyond the river—the world of clocks and schedules, of hurried pace and mounting crises—was far removed. There is a timelessness about that river that links the lives of all who have traveled its course or lived along its banks. I felt a growing kinship with the myriad and invisible stream of life that had for centuries been shaped and nurtured by the Mississippi.

The dawn hours were the most favorable for travel. With an early start and steady wind we could cover twenty to thirty river miles daily. It was just under 600 miles to the Gulf and we had no schedule to keep, so we flowed with a leisurely pace and stopped in each river town long enough to walk a bit among the people and feel the unique ambiance of each port of call.

The sun that we greeted with joy at dawn by noon seemed an adversary of unreasonable proportions. We were quite vulnerable beneath its harsh and reflected glare, especially when no breeze tempered its effects. We adopted Arab-style headdress and dark glasses and coated our exposed skin with generous amounts of sunscreen. In the late afternoon heat we would bucket up gallons of the cool brown river and douse each other with the cooling water.

"Olympic Fire" was a lightweight boat with a shallow draft. It was easy to beach her on a sandy shore and tether to a tree. Then we could camp in shore side tents and enjoy the space and privacy not available on board. If the shore was too steep, we would snag an overhanging willow branch with a grapnel hook and snug up close to the bank. Then we would have to find what sleep we could head-to-head, two to a hull, in our coffin-size berths.

Sunset always brought mosquitoes that tormented us mercilessly, driving us into our tents or under netting that covered the open hatches of the hulls. But the vexation of these tiny shore dwellers was tempered by the magnificence of the sunsets, the song of cicada and bullfrog, or the marvelous sight of shorebirds in flight over a river aswirl with eddies and whirlpools that reflected the fire of the sun and only hinted at the power of the flow.

Our craft was quite stable and if we didn't overfill the pot we could cook dinner as we sailed from a larder of dried beans, rice and easy-keeping vegetables like squash and cabbage.

We left Greenville, Mississippi, with sails flapping in the light airs as we drifted slowly downstream on the old river bend past mud banks lined with rusting barges. Ahead we noticed several working tugs breaking and reforming a barge tow. As we passed between the working tugs and the banked barges, one tug suddenly churned up backwash that pinned us against the down-sloped side of a banked barge.

We were frightened and confused. What was going on? Our fragile wooden vessel was scraping up and down against the rusting hulk of an iron barge. The sound was harsh and frightening. It startled Jessica out of the starboard hull. A mere quarter-inch of fiberglass and plywood separated her berth from the heavy barge. Our paddles were no match for the power of the backwash. We fended off as best we could, grimacing with each bow-crunching blow. It seemed like a very long time before the tug captain cut his engine and released us from the deadly hold. The damage to our vessel was minimal—a crack in the starboard bow above the water line and rough wood scraped bare along the rub rail of the starboard hull.

We were a different sort of crew as we rejoined the big river, shaken by the experience and sobered with the realization of how vulnerable our craft was on the commercial highway that the Mississippi has become.

Wide, Deep, and Muddy

All along our journey we would encounter people for whom the river was a way of life. We passed fisher folk in skiffs and Jon boats with catfish flopping wildly at their feet. We greeted travelers in canoes and houseboats. Twice the paddle-wheeler, "Mississippi Queen," her passengers lining the rails, churned past.

But sometimes we felt the river was ours. For hours on end no other traffic was visible. Through the wild lands of flood basin and past deep forests of bearded willow, we could imagine ourselves for a time as lone travelers in an unspoiled region.

Off the Grid

Despite the apparent calm, travel on the river called for constant vigilance. Around any bend, at any time, massive iron barges pushed by diesel-powered tow boats churned up wakes that rivaled an ocean swell. Sometimes the loads were six wide and as many as seven barges long— a massive bulk with little maneuverability. We had to dodge the tows coming and going as we tacked back and forth across the wind that seemed always to move upriver regardless of the turns and bends that snaked through the wilds of Arkansas, Mississippi and Louisiana.

Paul was a fearless Captain who judged his tacks close enough to nearly kiss the side of the approaching barge. I always breathed a sigh of relief when the order to "Come about!" turned us safely out of harm's way.

"Which side of the river do you want, Captain?" was our usual radio opening as soon as a tow came into sight. We had learned to be humble and to defer to these tows, planning our maneuvers to keep well out of the way. One captain answered our query with an observation:

"You see that buoy out there? Y'all ain't no bigger than it is on my screen." Another rounded a bend and upon sighting us exclaimed:

"Is that a sailboat I see? Oh Lordy! What next!" This same captain had just passed a pair of intrepid Frenchmen who had been making their way down river, swimming the length of it in wet suits.

Our arrival in Baton Rouge in mid-July marked the end of what we would remember as the easy segment of our journey. On the advice of local boaters, we traded excess gear and a little cash for a used three-horsepower outboard to carry us through the last stretch of river. Already industrial docks claimed every bit of the bank and ocean-going freighters loomed above us, their massive bulk silhouetted at sunset against an apricot sky.

Travel down river of Baton Rouge was a nightmare of screeching, grinding and slamming barges and tows breaking up and reforming; of harsh images of riverside industry with smoke stacks pouring filth into the summer sky; of acrid scents and the drone of diesel engines. But the river rolled on, undaunted by the industrial insult, reflecting with a swirling, shimmering, rippled and mirrored surface the setting sun that streaked pink and gray across the wide horizon.

The Half Life of a Free Radical

As we traveled along the crowded river corridor, our hulls pounded the surface in the wake of the monstrous vessels that passed. It was a harrowing stretch of river, especially when our not-so-trusty outboard sputtered to a halt, its fuel line clogged in the midst of some of the worst of the industrial traffic. Paul's calm was uncanny as he painstakingly disassembled the motor to dislodge the debris. All too often he accomplished this feat while Jessica bravely held steady the helm and I paddled mid-river across the path of an oncoming barge tow. The strain on our vessel was continual and the harmony of our relationships was difficult to maintain.

Jessica noticed it first on a stretch of river just below New Orleans. "Paul, is this beam supposed to look like this,?" she asked, pointing out a deep crack in the crossbeam that supported both the forward mast and the center deck.

"No, it isn't." was his calm reply. But despite his demeanor, I knew we had a major problem. We had just bypassed New Orleans and would have to navigate through the locks into Lake Pontchatrain before we could stop for repairs. The sheer fatigue of our month's journey on the Mississippi was taking its toll.

We were weary. Weary of the river and its hidden depths, weary of the industrial traffic that kept us under siege, and weary of the sun and its glaring heat. We detoured into the ship canal, unceremoniously turning our backs on the Mississippi to concentrate on the arduous passage ahead. We were low on cash, food, water and gasoline and in dire need of safe harbor and rest. On that final day of our river journey we were especially thankful for the tug crew who shared cool drink and fresh produce as we awaited our turn through the locks.

We arrived in Lake Pontchatrain as a storm gathered strength. A local yachtsman guided us to a marina slip for the night, and warned us against anchoring in the shallow lake where sudden squalls set a treacherous chop in motion. After some inquiries, we found safe harbor in the 17th Street canal among the Shrimp fleet at Bucktown, a fourth-and fifth-generation squatters' settlement on the half-mile peninsula bounded by the Lake and the Canal.

We found friendship and rest among these proud and self-reliant people as we repaired our cracked beam, re-stepped the mast, and prepared to continue our travels across the lake and into the Gulf where dolphins and salt spray, white sands and swaying palms would fill our days as the Gulf breezes carried us onward.

Off the Grid

And as we traveled, we carried with us a bond with the heart and soul of the Mid-South region and a reverence for the timeless Mississippi where we had lived for a while immersed in its beauty and strength, borne to the sea in the power of its flow, and touched by the kindness of her people.

At Anchor in St. Petersburg

A spry Aunt Regina, with her engaging laugh, met us at the dock in Madeira Beach, Florida, jumping aboard with open arms. Uncle Ray and his wife Helen offered gracious hospitality despite our rather unorthodox and unannounced arrival. Ray was a younger, sober version of my father, with a way and wit about him that reminded me of my brother Robert.

Our only currency was our story. Daddy's long-lost-to-me family listened avidly as we shared about our river adventure at the elegant table Aunt Helen set for Sunday dinner. She seemed a bit unnerved by this sudden intrusion of the rag-tag crew of Olympic fire. She pointed out the posted rules of the home-owner's association, and then she and Ray offered us a week's respite in a nearby vacant apartment they managed.

We were as fish out of water in the high rise condominium, but so tired and so much in need of respite that no other choice made any sense. Within a week we had found safe harbor among other cruising sailors in the Vinoy Yacht Basin on the edge of downtown and just across from the St. Petersburg Pier. Our tiny, colorful craft was just one among many coming and going in that harbor.

When we set anchor, we had forty-seven cents, a larder of food, and one of the best views in town. I paddled to shore at Straub Park and climbed up into the sheltering limbs of an ancient banyan tree and cried.

Life at anchor off the edge of a busy city is much more stressful than traveling on the wind to a new port of call each day. Our relationships, already strained by the difficult river journey, were at the breaking point.

Jessica was thirteen and at a time in her life when her needs for privacy and a community of friends was great. It was apparent to me that we could not long continue as we were. Paul was leaving. Jessica stood her ground. She was staying in St. Petersburg.

The Half Life of a Free Radical

"I had to be my own advocate," she later told me.

Jessica and I were left on our own in St Petersburg, living aboard a derelict wooden Yawl, while Paul sailed on to the Bahamas in the catamaran. Pride or shame or some combination kept me from reaching out to my Uncle Ray and Aunt Regina for help.

I found work cleaning charter yachts at a nearby marina. While I polished the brass and sanded the teak topside, Jessica worked on her home study courses in the comfortable salons of the luxury yachts. We found a way to make our way, and along the way we encountered many generous people, especially among the good Quakers at the St. Petersburg Friends Meeting.

We also reconnected with a Memphis friend, MarSea and her five children. They shared with us generously, even letting us stay for a time in the back of a school bus parked in their driveway when life at anchor in the bay was wearing thin.

At a soup line in the city park, we met John X. & Martina Linnehan of the Immanuel House Peace Community. With others in their intentional community, they maintained a vigil at the General Electric plant in nearby Largo that manufactured nuclear triggers and released radioactive tritium into the air. Both had spent time in prison for blocking entrance to the plant. Once again, I had landed among a community of peaceful and determined resisters to weapons and war and was challenged to act.

16

Solidarity & Resistance

"I have learned over the years that when one's mind is made up, this diminishes fear; knowing what must be done does away with fear." — Rosa Parks

Our life on the edge of St. Petersburg brought us in contact with women and children who also lived precariously in the midst of abundance. I brought my concerns for the plight of the homeless to the nearby Friends meeting and to the good people serving soup in the city park.

Within a year of our arrival, Jessica and I had founded and moved to a Catholic Worker-inspired house where we welcomed other displaced mothers and children with no safe and certain place to call home. We shared the small rooming house with a dozen or so women and children who came in need of shelter. We lived together as coworkers in a haphazard community, each contributing what she could to keep the doors open.

We survived from month to month on the donations of individuals, churches, and civic groups who responded to our appeal. Soon we expanded our work to offer showers and a change of clothing to as many as one hundred walk ins a day. When our shelter beds were full we had the awful task of saying "No" to vulnerable and frightened people who had few alternatives. We had to do this two or three times a week, sometimes more.

Many who came for help were the working poor who were priced out of the housing market and had overstayed their welcome with family and friends; others were evicted and displaced when the bulldozers demolished entire neighborhoods for new development; some were fleeing family violence, others were just old and tired and poor, broken in body, mind and spirit.

Haphazard Community

We said "Yes, come in" as often as we could and tried to understand and assist. Most of the children who shared our home were under five and clinging to young mothers who bore sole responsibility for their welfare. Many of our guests were sick with lingering colds and other chronic ailments. Some were pregnant, others had just given birth. All were in emotional and financial distress and were doing everything that they knew to find a way back home.

For those who we could not take in as house guests—for the single men or those who were struggling with alcohol and other drug addictions, or with serious emotional instability— for those homeless persons we could offer only a shower, a change of clothes, a kind word, and referral to a soup kitchen or counseling center.

Of the many hundreds of homeless men who came to the Drop-in Center, many had lost high-paying jobs in northern towns and were barely surviving as day laborers. Some were veterans, adrift and moving from town to town relying on the comradeship of their brothers on the street. They came when the city-supported shelters were full; they came when church doors were closed; they came when the police chased them from the benches where they sought rest in defiance of city laws making it a crime to lie down to rest or sleep in public after 11 p.m.; they came from the cramped back seats of cars, from under bridges, and out from the vacant and boarded houses where they lived furtively from day to day. And they came day after day. Men, women and children, their numbers increasing year to year.

Jessica and I were immersed in a 24-hour, seven-day-a-week labor, and the need was unrelenting. Calls for assistance rang into the night adding to the stress of life in a deteriorating neighborhood. And with each new face, of the many, many hundreds who came, I felt the frustration knowing that our efforts to help would do little to change the circumstances that brought them to our door. With each new guest I was challenged anew to find the ways and means to awaken others in the community to the crisis so that just solutions could be sought.

During this time our friend, Mitch Snyder, who we had met when we volunteered in Washington, D.C. with the Community for Creative Nonviolence, had initiated a campaign called "Take Off the Boards!" It was an effort to reclaim vacant houses for use by the displaced and un-housed poor. There were plenty such houses in our St. Petersburg neighborhood. Fine homes were being demolished for parking lots in the area near the University of South Florida. It didn't take much to convince my homeless guests to join in the action.

And I grew weary, drained of the emotional resources to meet each new guest with joy, and disheartened at inadequate community response to the crisis. There seemed to be no end to the need as the shelters overflowed, still the city-hired bulldozers rolled, demolishing the habitat of the poor.

With the help of the good Quakers, Jessica was accepted into Olney Friends School, a private boarding school in Ohio, not far from where her third great-grandmother, Catharine Huff Mayger, had lived when she first arrived from Germany. We took the Greyhound together to check out the school. It provided her with a loving environment that nurtured her in ways I never could have. Jessica worked part-time work on the campus to augment the generous scholarship assistance. Her paternal grandmother sent her a monthly allowance to help make up for her father's failure to pay child support.

I had peace of mind knowing Jessica was in such a safe and caring environment and though I missed her, it was the wisest choice we could have made. She made good and lasting friendships there, graduating *cum laude* and Valedictorian of her class. Robert, Vernua, Katrina and James made the very long journey to Ohio to join us on her graduation day.

Back in St. Petersburg I stayed on with the work until others stepped forward. Then I took up the offer from a kind friend, Bill Honey, the attorney who had successfully defended us in our efforts to reclaim vacant houses for the homeless. He provided me with a place of rest and distance from the inner-city in a desert foothills retreat near Phoenix, Arizona.

Layers of mountains surrounded me there and a reverent quiet settled about me edging out the concerns of the work I had left behind. No more would I jump at every phone call wondering if there was an empty bed to offer, nor would I look into the worried eyes of yet another young mother with children in tow who had no safe and certain place to call home. I found some peace there and the time to heal, to write, and to reflect.

Living now in Asheville, with a growing number of displaced and homeless persons sorely visible in the center of town, I have kept my distance from the struggles. Other young, idealistic and determined advocates work daily to alleviate the suffering and to call for systemic change, much as I did so long ago in my work among the homeless and mentally ill in Memphis and St. Petersburg.

Recently, as I went to Asheville's Pritchard Park to give more thought to this book, the space was almost fully occupied by homeless women and men, sprawled out on blankets beneath the tree, surrounded by backpacks and bags of donated food. They were taking up nearly all the available benches. I raised their ire when I tapped a man sprawled out on a bench and asked if he would sit up and share the bench. He angrily complied, accusing me of having no compassion for people without homes. His fellow travelers chimed in yelling harsh and accusatory words.

"Just because you have a home, you think you're better than us." Surrounded as we are by the growing affluence and gentrification of the city, I understood their anger.

"We have to find some way to share this space," I countered. So I sat reading amid their taunts as one after another approached me, first with a challenging posture, then sitting down and opening up with their story of woe, so similar to the stories I had daily heard in Memphis, in St. Petersburg, and in Alderson Federal Prison.

I had no answers for the felon whose conviction made him ineligible for public housing, or for the older woman, not quite the age of social security, whose weary and angry face showed the strain of her circumstance. She had nowhere to go, and waiting lists for available housing were many years long. I didn't dare engage the angry Iraq veteran who railed aloud about fighting the war to secure our "so-called freedoms," only to become another homeless person, competing for space on the street.

"I'm a veteran," he asserted. "Hell if I'm going to give up my bench."

Solidarity & Resistance

How well I know the stories of injustices heaped upon returning veterans and the displaced poor. I watched as the passing tourists averted their gaze and quickened their step, realizing how little has really changed in this country, and how deep the problems are that divide us by class and race and religion and politics.

As I pedaled home, I stopped to greet some friends living in the nearby Vanderbilt senior housing. Both are Viet Nam war veterans. One, an Apache raised out west on a reservation, wore a T-shirt with the slogan, "Fighting Terrorism since 1492." The other, a West Virginia musician, raised near the Alderson prison where I did time, wore his "Bronze Star" Viet Nam Veteran hat.

"We're still suffering from that Viet Nam War," he said.

Oh yes. Yes we are.

Finding My Home in Appalachia

Nearly nine months of the deep and healing quiet of the Sonoran desert, with its marvels of towering Saguaro, cactus blossom and coyote howl had restored me. It was time to move on.

Jessica and I traveled cross-country on a wing and a prayer from my retreat in Cave Creek, Arizona, to Burnsville, North Carolina, for an interview with the grassroots action group Rural Southern Voice for Peace. They were in need of an editor for their publication of the same name.

Rural Southern Voice For Peace (RSVP) gave voice to the struggles for justice of people living in the small towns and rural communities of the Southeastern United States. I had first learned of their work through the Mid-South Peace & Justice Center. Somehow word of their search for a new editor came to my attention in Arizona.

I didn't know what my next step would be had my interview been unsuccessful, but there was safe refuge with Eileen's family in her home in Surgoinsville, Tennessee, just two hours over the mountains from Celo, so I took the risk.

By the time Jessica and I made it to Memphis, about half-way into our journey, we were down to our last few dollars. Mama and Regina helped with enough cash to carry us to the Celo Community near Burnsville, North Carolina, and then on to Ohio, for Jessica's junior year at Olney Friends School.

The Half Life of a Free Radical

It was harvest time when we arrived in Yancey County, North Carolina. As we drove the narrow, winding Appalachian roads leading to Celo we passed squat tipis of brown and yellow tobacco drying in fields or hanging in weathered barns. The roadside was bright with the yellows of daisy and goldenrod and the purple hues of ironweed, clover, thistle and aster. Monarch butterflies were busy in the meadows where horses grazed. The clouds, heavy with the afternoon rains, cast a dense mantle over the many layers of surrounding mountains. The corn was high, the tomatoes a deep red and the potatoes ready for digging. From the deep forests where the barest hint of color tinged the dogwood came the cry of the crow. The season was turning in the land of the Cherokee, and once again in my own life. It seemed I had found my way to the best possible place to be.

Celo Community is the oldest land trust community in the country. There were no double locks. No window bars or alarms to secure loved ones or possessions, and no sirens blasting through the silence of the night. The windows opened wide to the sweet coolness of the coming Fall, to the voice of the river rushing over smooth stones and mossy boulders, to the cricket song and the wavering "whooo" of a night owl.

I attended the small Celo Friends meeting held in a restored goat barn and nestled in a quiet wood. It was a source of much spiritual nurture for me, as were the surrounding mountains and the supportive and cooperative community. I lived for part of my time there in a three-room cabin nestled in a rhododendron thicket just about a half mile from my workplace. Instead of the harsh inner city streets, I walked meandering paths through deep woods with mountain streams and wildflowers as companions.

I chose not to have a telephone in my new home. I needed the quiet and solitude that I found so healing. My rent was only $60 monthly and the costs for heating fuel and electricity brought the total to about $150 each month. My part-time wages were more than adequate to provide for these needs.

Not long after my arrival I decided to let go of the old car that we had traveled in from Arizona. It was costly to maintain and more and more seemed out of sync with the pace and rhythm of my new life. Besides, during all those years in St. Petersburg at the shelter and living on the boats, we had managed without an automobile. I drove

Solidarity & Resistance

it to the junk yard near Spruce Pine and let it go for scrap. I've been car-free ever since.

Soon after I began my work as editor of *Rural Southern Voice for Peace*, the U.S. was again at war.

On a cold January 16, 1991, as I was settling in for the night, the radio broadcast intruded with the news that a U.S. Military attack was underway in the war called Desert Storm. More than 100,000 persons were killed outright when the U.S. rained hell fire on the ancient city of Baghdad. Many thousand others would face decades of illness and death.

Desert Storm was the opening strike in the final dark decade of the gruesomely violent 20th century. The high-tech assault continued relentlessly for weeks, a spectacle broadcast into almost every American home. I listened on my bedside radio to the commentators' blow-by-blow accounts extolling the claimed precision of these weapons of mass destruction.

In my work as editor, I corresponded with and shared stories of peace and environmental activists in rural communities and small cities in the Southeast. This was in pre-internet days. Our newsletter provided a vital link.

Yet our voices for peace could not counter the massive propaganda for Desert Storm. Yellow ribbons seemed to decorate every tree in the nearby town of Burnsville, as blindly-brave local youth answered the call to war, much as my two brothers had done a generation before when they volunteered for the war in Viet Nam.

Throughout a dreadfully long and lonely winter night as the war continued, I drifted in and out of sleep. A deepening sense of despair hovered. Old prayers of intercession, drilled into my consciousness throughout my Catholic childhood, came to mind: *Deliver us we beg you, oh Lord, from every evil, past, present and to come.*

The prayer spilled out of me like a mantra as U.S. gun ships unleashed their aggressive fury on the people of Iraq. Prayers seemed all that I could do from my lonely cabin in the woods as the bombs exploded over Baghdad with relentless fury. Sometime during that dark night I had a remarkably lucid dream:

> *I awakened within my dream in an unfamiliar bedroom, strangely compelled to open a large bay window and step out into the balmy night.*

The Half Life of a Free Radical

I purposely left the bedroom door unlocked behind me. Then, of a sudden, I was borne aloft on a sweet breeze. I soared above the treetops, inhaling the fragrance of blooming mimosa. When I returned from my dream flight I noticed someone standing just inside the bedroom door.

A handsome young man walked slowly toward me smiling with a familiar warmth. I recognized my Daddy—not from how he appeared in the moonlit room, but from how I felt as he drew near. My long-dead father seemed healthy and whole again, with all the vitality and strength that a lifetime of alcoholism had drained from him.

Daddy wrapped his arms around me, taking me into a protective and loving embrace. Once again I was the frightened little girl awakened by a night terror who nestled safely in his arms. It was a comfort I remembered from so very long ago in the dim light of our Memphis living room as my Daddy softly sang the old Irish lullaby, "Too-ra-loo-ra loo ral," and rocked me back to sleep. Years of grief and pain washed away in that dream embrace. I felt my father's love as a healing presence even as I knew I must let him go.

Daddy did not come alone through the unlocked door in that lucid dream. Danny followed closely behind. He was only forty one when he collapsed on our Mother's floor, bleeding to death from a wound from cancer surgery. Daddy opened his arms to welcome Danny in the embrace, but I could not let this brother in, fearing perhaps an encounter with some painful truth between us yet unresolved.

"Go away," I said. "Leave me alone." More a strong thought than audible words. In that instant both Daddy and Danny were gone.

I came fully awake in the loft of my tiny mountain home, strangely comforted and deeply troubled. Now, twenty-five years since that dream, I feel only compassion and a deep sadness for the toll of war and alcoholism on my father, my brothers, my entire family.

It is said that the deeper our wounds, the more space is carved out for love and compassion. As I see Danny's face reflected in his own fine son, and in the smiles of his two lovely granddaughters, I am heartened by the continuities of life and believe that through his progeny, Danny's spirit must surely live again in fullness and wholeness, free of the illness and war that robbed him of life.

Solidarity & Resistance

"A Fool's Pardon"

In the late summer of 1992, I followed my heart across the sea to the island home place of my great-great grandparents. Jessica was a student then at Warren-Wilson College near Asheville, and I was ready for a change.

I volunteered with a Quaker project in Belfast in the British-occupied province of Ulster. For a few months I lived along the so-called "Peace line," where ugly walls of concrete, steel and barbed wire separated the housing estates of working-class Protestants from those of Irish Catholics.

The divided neighborhoods of Belfast were oddly similar to the North Memphis neighborhoods of my youth where the separation was determined by the color of one's skin, rather than one's religious heritage. As I wandered through the city with what locals called "a fools pardon," I felt the hatred in the warnings: "Irish Out" and "Kill all Taigs" scrawled on the gable-end walls in Protestant neighborhoods near the Shankill Road. The Nationalistic pride of Irish Catholics was depicted in murals along the Falls Road with themes commemorating such events as the 1916 Rising and the 1981 Irish hunger strike.

"Taig" I discovered is a term of contempt for Gaelic Catholics. Like the vulgar word "nigger," that I all-too-often heard as a child in Memphis, this word too denies the inherent dignity of a people by setting them apart as hated others.

During my time in Belfast, terrorist gunmen on both sides of the conflict were still engaged in brutal tit-for-tat murders and bombings, while Britain's teen soldiers patrolled the streets from massive fortresses dressed in jungle combat gear with automatic weapons at ready.

In the Republic of Ireland I visited The Public Museum in Fitzgerald's Park in "the rebel city" Cork, where my great-great grandparents in the Donnelly and Mahoney families had lived. One exhibit featured photos from the 1916 Easter Rising. *An tÉ irí Amach* (The Rising). The black-and-white photographs riveted my attention.

The most compelling photo was of Michael O'Hanrahan. His image was hauntingly familiar—as though a composite of the faces of my five Hanrahan brothers. This Irish revolutionary used the Gaelic form of his name–Micheál Ó hAnnracháin. He was a journalist and a novelist and a member of the Gaelic League, taking part in some of the more radical nationalist campaigns of the day. Several Irish nationalist newspapers, including *Sinn Féin* and the *Irish Volunteer*, published his articles.

Michael O'Hanrahan was thirty-nine years old when he was executed by firing squad May 4, 1916, in the stone breaker's yard at Kilmainham Prison for his part in "an armed rebellion and in the waging of war against His Majesty the King."

Though we share a surname, by the time of the 1916 Easter Rising, the Hanrahans in my ancestral line had long since left Ireland for America. Never during my childhood, at home or in class, did I learn of the "troubles" in Ireland. My journey there deepened my appreciation of my ancestral roots and the ongoing struggles for dignity and justice.

Inmate No. 90285-020

I returned from Ireland to find welcome in Asheville from my friends Kathleen McLoughlin and Jim Brown in the Montford neighborhood. Both then were active in justice and peace work, particularly around the U.S. interventions in Central America and were active with Witness for Peace.

In 1990, Kathleen asked me to accompany her to Fort Benning, Georgia, where we participated in a peaceful gathering at the gates in support of the recent arrest there of Father Roy Bourgeois, a Maryknoll priest. Kathleen and I were both arrested for crossing the line onto the military base that was home to the notorious U.S. Army School of Americas (SOA). Over the next two decades we returned many times as part of the SOA Watch Movement.

In November, 2000, I was one of twenty-six persons from fourteen states selected for prosecution for peaceful protest at Fort Benning. After trial, I received the maximum sentence, and surrendered to the Federal Bureau of Prisons at Alderson Federal Prison, the oldest and largest federal prison for women in Alderson, West Virginia, not far from where my great-great grandmother, Catharine Huff Mayger, had lived. It was July 17, 2001.

For six months I occupied the top bunk of cinder-block cubicle 042— a nine-by-twelve feet stall in a concrete prison warehouse. I

Solidarity & Resistance

was inmate number 90285-020, just one more number in a criminal justice system that has ensnared over two million U.S. Citizens.

I was imprisoned with mothers, grandmothers, and great grandmothers, women from eighteen to almost eighty-years old. We were Muslims and Christians, Buddhists and Pagans, gay women and straight women, old and young women, pregnant and dying women. And nowhere else, I think, but prison could I have shared living space with such diversity of American women.

Night after weary night we slept closely stacked in our prison bunks breathing together in the dim florescence. We endured the deadening monotony and demeaning control of prison routine. Each day we found, somehow, the simple grace to endure the indignities and privations of prison life despite the punitive system that sought to divide, denigrate, disempower, contain and control us. Among us were convicted embezzlers, thieves, bank robbers and con artists. But most, as many as eighty percent of Alderson's nearly 900 captives, were convicted violators of America's draconian drug laws, accounting for more than a one-hundred percent increase in women felons since 1990.

Prison was a hard situation for me. I had been vocal in my dissent for so long, and always quick to the defense of others. In prison I learned a little bit about the survival tactic of outward acquiescence while maintaining an inner resolute resistance to the injustice. We were a profitable commodity in that prison work camp. Many women worked long hours locked in the UNICOR Federal Prison Industries building, sewing army jackets for pennies an hour.

I wrote about my experiences, published in two books: *Jailed for Justice: A Woman's Guide to Federal Prison Camp*, intended to help other women who may engage in civil resistance, to understand something of what the prison experience might be. The other, *Conscience & Consequence: A Prison Memoir*, detailed my own personal journey inside.

Jessica was able to make the trip to visit me in prison just after the fall of the Twin Towers. She traveled with my two Celo Community friends, Quakers Judy Conrad and Judy Scheckel. Their visit lifted my spirits.

My brave daughter expressed her feelings in a poem she wrote in July, 2001, as I reported to prison:

The Half Life of a Free Radical

Torn

On the occasion of her mother's six-month incarceration for nonviolent action opposing U.S. Army counterinsurgency training at Ft. Benning, Georgia.

Life's Passions and Pain rolled up into one
Images of a loved one curled up in a ball.
Pride for a road so hard to travel for so long.
And yet so valiant and so strong.

Tears of a child so long ago
Fall from the face of one who really does know
That all is as it should be today
And yet I wait and I cry and I pray.

Too Many Mothers, disappeared,
Will not return
Too Many daughters will never know
The Welcoming embrace which I await

My tears blend with theirs,
My fears pale in comparison
And yet, I remain
Afraid, Aware, and mostly Proud.
   —Jessica

17

Requiem Aeternam

Though we need to weep your loss,
You dwell in that safe place in our hearts,
Where no storm or night or pain can reach you.
   —John O'Donohue, *Benedictus*

Daddy's in the VA hospital again. He's dying. Can you come? It was Robert, my sober brother, who reached me in Key West with the news.

I sat down on the steps of the elegant house where I was staying. The palm trees swayed in the fragrant summer breeze and the charms of the island were particularly beguiling that day. I did not want to go back to Memphis. I needed time to think.

Over the years I had come to some measure of peace with my father, accepting, finally, that he could never be the sober, reliable pillar of support I had yearned for him to be. I had let go of him long before illness took him, holding in memory only his bright smile and dancing eyes. I had nothing more to say to him.

I called Robert back and said I could not come. I can hear Daddy's voice now, singing "Too-Ra-Loo-Ra-Loo Ral" as he rocked me back to sleep in the dim memory of long ago when night terrors awakened me.

But in his last days, when he called on me, I could not be there for my Daddy.

The Half Life of a Free Radical

"Hush Now, Don't You Cry"

Daddy died at the Memphis VA hospital on July 28, 1979, just ten days after his 68th birthday. For Mama's sake, Jessica and I went back for the funeral, thanks to a loan for airfare from Michael.

Daddy's body was displayed in an open coffin as friends and acquaintances paid a final visit. I hardly recognized his powdered and wax-like visage. When I dared to comment on how unlike himself our Daddy looked, Danny flew into a rage. He had arranged the costly and maudlin display. He would brook no criticism.

Tommy, also lost in drink, was particularly morose in his grieving.

"The next time we're all together we'll be burying Mama," he lamented.

"If you don't put that bottle down, brother, you'll be the next in line," I shot back. I had learned to keep an emotional distance from my brothers. Caring and compassion, cajoling and complaining was useless in the face of that addiction.

I stood at Mama's side as she said her last goodbye to Daddy as he lay in the open coffin. She reached down and gently laid her hand on his forehead. It was a most tender gesture of farewell, the most loving expression I can remember ever witnessing in their tragic relationship.

The funeral Mass at Sacred Heart was held in the sanctuary where Daddy and Mama married nearly thirty-five years before. My three sisters' read from the scriptures. It was difficult to sit through the Mass. Tommy elbowed me in the pew as the others stood to go to the Communion rail: "Fake it like I do," he whispered. But I could not. Would not.

After the funeral, we gathered on Faxon Avenue. Some friends brought by platters of food, but others, still skittish about the neighborhood, did not come. At dusk, two men walked up to the porch carrying a fifth of Irish whiskey.

"We came to drink a toast to Danny," one of them said. We invited them inside.

"We've known Danny for years," one of them told me. What they seemed surprised to learn was that the Danny they shared drinks

Requiem Aeternam

with at Greer's Sandwich Shop, night after night, walked home to a house full of children and a very tired wife.

There was so much that I did not know about my Daddy. He so rarely shared his feelings. Years after his death, in 2003, I published an anti-war article in the Asheville *Mountain Xpress*.[102] It was shared widely on the Internet. I received a flood of positive responses, including this one from a person who remembered our Daddy.

> *I am a native Memphian and worked with Daniel Hanrahan at Aetna Casualty & Surety in the late 1950's. He was quite a character and could always come up with something to make us laugh during the workday. Folks like that are always nice to be around and people like them as they did Mr. Hanrahan. I thought you might like to know that people fondly remember your dad.*

Johnny's "Blaze of Glory"

Jessica and I were living in St. Petersburg, Florida, in 1985 and deeply involved in organizing for our dream of a Catholic Worker-inspired homeless shelter and drop-in advocacy center.

We arrived home to our apartment not far from the Friends Meeting House one evening to find a note on the door:

"Call home at once."

We didn't have a home telephone, so we walked to the corner convenience store and called Mama. She was matter of fact, but her grief was deep. Johnny was dead.

John Vincent was only thirty-two when he fell three floors to his death November 5, 1985. He was a laborer in the construction of The Club apartment complex in Germantown, Tennessee.

"I'm going out in a blaze of glory!" Johnny predicted, talking with Vernua just days before his death.

Johnny was the seventh of we nine, and a handsome blues-singing rebel who took up numerous occupations in his short life, including a stint in the Memphis rail yards. He studied television production at Northside high school and at Shelby State Community College and then in Texas at Austin Community College. He produced programs for WQOX, the Memphis Board of Education television channel, and produced and directed a series of programs for Cable Channel 32 featuring Blues and Rock 'N Roll music.

The Half Life of a Free Radical

I loved Johnny with a love reserved for wandering and lost gleemen born out of their time. He was a minstrel of sorts, traveling about with music in his heart and many a story to tell. When Johnny died, falling backward into a pile of construction rubble, it was again Danny who negotiated with the undertakers. I was forewarned by family peacemakers to keep quiet, so I stood at the back of the funeral parlor, observing from a distance as a parade of familiar faces filed past the open coffin.

The day was marked with the sentimental funeral music, the swollen and tearful eyes of visitors, the delivery of dozens of sprays of flowers, many from local bars, and the repetitious drone of the Rosary recited by the still-loyal Catholics among us. I bade Johnny farewell and placed a small poem in his coffin. I was raging inside at the loss of my fine young brother.

Young and handsome brother
 Good bye, good bye.
You shared your truth With humor wry.
Why, for wages cheap
Did you have to die?

Johnny's Native American friend, Richard Galvin, was the first to reach our brother after he fell. He held Johnny as he slipped away. At the funeral parlor, Richard stood tall in silent tribute beside the coffin.

"I'm carrying Johnny's spirit for you," he told us, and with his hand to his heart assured each of us, "Johnny is here." I had no doubt that he was.

One time, as I railed against the pollution of automobiles and the incessant road building that destroyed our neighborhood and made pedestrian travel so difficult, Johnny challenged me.

"If you don't like all the busy roads and gas fumes, why do you keep using a car?" So in his honor, not long after his death, I sold my old beater of a car to the scrap yard. Since then I have relied on bus and barter, foot and pedal to make my way.

Johnny enjoyed his many nieces and nephews. Jessica remembers: "Uncle Johnny always wanted us to think for ourselves, to get away from the TV and to read a book. But he did like to get his chance to watch the music programs on MTV."

Requiem Aeternam

Johnny had been living on Tutwiler in a small back apartment. In addition to finding work on various construction sites, he was occasionally employed as a nude model at the Memphis College of Art. While there he heard of a covert plan to turn the 1937-era Overton Park band shell into a parking lot for the Brooks Art Gallery.

Johnny began making the rounds on his bicycle with a petition to save the shell. He was determined to prevent destruction of the amphitheater where a nineteen-year-old Elvis Presley in 1954 had played what some have called the first "Rock 'N Roll" show.

I still have a postcard that Johnny sent to Jessica and me just days before his death. It pictures a North American Indian dancer in full ceremonial dress leaping over high flames. In his cursive handwriting Johnny's last words to Jessica and me were full of love:

Hello, I was missing you so I thought I would drop you a line.
Hope everything is going O.K. Love and kisses,
Your Brother/Uncle, John

During his wake after the formal funeral, family and friends decided to take action in Johnny's name. The Overton Park Shell was part of Memphis music history. Carl Perkins, Johnny Cash, Waylon Jennings and many others had also made their first public appearances on that stage. As children, my siblings and I would walk the few miles in the hot summer nights to hear Memphis musicians in open-air concerts there.

So we formed the "Save Our Shell" committee and adjourned to the deteriorating band shell in Overton Park. With hammers in hand we began the work of reclaiming the Memphis landmark. We decorated the stage with Johnny's funeral flowers and painted a new sign: "The John Hanrahan Memorial Shell."

We piled rotted wooden seats in the street. I remember that we set them afire, but Eileen says we didn't. Perhaps I just wished we had. Nonetheless, the SOS movement, Save our Shell, was ignited. By the next summer the campaign was well under way.

An article in *The Commercial Appeal* featured a full-color, full-page photo of some of the volunteers, including Eileen. John's friend David Leonard, a disk jockey for the community radio WEVL, became president of Save Our Shell, Inc. He spoke well of our brother:

The Half Life of a Free Radical

> *John put out one newsletter and did lots of historical research. He was onto the fact that some people with Brooks and the city wanted to tear the shell down for a museum expansion. Now John wasn't an organizer or a man of wealth and power. But he was a dreamer, and he saw the importance of this before the rest of us. Damned if it didn't take his dying for us to realize how important it was.*[103]

The grassroots campaign took hold, and the Overton Park Shell reopened in 1987 for its Fiftieth Anniversary. The Mayor presented Mama with a Key to the City and the band played "When Johnny comes marching home again."

Many years later, I wandered over to the Overton Park Shell for some quiet moments, pen in hand:

Back in Memphis where memories come hard,
Thinking of Johnny, lost brother and bard.

A pick-up blues band in Overton Park Shell,
Practices the rhythms you loved so well.

You are everywhere brother as the fall breeze blows,
Across weathered plank benches in long empty rows.

The silver light gilds the long-leaf Pine,
Your rainbow stage brightens visionary brother of mine.

For the next twenty years, the "Save our Shell" committee managed the venue, offering as many as forty music concerts a year. The Overton Park Shell is now well-funded and professionally managed by the Levitt Foundation, but it would not have been preserved as a beloved Memphis landmark without Johnny's efforts, and those of many others who loved and missed him.

Peter L. Sides and Katie Rhodes, wrote a poem for our family:

The Hanrahan clan is A valiant bunch
They don't lose heart and they don't tire much
They just keep fighting with might and main
With Irish pluck and an active brain

Requiem Aeternam

With sinews and a will to win
They get back up and fight again
Their women handsome their brothers strong
They're worth a cheer or a battle song.

Danny's Last Waltz

I don't remember now just which sibling had the task to tell me of Danny's death. Perhaps it was Michael. I was in St. Petersburg where Jessica and I managed the ASAP woman's shelter and drop-in center with our homeless friends.

"Danny's dead."

Michael's voice was somber. It was July 29, 1988. Danny was only forty-one. He had not been well for some time. He contracted Malaria in Viet Nam, and developed thyroid cancer from exposure to some of the millions of gallons of Agent Orange dumped on that besieged country.

Later I learned that surgeons had cut out much of Danny's tongue and into the lymph glands of his neck, then released him too soon from the hospital. Any healing was hindered by his drinking. He hemorrhaged from the wound, bleeding out in our mother's apartment.

Mama was frantic in her efforts to save him and ran down nine flights of stairs seeking help. Blood transfusions at the hospital came too late. Mama later had to engage in a difficult legal struggle with the hospital which attempted to charge her for blood transfusions dated days after Danny had been declared dead.

Danny's death forced me to confront feelings I had long buried. We hadn't agreed on any topic in years. Our chance meetings at a sibling's house or family gathering were strained. Alone in my room when I heard the news, I sat down, trying to absorb the shock.

I was taken by a strong impulse to turn on the radio. The Lettermen were singing "Theme from A Summer Place." It had been one of Danny's favorite songs. I was rushed with memories, not of our differences or of the barriers that kept us apart, but of that last summer we teenagers spent together before our brothers went off to the war.

The Half Life of a Free Radical

It was the summer of 1965 when the gang of us gathered. Teenagers waltzing into life and love, alive with the promise of youth, and ignorant of the toll the war would take.

My brothers were hard-drinking men, especially after returning from Viet Nam. While I struggled to keep my head above water as a single mother, Danny and Tommy were drowning in the alcohol that was no antidote to the moral damage and poisons of war. Danny had really tried, I believe, to get back in charge of his life. Like his brother Tommy, he spent time in and out of alcohol rehabilitation centers, but he could not beat that insidious curse.

Danny's only child, also Daniel, was not yet three when his parents divorced. Danny by then had lost his job and his home and was living with Robert and Vernua in the small and crowded house on Faxon where we were raised.

Back in St. Petersburg, Jessica and I had just been through an intense crisis at the homeless shelter. We had nearly lost our friend and co-worker Bruce to a terrible assault. He had been on duty at the Drop-In Center desk when a mentally-ill woman pulled a knife and began stabbing. His blood pooled on the floor as she fled to the street.

As Bruce lay near death at the hospital, we got the call about brother Danny's death. Jessica decided to stay in St. Petersburg to be with Bruce, who loved her like a father should. This gentle man had been a mainstay of the drop-in center, managing the day-to-day operations and keeping a kind and loving eye out for us. I needed to stay, but I had to go.

I took the Greyhound the next morning from St. Petersburg to Memphis, winding through the deep South, passing from a landscape of palmetto shrub and royal palm into fields of soy and cotton. The kudzu vines choked the life out of the tallest roadside trees, like that war and its insidious poisons had finally choked the life out of my strong, handsome brother.

The journey was surreal. In the half sleep of the Greyhound night we were rousted off the bus in every station, to line up again at the doors, weary, disheveled, and caught in the harsh white fluorescence.

As the bus rolled into the night through Alabama, Mississippi, and into Tennessee, Danny's life and our lives together in our long-ago childhood passed across my mind. Amid the coughing and snoring, and the few quiet conversations among riders, I felt how vulnerable we all were jostling down that dark highway, bodies

Requiem Aeternam

sprawled out or curled tight, strangers falling into restless sleep in those few quiet hours between the station stops. Strangers with our private thoughts, our secret pains, cramped and crowded, yet oddly connected with an unspoken bond.

Will Danny connect? Will he find ease and comfort at the end of his journey? Finally, will he walk into the light again, the healing light? I remember the twenty-year-old Danny before he rode into the hellish night of that goddamn war, and now, the forty-one year old, finally finding rest from his torments. He had been a proud Marine, following Tommy to Viet Nam, he participated in the war in ways that utterly changed him.

By the time I arrived home, funeral arrangements had been made. Danny would've liked it, I suppose. Five or six priests celebrated a Requiem Mass at Sacred Heart Church. Danny had been attending services there before he died. The pews were filled with grieving friends, including both of his ex-wives and his young son.

At the funeral parlor Tommy took my hand and we walked together to the open coffin. It was difficult to stand beside Tommy as he viewed his twin lying dead. My own feelings were tumultuous. I was surprised by the sudden urge to pummel Danny as he lay there helpless before me. There was so much unsaid and unfinished between us. Now he was gone before we could find our peace with one another.

Tommy arranged a six-gun salute at Memphis National Cemetery with Marines in dress-blue uniform. They fired a round into the sky in tribute, and then carefully folded the flag that draped our brother's coffin and handed it to Mama. I could barely contain my rage. Tommy held me back.

"Danny would have wanted this," he said.

We had a final gathering at Tommy's home where the Irish whiskey flowed and everyone shared the good memories they had of Daniel Joseph while taking a nip of the dog that had so fiercely bitten him.

I don't even remember the last time we tried to talk with each other, perhaps it was at Johnny's funeral where he railed against his younger brother's death as they lowered his coffin into the ground.

Eileen said Danny had intended to make peace with me and had talked about coming to visit before he became so sick.

Whatever the hurt that separated us, it is better put to rest, as Danny is, in that cool Tennessee dirt where we grew up, doing the best we could.

Tommy's last Climb

Like his twin, Tommy never recovered from that war and the Agent Orange poisons that coursed through his system. He suffered especially from the peripheral neuropathy that limited his ability to walk. He died alone in his mid-town Memphis apartment. The last to see him alive were the homeless veterans he visited at the nearby Vets Center.

It was early March, 1996, when the telephone call came, and still cold and gray outside.

"Tommy's dead." Michael's voice was terse. It carried a chill finality.

"When?" I asked.

"We don't know," Michael replied. "They found him in his apartment. He had been dead a few days."

It took a moment for this grim message to move from my head to my heart. I asked a few questions about the funeral and when we were to gather in Memphis. A deep level of sadness settled in over me, muffling a rage that could not break free. Tommy was gone. It was time to bury a third brother.

I went outside to my garden and picked up the shovel to plant some seed potatoes. As I worked, memories of one of my last visits with my brother were with me.

"I have everything I need within a few blocks," Tommy had said as we stood together on the roof of his mid-town apartment in the summer of 1995. The rooftop breeze was a refreshing change from the hot pavement below.

"I can walk to the grocery store, to a restaurant, and to the library," he said, pointing out the directions as he spoke. But I don't think he had been doing much walking lately. He struggled with a cane and moved slowly as we took the steps to and from the roof. It was hard to see him so infirm.

Tommy's last paid employment had been in the reference department of the Memphis Public Library. He seemed to thrive in the midst of books. But Tommy could not put down the bottle. He

Requiem Aeternam

lost his job with the library, likely due to his alcohol dependence. It must have been a hard blow.

He kept a neat apartment. He had a TV, a single bed, a small table with books stacked nearby, and a few chairs. The kitchen and bathroom were tiny. His large storage closet was filled with camping equipment from his more active days.

The apartment was just a few minutes' from Mama's apartment, and she often walked over to have lunch with him. She never gave up on her war-wounded sons.

After his death we discovered some handwritten notes on Tommy's desk. A tragic litany of the emotional and physical toll of the war, and of his years trying to overcome the trauma. Three separate times in treatment facilities for alcoholism, the PTSD group he attended twice weekly, and the help he received from the Vet Center in Memphis with counselors Ed Wallen and Claire Garcia.

All of this, tragically, was not enough to counter the burden he carried. In the papers he left on the table, he wrote of his "fears, apprehension, and self-doubt," and of his "inability to maintain a relationship."

"No one seems to understand where I am coming from, and I no longer have any idea of where I am going," he wrote. "I am unable to hold jobs for any sustained length of time ...I feel that I do not fit in society. ...most friends are dead."

The notes are sparse. Merely an outline of a life stolen by that filthy, rotten war machine. He had become "a recluse," tormented by "sleeplessness, dreams, flashbacks, distrust of authority, lack of concentration, isolation, inability to feel at ease around others."

Then he lists the physical challenges of the peripheral neuropathy from the Agent Orange toxins that make it difficult for him to walk, to button his shirt, to operate simple machines.

I can barely write this account. The rage I still feel at the loss of my fine brothers wants to spill out over the page. It is my defense against the grief still buried.

Many years before his death I had one of my clearest dreams with Tommy:

> *I came upon my brother sitting inside one of the two large oak trees that grew in the small front yard of our childhood home. He carried an aura of authority and wisdom about him like a Druid priest. The tree*

The Half Life of a Free Radical

was immense. Tommy held forth in a cozy nook in the hollowed-out center surrounded by ancient leather-bound books. He looked up and said: "There are only a few books worth reading."

It's just a fragment of a dream. But it seemed to reflect a deeper truth about Thomas Joseph Hanrahan. Though he may have told me which books were "worth reading," I don't remember now what they may have been. The alcoholism, combined with the horrible burden of pain he carried from his Viet Nam War experiences and the Agent Orange toxins were the death of him.

"That's how they've kept the Irish down," Michael quipped once as we talked about the ravages of alcohol. "Otherwise, we'd rule the world."

I am still haunted by the image of Tommy's cane hanging on the inside knob of his front door. It was the day after his funeral. He would not have minded had I taken it then. I sensed that he was somehow present as my gaze rested on the simple wooden stick that had helped him walk.

Tommy was dead. His blood spilled and dried in a dark pool on the kitchen floor where his body may have lain for days before it was discovered. No one in the family had been notified when the building caretaker, his friend, unlocked his apartment to check on him and found him dead. The police forgot to follow up.

Tommy's body lay in the city morgue, unclaimed for days, until Mama and Robert's daughter Katrina walked over to check on him at his apartment. They wanted to take him to lunch. Tommy had no phone so they could not call. The office staff in the apartment offered Mama their condolences as she came in.

"What do you know that I don't know?" she asked. It was the first she had heard of his death. Dear Vernua went to the morgue to identify the body. Tommy's missing middle fingers on his right hand, lost so many years ago on a battlefield in Viet Nam, was all she needed to tell them:

"Yes. This was our brother, Thomas Patrick."

Eternal rest grant unto him, oh Lord, and let perpetual light shine upon him. May he rest in peace.

The funeral Mass was held at the chapel on the grounds of the St. Peter Manor. Mama had helped raise the funds that built the chapel. Regina and I asked to have time to speak. Childhood friend

Requiem Aeternam

Ricky Gantert, now in priestly robes, said the Mass. His parents had come often to our home when we were young. Ricky tolerated well the impropriety when I seized the pulpit and lectured the congregation about the evils of war. Jessica came to stand with me. I spoke of my brothers' service as altar boys, and of their time in the Marines in Viet Nam going from altar boys to boy soldiers trained to kill.

"The next time you hear the drums of war beating, remember my brothers," I said. "How many more must die?" When we made our way back to our seat, Mama leaned over to whisper in my ear:

"Tommy would have liked that." Then she added, "Don't you make a recitation at my funeral."

One December 5th, many years later, Tommy was heavy on my heart when I went to sleep and fell into a dream:

My sisters and I are trying to hold steady a wooden ladder that reaches high beyond the tree tops. Tommy is climbing, climbing, trying to hold his balance and make it to the top. The ladder is leaning as he climbs, and we try, we try so very hard to lean it against something solid, a tall building, so he can reach the roof and safety. But no, the gap is too wide. He leaps and falls, too far, too far, he falls. And so close to the edge of safety when he falls.

Now Tommy too lies dead and buried in that cold Tennessee dirt, buried in his mother's grave, because the Memphis National Cemetery was full.

"No ma'am, he can't share his brother's grave."

But Mama said, "That's how they came into the world. Why? Oh why can't they be buried together?"

"We don't bury men on top of men," they told our Mother, but they gave her the flag, and fired a salute to that rabid dog of war that killed her two handsome sons.

Emotions were raw between my sisters and me. Mary and Regina were at Mama's apartment when Eileen and I asked who was going over to clean our brother's apartment. Eileen said she would help. Mary and Regina did not respond. Eileen and I left and arrived about a half hour later at our brother's apartment. When we asked at the office for the key, they said our sisters were already there. We knocked at the door and when Regina opened it I confronted her.

"Why didn't you tell us you were coming here?" I asked.

The Half Life of a Free Radical

The resulting shouting match was unparalleled in our adult lives. Regina exploded in shrill anger and left. Eileen became quiet and sat down. Mary seemed fragile and vulnerable.

"Why are you accusing us?" she asked. "I just wanted to come and be quiet here in my brother's home. Holding his blanket to her breast she was shaking with grief and emotion.

It has been too hard to sort through all the emotions unleashed that day. Mary left the apartment soon after Regina did. It was dusk and she was not used to walking city streets on her own. Eileen and I stayed. As I mopped up our brother's blood, Eileen sat reading from the notebook he had left on the table.

Mama was so worried about Mary that she ran out in the rainy dusk of that March evening to find her. Later that night, when we all gathered at a nearby restaurant for dinner, I approached Mama for a hug. She stiffened and turned away.

Still, after all these intervening years, I have been unable to work out just what happened that day. We just could not find the comfort we needed in one another. It was the last time we four sisters were all together. Grief takes a harsh and dreadful toll.

Endless Wars

In 2003, with yet another war imminent, I was asked to speak at an anti-war rally in Asheville. I wrote Michael and asked advice:

"What shall I say?" Writing back, Michael advised:

> *Tell them of our yard in Memphis—full of broken men and dreams. Of Gus the sniper who went to Canada because they wouldn't let him go back after two tours; of Charlie who sang better than Roy Orbison missing two inches from the middle of his leg. Of Bill the virgin who left his testicles on a field.*
>
> *So many crips filled that summer of '68. I wish I could remember them all. They felt at home on Faxon far from the war yet still far from home. They were only wounded, they did not really count. You know every year or so one of them calls our mom and tells her "thank you."*
>
> *The last person to see our brother Tom was the head of the Vet center in Memphis. Tommy had dropped in to talk to some of the homeless vets. He handed out a few dollars. Then went home and died alone.*

Requiem Aeternam

> *I do not feel he died alone. I feel he died part of an orchestra of pain singing in the choir of never again. Let your speech resound with their pain. Tell them you will welcome the soldiers home however they return. But just maybe this time they won't be maimed in body and soul.*
>
> *God bless the Bill of Rights and the Constitution of the United States.* –Michael Hanrahan

The Veterans' Truth

Many veterans shared their stories at that peace rally in Asheville in 2003. It was a powerful plea for another way.

No more war.
No more spending young lives in the horror of slaughter.
No more distorting noble ideals to the cold, calculated strategy of generals.
No more killing enemies who shift and change at politicians' whim.
No more profit to the weapons merchants.
No more flag-draped coffins for the mothers, and sisters, brothers and wives and children.
No more war!

It was the veterans' voices that were most compelling that day— especially the one who sat in the center of our peace rally— the late stage, end stage alcoholic. His face was rough, puffy and red, his clothes soiled and ill fitting, his eyes tormented, his visage that of a soul lost.

What I need to say is how much this broken, discarded, homeless Viet Nam veteran has touched me.

I watched as he mouthed the words of the Constitution as a Gulf War veteran recited it from the speakers' platform. This tormented soul knew every word.

I struggled with some aversion when this discarded warrior approached me after the rally. What maudlin tale of woe would he relate in slurred incoherence? What disruption to my afternoon plans?

"I served in Nam. I was there," he began. Then his face contorted in a pain I'd seen on my own brothers' faces— a flashback to a lost youth spent in that jungle war.

"I ran," he said. "I was afraid and I turned and I ran."

I put my hand on his shoulder as I listened.

"I'm so sorry," I said, as he stumbled away, bleary eyed and immensely sad.

What I need to say is how much this broken and defeated man reminds me of my own dead brothers. Viet Nam's bloody jungles took their youth. Drink and battlefield toxins took their health. They bore the burden of that war, a war whose horror we still cannot face.

Now this man—this lone, remnant soldier sitting in our midst in this rally for peace—this once proud soldier listens, teary-eyed, as other veterans from more recent wars tell their stories.

This late stage, end stage, homeless alcoholic may never recover his voice, or his clarity, or his health, but his presence among us speaks the truth of war in a way no other voice can. He bears witness to the ongoing costs and the unfinished healing.

I want to turn away. Don't make me look. Don't remind me now of my own late stage, end stage alcoholic veteran brothers, now dead and gone—too soon dead and gone. Their idealism spent, and all but forgotten as we rush forward into yet another war.

We have not yet fully grieved the past wars, not yet really looked into the faces of those soldiers who three decades ago lost youth, innocence, hope, and future on the killing fields of Viet Nam.

That homeless alcoholic in our midst, reciting the Constitution by heart. He too, with his unsightly presence, speaks the truth about war. Will we listen?

Mama's Last Goodbye

The voice in my head was matter-of-fact and clear: "Pack like you're going tomorrow."

I had been wide awake through most of the night worrying about Mama and how I would get enough money to make it back to Memphis. I knew if I did not heed the prompt, I would likely not be able to fall asleep.

I went to the closet and pulled out the thrift-store suitcase. I had been putting off trying to mend the lining. It had been ripped from the backing and the zipper broken. Feeling around in a corner I was

Requiem Aeternam

astounded to find a handful of colorful twenty-pound notes stuffed inside. They were illustrated with a likeness of the Queen of England, and looked like play money to me. I finished packing, still marveling at what I had discovered, and then fell into a deep sleep.

Early the next morning I showed the money to my neighbor, the folk singer Peggy Seeger. She often traveled to England and would recognize the currency.

"Are these real?" I asked. She assured me they were and then offered to check the exchange rate and give me the equivalent in dollar bills. It was just enough cash for the round-trip Greyhound ticket. Just enough.

I took the next bus out to Memphis. Mama's frequent mantra, "God provides," echoed in my mind as the bus made its way along the familiar Interstate route from Asheville, over the mountains and through Knoxville, Nashville, Jackson, and finally, after a long and restless night, rolled into the Memphis station.

Mama was living then at St. Peter Villa, a Catholic nursing home adjacent to her apartment at St. Peter Manor. Twice when I visited with her before her memory failed, she had asked that I walk with her to the Villa to check that she was still in line for a room. She had placed her name on the waiting list several years before she needed the care. Looking back now, I am grateful. Mama made it clear to me that this had been her intention all along for the time when she could no longer live alone.

The red-brick, four-story building is the final home for many of Memphis' low-income Catholics and Medicare-supported elders. The inter-racial living quarters are a stark contrast to the apartheid Memphis most residents had known in their younger days. Separated once by Jim Crow's cruel dictates, these keepers of much of the rich history of the Mid-South shared bedroom and bath, day room and dining tables and the last years of their lives.

When I arrived, the Villa was busy with the goings and comings of employees, residents and visitors. I found Mama in the day room among other residents parked in their wheelchairs, nodding and dozing in front of the nurse's station, or just staring ahead, paying little heed to the incessant drone of the television. Light poured in through the open blinds and rested here and there on the tiled floor, a blessed relief from the harsh fluorescence of the hallways. The day

The Half Life of a Free Radical

was warm so I quickly wheeled Mama outside where we could sit beneath a shade tree looking out across the landscaped grounds.

Mama was always gracious, never demanding in her welcome when I arrived. But I felt deep regret during my visits that my own lifestyle choices to live below a taxable income as a war-tax refuser had left me unable to take her home with me. It would have been impossible to properly care for her in the bartered-for, wood-heated, dilapidated house where I lived far from Memphis. It was then that my appreciation for Vernua and Robert was strongest. They were our Mama's every-day visitors and loving care-takers to the end. All her other children had fled Memphis long ago, and returning was both financially and emotionally too hard for frequent visits. When they could, they came.

Mama's first roommate, who I knew only as Mrs. Ollie, wore her gray hair pulled tight into a top braid. She held forth with kind authority. Mrs. Ollie had the window side of the room. She filled her corner with bright plastic flower arrangements and her tiny dresser with photos of her large family, "all college graduates," she proudly announced.

"I look out for your Mama at night," she told me once. "She gets to scooting around. We don't want her to get all broke up."

Throughout most of her stay at the Villa, Mama could get around independently in her wheelchair. She moved up and down the hallways looking in on her neighbors, much as she had done when we lived on Faxon Avenue.

Mrs. Ollie's reminiscences were from the other side of the Memphis color line. Her father had been a railroad man she told me, and an old-time preacher who "sold his land for a song and a dance."

"I'm here to stay," she declared one afternoon, "So I'm going to have to change my address so I can vote from this precinct."

Mrs. Ollie had been a registrar of voters and a ward and precinct clerk for the Democrats of Shelby County for decades.

"I am known throughout the state of Tennessee by the Democrats. I worked for all of them," she told me.

Later Mama shared a room with Miss Addie. The companionship they kept was subtle and poignant. Miss Addie was much, much younger, but she couldn't see, hear, or speak clearly. Neither could she tend to her most basic needs beyond the rudimentary way she

Requiem Aeternam

ate, pushing the food into her mouth with both hands while making many and varied sounds of satisfaction. It seemed her only pleasure.

Mama was well tuned to Miss Addie. Sometimes, when I was sure both were making only the quiet sounds of sleepers, Mama would stir, her silky thin silver hair sliding across her pillow. Gaining my attention she would whisper:

"Check to see if Miss Addie needs something. She might want water." Mama understood Miss Addie in ways, it seemed, that even the long-time attendants could not.

The metal beds in the small rooms were separated by a textured plastic curtain. A small cork bulletin board held large-print phone numbers of family. I pinned a photo of our Mama there: a news clipping from her college days when she won an award for "journalistic excellence" as editor of *The Flame*, the Siena College student newspaper. She was a beauty then, and her beauty seemed never to fade.

At the Villa, middle-age or older daughters tended to their mothers, and provided some relief to the overworked staff, mostly women of color, whose motions seemed tired, perfunctory, but always kind. They wore brightly-patterned uniforms and spoke in the distinctive vernacular of Memphis' black working poor.

The noise was incessant: slamming doors, the clanking of meal carts, televisions blaring on competing channels, nurse's sneakers squeaking and wheel-chaired feet skimming up and down the linoleum halls, blaring buzzers and beepers. Amid the noise and the smells, the fluorescent harshness exposed the drooling, slouching, moaning, crowded, dying poor. It was hard to be there, and hard to leave.

The nurses' station reminded me of the guards' station in my barracks at Alderson Federal Prison. As it was with my fellow prisoners, many residents had been long cut off from family by distance and circumstance. There was resignation in some, determination in others, and the balm of kindness and solidarity among them.

Large photos of the current Bishop and the Pope, dressed in their ceremonial garb, hung in the reception area. A gilded statue of the Little Infant of Prague stood just beside an elevator that groaned its way up to the residential floors. In his left hand, the infant Jesus held a tiny globe topped by a cross. His right hand was raised in

The Half Life of a Free Radical

blessing. The statue was decorated with an ornate embroidered cloak and a jeweled crown.

In old Ireland, smaller versions of the Infant of Prague were placed under hedge rows or buried in the garden to ensure good weather and to keep the family free of want. That was a particularly important appeal during the years of The Great Hunger. But there was a different kind of hunger here at the Villa, where so many of Memphis' poor lived.

On one visit in her last months, I found Mama sitting in the corner of her room, her frail body leaning to one side, her head bowed. Her bed was made up and her water pitcher had been filled. The window blinds were open to a view of a sycamore leafing out. Sunlight brightened the room. Vernua had been there. She came every day. Her romance novel was still open on the window sill next to the philodendron. Its roots were matted in Mama's emerald-green, cut-glass vase, a long-ago gift from Daddy.

Standing behind Mama's chair, I stroked her damp, freshly-shampooed hair and announced myself.

"Mama, It's Clare. I'm back." She stirred, then looked up as a quiet smile crossed her face, as if she had expected me all along.

"It is so good to see you, Mama. Can I help you with anything?" Her voice was barely audible. I had to lean in close to hear her reply.

"I want to lie down," she said. It had been over a month since my last visit and she had not been able to stand alone then. The nurses were busy with others, so I moved the chair close to the bed, locked the wheels and helped her to her feet. In a waltz-like maneuver we danced to the edge of the bed and I sat her down. Resting for a breath, I scooped her legs in my arms, pivoting her around as I lifted her swollen feet. God, she was frail. I could feel each bone.

As soon as her head settled on the pillow, she closed her eyes and fell asleep. I closed the blinds. In the dim light beside Mama's bed, keeping vigil as she slept, I thought of my own life and how it might be for me in my last years.

Every six weeks I came to be with Mama, spending a week of days at her side. We found our way out of doors as often as we could to sit beneath the tall oaks and look up at the blue, blue sky. She called it "cerulean blue." Some of the trees there were so old that Mama remembered sitting beneath them as a child.

Requiem Aeternam

We lived in the moment. Watching the robins prance across the wide expanse of lawn, feeling the breeze, listening to the bird song. I experienced so much healing in those sacred moments with my Mama in her last days. It was her final gift.

Mending Mama's Quilt

Mama's crocheted quilt is one of the few family heirlooms to survive over the years, and barely so. The quilt has been snagged on door jambs, dragged over the wooden floors, heaped in the corner, spilled on, peed on, and otherwise ill used to the point that many of the multi-colored wool squares have unraveled and been pulled apart from the whole.

Mama kept the still-ragged relic with her when she moved to her mid-town apartment. I have that quilt now, though not the needle crafting skills to properly restore it. So as best I can, I have patched the squares and woven the loose strands, attempting to make it whole again. It seems a fitting metaphor for this years-long project recounting stories of my life and of my family. Many threads are missing, hopelessly unraveled, as memory can become.

The story is stitched together with the limitations of my own perspective and skill. Sometimes while I write, I pull Mama's old quilt up over my legs and onto my lap. It is nearly eighty-years-old now, and still warms me.

On her eightieth birthday, October 29, 1997, Mama wrote me from her email account: Hunigram@prodigy.com

> *Dear Clare, Thanks for your great letter. It does my heart good to know you remember the good things, like dandelions that always brightened my outlook when they came unbidden to smile up at me when I bowed my head in sorrow. Little bits of sunshine scattered at my feet.*
> *Mama*

I am grateful for the times I could be with Mama in her last years. Just being there, quietly sitting. Without words. I saw many emotions play across her face. Sometimes she seemed like a little girl, crying for her long-lost mother. Another time, she would brighten with the confident smile of a young woman. Now and then a worried look would appear, later a serene one. Sometimes she cried, softly, as some old sorrow passed through. So many aspects of my Mama were visible as she moved in silent memory from place to place through time, or no time.

During a visit at Eileen's home near Rogersville, Tennessee, on Thanksgiving Day in 1996, I encouraged Mama to write about her life. She had kept so much of her story to herself. As we talked I could feel her pain and could understand how hard it must have been for her throughout her thirty-four-year marriage.

She wrote of her early life, of her grandmother and father, and her life and work before she married. That is where she ended her story. When I gathered her essays and published them into a small book, I brought it to her at the nursing home. She ran her fingers over the cover, and lingered a while on her name: Alice Donnelly Hanrahan.

"I don't really know that person anymore," she said, turning to the window to point out how the light played on the lawn outside. Mama slipped away quietly sometime in the night of March 30, 2007. Robert had tucked her in before she fell asleep. He was the one who called me with the news of her passing.

We buried Mama in Memphis National Cemetery, in that cold Tennessee dirt, on top of Daddy's grave. She had long before given her own grave to bury her son, Thomas Patrick, when the cemetery refused to allow him to be buried in the same grave with his twin. "We don't bury men on top of men."

I had so much that I wanted to say about our Mama before they lowered her casket into the ground, but I held my tongue, keeping in mind what she told me at Tommy's funeral Mass: "Don't make a recitation at my funeral."

Jessica stood to the occasion, sharing a poem she wrote for her "gorgeous, lovely, perfect, wonderful, magnificent, marvelous, Grandmama," as Jessica and her cousin Katrina lovingly described their Grandmother.

The dandelions were in bloom when Mama died. Her children, scattered like seeds on the winds, could scarcely believe she was gone. Separated by death and geography and unhealed hurts, we and our progeny have bloomed in the crevices and broken places of our lives to brighten the world in ways that would make our parents proud.

The dandelions are blooming again today as I write these last words of my story. The "Little bits of sunshine scattered at my feet,"

Requiem Aeternam

that our Mama so loved. My siblings now are grandparents and great-grandparents, with several generations of the Donnelly-Hanrahan clan finding their way and holding the ground the length of Tennessee from the mighty Mississippi to the Great Smokey mountains and beyond.

Despite all the hardships, our parents imparted in us all an appreciation of the every-day graces and simple pleasures of life, and a respect for the dignity and worth of all. No small accomplishment, and one that is bearing the fruit of right action in diverse ways.

The Half Life of a Free Radical

"May you have the commitment to harvest your life, to heal what has hurt you, to allow it to come closer to you and become one with you."

–From *A Blessing for Old Age*, John O'Donohue

The Half Life of a Free Radical

Appendix

Heaven's Angel
(Jessica's graveside poem for her grandmother)

Heaven gained a precious angel,
On this day when we all cry.
As we mourn the greatest loss,
There is rejoicing in the sky.

So feel the pain,
We miss her so.
But soon it's time,
To let her go.

She's free. She's free. Her time has come,
To reap what she has sown.
The seeds of love she planted,
Look around see what she's grown.

Our faith, our families,
Our love for all.
She planted these values,
Within us all.

Rejoice, rejoice and weep no more,
She's with the angel's who've gone before.
She's bathed in light from God above,
And with us always in the form of love.

The Half Life of a Free Radical

Let's Really Support Our Soldiers

Feb 26, 2003 / vol 9 no 29,
Mountain Xpress, Asheville, North Carolina

by Clare Hanrahan

"The time for dissent is passed once the war is declared," one Asheville resident wrote in a recent letter to the editor of a local publication, echoing the sentiments of many who fear for the lives of their loved ones in this coming war.

"Don't undermine the morale of our troops now that they're deployed," is another caution, skillfully manipulated by a government determined to go to war despite calls by millions of mainstream people worldwide for restraint, diplomacy and genuine efforts to avoid another barbaric assault on the people of Iraq.

This war is wrong. It is an immoral and illegal act of terror. It will continue to be wrong throughout its bloody course. The men and women in the U.S. military – armed with the most terrible weapons ever devised, and deployed to toxic battlefields – are now awaiting orders to unleash hellfire on a country and a people already devastated and starved. Throughout Western North Carolina, this military call-up has torn asunder family after family. Already the human collateral damage of past wars and of the ongoing domestic war on the poor fills our streets, while funds for health care, housing, education and transportation are cut to the bone.

If this war continues, many of our sons and daughters, husbands and fathers in the military will be returned to us only as ashes (a measure proposed by Pentagon war planners to limit contamination from soldiers exposed to anthrax, smallpox or other toxins), and we may never even hear about the hundreds of thousands of Iraqi people – most of them noncombatants – who will also die.

Those who have called a "Support Our Soldiers" rally in Asheville attempt to equate dissent with disrespect for the men and women who have chosen the military path. This is deceitful, divisive and dangerous. Many among the nearly 2,000 people who gathered in Asheville on Feb. 15 to say no to this war are veterans; others have lost loved ones in previous conflicts and would not wish this grief on any other family.

We oppose this war because it is wrong and unnecessary. We oppose this war because it violates the very Constitution our soldiers have sworn to uphold. We oppose this war because we fear our government's unchecked power far more than we fear the dangerous dictator in Iraq. We oppose this war because we believe that the best way to support our soldiers is to refuse to consent to the wanton exploitation of their noble impulse, and the reckless abuse of their precious lives.

When I was a teenager in Memphis, "Back our Boys in Vietnam" was the only bumper sticker my parents ever allowed on our family car. This was after my older brother, Tommy, joined the Marines just out of high school. In solidarity, my sister Eileen and I joined the USO. We wanted to show our support and express our patriotic sentiments. We wanted to do what was right in a time of war, as we believed our brave brother had done when called on by his country.

I was naive, blindly patriotic, and deeply concerned for my family and friends in the military. I would have waved the flag in any "Support our Soldiers" rally.

As a USO volunteer, I met hundreds of young men in transit to Vietnam. Most were too young to vote; too young to drink in the nightclubs; too young, really, to even know why they were drafted to fight, kill and die in Vietnam. Some of them were African-American soldiers, many from Northern cities; even on their way to war, they still had to contend with the ugly racism rampant in Memphis, my hometown.

Brother Tommy made it home a few days before Christmas, 1967. He was wounded and broken in ways only the years would fully reveal. At the VA hospital, I visited with other casualties of that war. Many of these men had no family nearby, so they came to our home on weekends – some on crutches, some missing limbs or with wounds still bandaged. Some just sat on the porch and stared out into space.

It wasn't long before Tommy's twin, Danny, stepped forward. He was in the recruiters' bag before my parents could intervene.

"There was nothing I could do to stop him," my mother lamented. I stood with her the day he left, and I joined her at a local Marine Corps Mothers' Club gathering where women offered one

The Half Life of a Free Radical

another support as their not-quite-grown sons fought and died in Southeast Asia.

One after another, my fine young brothers – bright, handsome and brave – went off to war. One after another, they returned – wounded, poisoned and broken. And one after another, they died – carrying to their early graves the memories of that war and the Agent Orange toxins that coursed through their systems. Their names were never etched on that Wailing Wall in Washington, D.C. Nor were the names of their brothers in arms whose suicides exceed the number of combat deaths, or the names of the many others who still suffer from the delayed stress of that criminal war.

These veterans, forgotten by their country, are joined now by the many spent-and-discarded soldiers from the first Bush's Gulf War – soldiers still seeking the acknowledgment and treatment of their war-induced illnesses while the son of a Bush who called them to war cuts funding for the veterans' hospitals. Is this what we mean by "Support our Troops"?

I will not stand by and wave a flag as this next generation marches off to war. I will not repeat trite platitudes as these men and women are used up and then abandoned by a U.S. government that has broken faith with its noble principles, that fails to protect its citizens – a U.S. regime that threatens the world with the use of first-strike nuclear weapons.

This president who calls for endless war never stood in battle, never struggled for a livelihood, never learned the lessons of the Christianity he claims – nor of the God he invokes in his power-hungry quest for domination and control. It is he – and the other politicians, generals and armchair warriors – who truly undermine the safety and security of our men and women in the military and who constitute the biggest threat to peace in this world.

Last month, I shared a Greyhound journey with some young marines who boarded the bus in Knoxville. They were on their way to Camp Lejeune, and as the night deepened and the bus rolled on through the mountains, I listened to their conversations. They talked about the families they'd left behind, about the pay packet that didn't quite cover their expenses, about their girlfriends and the buddies they'd made in boot camp. One wore a new jacket boldly embroidered with the slogan, "Trained to fight, learned to kill, ready to die, but never will." They were not sophisticated men, just country boys setting off on heroes' journeys – cocky and sure of themselves, and full of the rhetoric instilled by their military indoctrination. Listening to them, I understood my mother's lament: There was nothing I could do to stop them. They could have been the two brothers whose loss I still grieve.

I will continue to voice my opposition to this war – it is my moral and civic duty. And I will continue to support our soldiers with my ongoing, outspoken, risk-taking refusal to cooperate with this government in yet another criminal war.

Clare Hanrahan lives in Asheville. A conscientious objector to war and to paying for war, she is the author of Jailed For Justice: A Woman's Guide to Federal Prison Camp.

Reference Notes

1. Brown, Robbie. "Memphis Drops Confederate Names From Parks, Sowing New Battles." *The New York Times*, March 28, 2013.
2. Bolton, Felicia. "Mayor A C Wharton calls for removal of Confederate monument." WMCActionNews5.com. June 25, 2015.
3. www.memphistn.gov/Visitors/MovingtoMemphis/MemphisChronology/1900s.
4. Roosevelt, Theodore. *The Winning of the West, Part I, The Spread of English Speaking Peoples*. G.P. Putnam's Son, 1889. P. 134.
5. Wright, Muriel H. Chronicles of Oklahoma, Volume 6, No. 4, December, 1928. "The Naming of the Mississippi River." page 529.
6. http://historic-memphis.com/memphis-historic/mainstreet/ mainstreet.html.
7. Atkins, Joseph B. "Memphis and the 1878 Yellow Fever Epidemic: From "Casablanca on the Mississippi" to "City of the Dead." February 5, www.laborsouth.blogspot.com.
8. "An excerpt from the diary of 15th Illinois Infantry soldier William M. Reid concerning his experience at the Battle of Shiloh in Tennessee during the U.S. Civil War." *Civil War Times*. Apr2012, Vol. 51 Issue 2, p50-56. 6p.

9. Hardwick, Kevin R. "Your Old Father Abe Lincoln Is Dead and Damned": Black Soldiers and the Memphis Race Riot of 1866." *Journal of Social History* (1993): 109-128.

10. Waller A. "Community, Class and Race in the Memphis Riot Of 1866." *Journal of Social History* [serial online]. Winter84 1984; 18(2).

11. Forehand, Beverly. "Striking Resemblance: Kentucky, Tennessee, Black Codes and Readjustment, 1865-1866" (1996). Masters Theses, Western Kentucky University, 1966.

12. Ignatiev, Noel. "The Divide Between the Blacks and the Irish." www.theroot.com.

13. Patrick McKenna. "When the Irish Became White: Immigrants in mid 19th century US." www.irishtimes.com/blogs/generationemigration/2013/02/12.

14. Murphy, Angela F. American Slavery, *Irish Freedom: Abolition, Immigrant Citizenship, and the Transatlantic Movement for Irish Repeal*. Baton Rouge: Louisiana State University Press, 2010.

15. Ignatiev, Noel. *How the Irish Became White*. Routledge. New York. 1995, Pg. 140.

16. Knobel, Dale T. *Paddy and the Republic: Ethnicity and Nationality in Antebellum America*. Wesleyan University Press, 1986.

17. Callahan, John F. "About Lynching," *The Oxford Companion to African American Literature*. Oxford University Press, 1997.

18. Padgett, Kenneth. *Blackface! The History of Racist Blackface Stereotypes*. www.black-face.com.

19. Bay, Mia. *To Tell the Truth Freely: The Life of Ida B. Wells*. Macmillan, Feb 2, 2010.

20. Wells, Ida B. *Memphis Free Speech and Headlight*. May 25, 1892.

21. Ramsey, Donovan X. "Police Killings Picked Up Where Lynching Left Off." NewsOne.Com. Aug. 29, 2014.

Reference Notes

22. The Mystic Society of the Memphi. www.memphi.com.

23. Martin, Harold H. "The Cities of America: Memphis" *Saturday Evening Post.* November 16, 1946.

24. Gorm, Elliot. *Mother Jones: The Most Dangerous Woman in America.* New York: Hill and Wang, 2001.

25. "Back to Burke." *The American Conservative.* Volume: 10. Issue: 9. September 2011, P 5.

26. Donnelly, Jim. "The Irish Famine." BBC British History, 2-17-2011. http://www.bbc.co.uk/history/british/victorians/famine

27. Mahony, James. "Sketches in the West of Ireland." *Illustrated London News* (1847).

28. Whyte, *Robert. Robert Whyte's 1847 Famine Ship diary: The Journey of an Irish Coffin Ship.* Irish American Book Company, 1994. www.irishgenealogy-tookkit.com.

29. "Coffin ships: feath and pestilence on the Atlantic." www.irish-genealogy-toolkit.com.

30. Whyte, Robert.

31. The Pogues. *Poor Paddy Works on the Railway.* www.pogues.com.

32. *Our Grandpas Civil War.* "Teachable Moment– Civil War "Impressed" https://ourgrampascivilwar.wordpress.com

33. Park, Martha. "Memphis Burning." *Memphis Flyer*, February 4, 2016.

34. Obituary, *The Commercial Appeal*, Memphis, Tennessee, January, 1922.

35. Hanrahan, Alice Donnelly. *In the Pinch: Memphis Memories.* . Celtic WordCraft, 2006.

36. Blind Lemon Jefferson. *Rising High Water Blues* www.Oldielyrics.com.

37. R.A. Lawson. *Jim Crow's Counterculture: The Blues and Black Southerner*s, 1890-1945. Baton Rouge: Louisiana State University Press, 2010.

38. Hanrahan, Alice Donnelly.

39. Saxon, Elizabeth Lyle. *A Southern Woman's War Time Remembrances*. Press of the Pilcher Printing Company, 1905.

40. Lauderdale, Vance. "Crash in Crosstown, 1944." *Memphis Magazine*, June 2008.

41. "Irish Ancestry, Pre-Famine Emigration." *The Irish Times*. www.theirishtimes.com.

42. "Watchman killed in BRT yard. Fell on Track of L Train." *Brooklyn Daily Eagle*. July 27, 1907.

43. Lyon, Peter. "The Honest Man." *American Heritage*. February, 1959.

44. Hanrahan, Alice. "Ladies' Fare." *Tennessee Register*. (undated press clipping).

45. Honey, Michael K. *Southern Labor and Black Civil Rights: Organizing Memphis Workers*. University of Illinois Press, Urbana and Chicago, 1993.

46. Honey, Michael K. *Going Down Jericho Road: The Memphis Strike, Martin Luther King's Last Campaign*. W. W. Norton and Company. New York and London. 2007.

47. Honey, Michael K. *Black Workers Remember: An Oral History of Segregation, Unionism, and the Freedom Struggle*. Berkeley: University of California Press, 1999.

48. Roark, Eldon. "Strolling." *The Commercial Appeal*, September 3, 1959.

49. Booker, Simeon. "To Be a 'Negro' Newsman—Reporting on the Emmett Till Murder Trial." *Neiman Reports*, Sept. 7, 2011.

50. ibid.

51. Connelly, Richard. "Recall Old Lady In Shoe? Well, Meet The Hanrahans." *The Commercial Appeal*, March 30, 1960.

52. "Chicago Archbishop Raps Rock and Roll." *Sarasota Journal*, March 1, 1957.

53. Handy, W.C. Lyrics to "The Memphis Blues" 1912.

54 Butler, Alban. *Butler's Lives of the Saints*. Complete Edition. Ed., rev., and suppl. Herbert Thurston, and Donald

Reference Notes

Attwater. 4 vols. Westminster, Maryland: Christian Classics, 1956.

55. *The Official Handbook of the Legion of Mary*. Concilium Legionis Mariae. 1962.

56. Pope Pius XII. "Address to Tertiaries." Acta Ap. Sedis, 1956.

57. Queener, Eileen. "They Were Filled With Love." *The Greeneville Sun*, December 24, 1980.

58. ibid.

59. Bridges, Patti. "Homeless now have a place to shower, pick up their mail." *St. Petersburg Times*, July 4, 1986. 295

60. Dries, Bill. "Court Gives Thumbs-Down to Sex Abuse Case." *The Daily News*, VOL. 125 | NO. 105, June 01, 2010.

61. Buser, Lawrwence. "Church Secrets: Memphis court documents unsealed in Catholic sex-abuse lawsuit: Offending priests were moved to avoid scandal; diocese admits mistakes, says it's responding." *The Commercial Appeal*, April 7, 2010.

62. ibid.

63. Hanrahan, Alice. "Ladies' Fare." *Tennessee Register*. (undated press clipping).

64. "Citizens Launch Political Group on Wide Basis." Clark Porteous. *Memphis Press Scimitar*, August 28, 1959.

65. "Churchhill, Boyd Appear Headed For Nov. 6 Rematch." *The Commercial Appeal*, October 10, 1975, Pg. 25.

66. "Memphis Girl is Finalist in National Contest for Junior Cook of The Year." Mrs. Alice Beatty Pitts. *Memphis Press Scimitar*, 1958.

67. Market News: "From Pillsbury: Quick Bread Mixes." *Memphis Press Scimitar*. January, 1961.

68. "Junior Cook of Year Contest Under Way." *Memphis Press-Scimitar*, October 1, 1959.

69. Hanrahan, Alice D. "Dual Role of Some Mothers." "Ladies' Fare." *Tennessee Register*, (undated press clipping).

70. Emilye Crosby. *Civil Rights History from the Ground Up: Local Struggles, a National Movement.* University of Georgia Press, 2011.

71. Green, Laurie B. *Battling the Plantation Mentality: Memphis and the Black Freedom Struggle.* The University of North Carolina Press: 2007.

72. AFSCME. "More than a Garbage Strike: The February 23 March." *Our Union History.* www.afscme.org/union/history/mlk/in-memphis.

73. ibid.

74. Strub, Whitney. "Black and White and Banned all Over." *Journal of Social History.* Vol 40, Issue 3, Spring 2007, Pg 685-715.

75. Finger, Michael. "Banned in Memphis The dark days of Lloyd T. Binford, known from coast to coast as the toughest censor in America." *Memphis Flyer*, May 8, 2008.

76. "Near Miss." *The Commercial Appeal.* Special Edition, Wednesday, May 11, 2011.

77. Hope, Laura Lee. *The Bobbsey Twins In The Land of Cotton.* Grossett & Dunlap. New York, 1942.

78. DeLong, Amy. "Supremely Human: The Civil Rights Activism of Memphis Catholics, 1961-1968." Memphis, Tennessee: Rhodes College, 2006.

79. Charlier, Tom. "Memphis named poorest metro area." *The Commercial Appeal*, October 20, 2013.

80. Day, Helen C. *Not Without Tears.* Sheed and Ward. 1952.

81. ibid.

82. Day, Dorothy. "On Pilgrimage-November 1952." *The Catholic Worker*, November 1952, 1, 4.

83. www.bishop-accountabilit Murphy-James-W.htm.

84. Gifford, Betty and Bill. *Catholic Worker Daze.* Xlibris Corporation, 2008

Reference Notes

85. Hanrahan, Clare. *Looking Things Over—Again, Memphis Catholic Workers in the 1950's & the Blessed Martin House of Hospitality,* 2nd edition, revised. Celtic WordCraft, 2000.

86. Guthrie, Rev. Milton, et. al. "Between the Rivers: The Catholic Heritage of West Tennessee," 1996.

87. Olmstead, Frederick Law. *The Cotton Kingdom.* New York: Mason Bros. 2nd Edition, Vol. I, 1862. p. 276.

88. Hillman, Jacque and Jimmy Hart. "October 1960, The Untold Story of Jackson's Civil Rights Movement." *The Jackson Sun*, 2003.

. Sallie Willis. "Cleric Pursues Fight Against Communism." *Whitehaven Press*, 22 October 1964.

90. DeLong, Amy.

91. Valencia, Nick and Marlena Baldacci. "Arrests sought after noose put on statue of James Meredith at Ole Miss." *Cable News Network*, February 21, 2014.

92. Porteous, Clark. "Marine Salutes $1 Lighter." *Memphis Press Scimitar*, December, 1967.

93. Daly, Mary. Gyn/Ecology. *The Metaethics Of Radical Feminism.* Beacon Press: Boston: 1978.

94. Wendi C. Thomas. "Site of 1968 sanitation accident earns fitting spot in history." *The Commercial Appeal*, Jan 19, 2014.

95. King, Jr., Martin Luther. "I've Been to the Mountaintop." delivered April 3, 1968, Mason Temple (Church of God in Christ Headquarters), Memphis, Tennessee.

96. "Miss USO." *Memphis Press Scimitar*, May 5, 1969.

97. Hanrahan, Clare. *FATE* magazine, September, 1981.

98. "Asheville women sentenced in U.S. Army protest case." *Asheville Citizen-Times*, May 24, 2001.

99. Van Biema, David H. "Radical Catholic Jim Douglass Fights A Grass-Roots War Against A Train Full Of Nuclear Weapons." *People.* May 21, 1984, Vol. 21 Issue 20, p50. 3p.

100. ibid.

101. Hanrahan, Clare. "Private Lives:" *St. Petersburg Times*, October 12, 1988.

102. Hanrahan, Clare. "Let's Really Support Our Soldiers." *Mountain Xpress*, Asheville, NC, February 26, 2003.

103. Smith, Whitney. "The Shell: Volunteers find a cause in restoration, A bequest of dreamer," *The Commercial Appeal*, July 27, 1986.

104. "Strike Up the Band," *The Commercial Appeal*, June 29, 2008.

Index

Index

A
Adrian, Bishop William 158, 163-64
Agent Orange 71, 192, 196, 279, 283-84
Alderson Federal Prison 15, 71, 216, 264, 270, 291
American Lebanese Syrian Associated Charities 144
American Snuff Company 33, 35, 39, 47, 52, 54, 239
Anderson-Clayton Cotton Company 186, 201, 205

B
Battery Park Apartments 43
Battle of Shiloh 21
Beale Street 26, 5, 95, 147, 149, 207, 250
Binford, Lloyd T. 146
Birth of a Nation, The 162
Black Code 23
Black Lives Matter 58
Blessed Martin House 59, 157-59, 250, 301
Bon Ton Cafe 211
Bureau of Refugees, Freedmen and Abandoned Land 38
Burke, Edmund 29
Burkes Book Store 140

C
Celo Community 265-66
Christian Brothers College 158-59, 184
Citizens to Preserve Overton Park. 88
Clayborn Temple 157, 203, 206
Coffin Ship 30, 31
Community for Creative Nonviolence 97, 263
Crump, E. H. (Boss) 34, 86

The Half Life of a Free Radical

D
Davis, Jefferson 17, 147
Day, Dorothy 156, 158, 236
Day, Helen Caldwell 156-59
Douglass, Jim and Shelly 253

E
Easter Rising (1916) 269-70
Elaine Massacre 151

F
Firestone Tire & Rubber Company. 54
Forrest, General Nathan Bedford 1117, 18
Forrest Park 26, 83
Fort Pickering 20, 22
Fred P. Gattas Co. 102, 142, 144, 183, 204

G
Gandhi, Mohandas 236
Gandhi-King Conference 155
Gifford, Charlye & Betty 158, 250, 252
Graceland 85

H
Hambone's Meditations 145
Handy, W. C. 26, 86, 149
Harris, Mary (Mother Jones) 28
Hernando De Soto Park 20
Hoffstetter, Sister Adrian Marie 59
Hotel King Cotton 212
Humes High School 83-85, 119
Hunthausen, Archbishop Raymond 235

I
Ingram, Mayor William B. 134

J
Jackson, President Andrew 19-20
James S. Robinson Apothecary 53
Jim Crow 12, 25, 145, 149, 158, 163
Johnson, President Lyndon B. 72, 168, 203

Index

K
Kennedy, President John F. 72, 166-67, 169
King, Jr., Dr. Martin Luther 12, 54, 153, 162, 201-03, 251
Klein, George 84
Ku Klux Klan (KKK) 162

L
Lawson, Rev. Jim 206
Lee, Tom 146-47
Legion of Decency 146
LeMoyne Owen College 158, 164
Leppert, Msgr. Joseph 58, 92, 158, 165-65
Lewis, Jerry Lee 85
Lions' Open Air School 36
Little Flower School 55, 89, 92, 107, 125, 139, 178
Loeb, Mayor Henry 59, 67, 134, 167, 201
Lorraine Motel 142, 204

M
McEwen, Humphreys County, Tennessee, 30-33
Memphis Catholic High School 144, 174, 176, 185, 189-90, 211
Memphis Committee on Community Relations 127
Memphis Cotton Carnival 149, 167, 210
Memphis Daily Appeal 26
Memphis Invaders 202-03, 207
Memphis Irish Society 53
Memphis National Cemetery 281, 285, 294
Memphis Press Scimitar 57, 58, 82, 127, 137, 140, 192
Memphis T. Mississippi 255
Memphis World 158
Memphis Yacht Club 238
Meredith, James 58, 165
Mid-South Peace & Justice Center 251, 253, 265
Millington Naval Air Technical Training Center 42, 191, 210
Monk 63
Mud Island 238, 244-45
Murphy, James W. 106, 158

N

NAACP 143, 160-61, 164
Nashville and Northwestern Railroad 32
New York Draft Riots 23

O

Ó hAnnracháin, Michael 269
Oak Ridge Environmental Peace Alliance 73
O'Connell, Daniel 23
Orgill, Mayor Edmund 127
Overton Park 76-77, 86-88, 141, 196
Overton Park Shell 84, 227-28

P

Parks, Rosa 160, 206, 261
Peabody Hotel 178
Persons, Ell 34
Pillsbury Bake-Off 49, 139, 181
Pinch, The 27-28, 33-34, 37-38, 54, 196
Pink Palace Museum 61, 84
Plessy v. Ferguson 25
Poplar Tunes 84
Porteous, Clark 57-58, 96, 157, 192
Presley, Elvis 26, 59, 83-85, 119, 147, 178, 277
Prince Mongo 63

Q

Quality Stamps Redemption Store 48

R

Roark, Eldon 57
Roosevelt, President Theodore 20
Rural Southern Voice for Peace 265, 267

S

Sacred Heart Catholic Church 42-43, 281
Sacred Heart High School 176, 178, 183, 185, 199
Sanitation Workers' Strike 54, 59, 134, 144, 157, 165, 201, 202, 207, 236
Saxon, Elizabeth Lyle 38
Seeger, Peggy 289

Index

Siena College 39, 59, 151, 158, 191
Snyder, Mitch 97-98-263
St. Jude Children's Research Hospital 143, 144, 163
St. Patrick's Catholic Church 32, 95, 157, 250
St. Peter Villa 74, 88, 105, 144, 289-92
St. Petersburg Times 254
St. Rose Catholic Worker 158, 250-51
St. Vincent de Paul Society 39, 110
Sultana 22
Sun Records 83
Suzore Theater 83, 146

T

Tennessee Register 45, 92, 137, 146
Tennessee Suffrage Movement 38
The Catholic Worker 156, 158
The Christian Sentinels 39
The Commercial Appeal 35, 53, 57, 106, 137, 139, 145, 155, 201, 277
The Cooper-Union 41
The Cotton Makers' Jubilee 149
The Great Hunger 28-30, 292
The Memphis Free Speech and Headlight 25, 27
Till, Emmett 57-58
Trail of Tears 20

U

U.S. Army School of Americas (SOA) 270
United Service Organization (USO) 42, 198, 208-211

V

Veterans for Peace 196
Viet Nam 71, 105, 183, 188-198, 200, 203-04, 209-10, 265, 267, 279-80, 284-85, 287-88

W

WDIA 61, 85, 188
Wells, Ida B. 25-26, 28, 156
Wharton, Mayor A. C. 18, 128
Withers, Ernest 87

X
Y
Yellow Fever (Yellow Jack) 21, 25, 27, 33
Z
Zippin Pippin 122

Crossing The Color Lines

www.ingramcontent.com/pod-product-compliance
Lightning Source LLC
Chambersburg PA
CBHW030434300426
44112CB00009B/999